Black Is White

by

George Barr Mccutcheon

Black Is White
by George Barr Mccutcheon

Copyright © 2023

All Rights reserved.

ISBN: 978-93-59952-27-7

Published by

DOUBLE 9 BOOKS

2/13-B, Ansari Road
Daryaganj, New Delhi – 110002
info@double9books.com
www.double9books.com
Tel. 011-40042856

ABOUT THE AUTHOR

George Barr McCutcheon was a famous American author who lived from July 26, 1866, to October 23, 1928. A group of books set in Graustark, a made-up country in East Europe, and the book Brewster's Millions, which was turned into a play and several movies, are his most well-known works. He was born in Indiana's Tippecanoe County. Even though he didn't go to school, his father stressed the value of literature and encouraged his boys to write. During McCutcheon's childhood, his dad had a few jobs that needed him to go to different places in the county. McCutcheon went to Purdue University and shared a room with George Ade, who would later become a comedian. He was editor of the newspaper Lafayette Daily Courier and wrote a satirical serial book about life on the Wabash River while he was in college. He died in Manhattan, New York City, New York. His brother was the famous artist John T. McCutcheon of that name. A lot of Indiana writers from the same time as McCutcheon are thought to be part of the Golden Age of Indiana Literature.

CONTENTS

CHAPTER I 7

CHAPTER II 16

CHAPTER III 28

CHAPTER IV 36

CHAPTER V 47

CHAPTER VI 57

CHAPTER VII 68

CHAPTER VIII 77

CHAPTER IX 89

CHAPTER X 99

CHAPTER XI 108

CHAPTER XII 117

CHAPTER XIII 128

CHAPTER XIV 139

CHAPTER XV 153

CHAPTER XVI 164

CHAPTER XVII 174

CHAPTER XVIII 186

CHAPTER XIX 197

CHAPTER XX 208

CHAPTER XXI 216

CHAPTER XXII 229

CHAPTER XXIII 234

CHAPTER XXIV 240

CHAPTER I

The two old men sat in the library, eyeing the blue envelope that lay on the end of the long table nearest the fireplace, where a merry but unnoticed blaze crackled in the vain effort to cry down the shrieks of the bleak December wind that whistled about the corners of the house.

Someone had come into the room—they did not know who nor when—to poke up the fire and to throw fresh coals into the grate. No doubt it was the parlourmaid. She was always doing something of the sort. It seemed to be her duty. Or, it might have been the housekeeper, in case the parlourmaid was out for the evening. Whoever it was, she certainly had poked up the fire, and in doing so had been compelled to push two pairs of feet out of the way to avoid trampling upon them.

Still they couldn't recall having seen her. For that matter, it wasn't of the slightest consequence. Of course, they might have poked it up themselves and saved her the trouble, but these ancients were not in the habit of doing anything that could be done by menials in the employ of Mr Brood. Their minds were centred upon the blue envelope that had arrived shortly after dinner. The fire was an old story; the blue envelope was a novelty.

From some shifting spot far out upon the broad Atlantic the contents of that blue envelope had come through the air, invisible, mysterious, uncanny. They could not understand it at all. A wireless message! It was the first of its kind they had seen, and they were very old men, who had seen everything else in the world—if one could believe their boastful tales.

They had sailed the seven seas and they had traversed all the lands of the earth, and yet here was mystery. A man had spoken out of the air a thousand miles away, and his words were lying there on the end of a library-table, in front of a cheerful hearthstone, within reach of their wistful fingers; and someone had come in to poke up the fire without their knowledge. How could they be expected to know?

There was something maddening in the fact that the envelope would have to remain unopened until young Frederic Brood came home for the night. They found themselves wondering if by any chance he would fail to come in at all. Their hour for retiring was ten o'clock, day in, day out. As a rule they went to sleep about half-past eight. They seldom retired unless someone made the act possible by first awakening them.

The clock on the wide mantelpiece had declared some time before, in ominous tones, that half-past ten had arrived, and yet they were not sleepy. They had not been so thoroughly wideawake in years.

Up to half-past nine they discussed the blue envelope with every inmate of the house, from Mrs John Desmond, the housekeeper, down to the voiceless but eloquent decanter of port that stood between them, first on the arm of one chair, then the other. They were very old men; they could soliloquise without in the least disturbing each other. An observer would say, during these periods of abstraction, that their remarks were addressed to the decanter, and that the poor decanter had something to say in return. But, for all that, their eyes seldom left the broad blue envelope that had lain there since half-past eight.

They knew that it came directly or indirectly from the man to whom they owed their present condition of comfort and security after half a century of vicissitudes; from the man whose life they had saved more than once in those old, evil days when comforts were so few that they passed without recognition in the maelstrom of events. From mid-ocean James Brood was speaking to his son. His words—perhaps his cry for help—were lying there on the end of the table, confined in a flimsy blue envelope, and no one dared to liberate them.

Frederic Brood deserved a thrashing for staying out so late—at least, so the decanter had been told a dozen times or more, and the clock, too, for that matter, to say nothing of the confidences reposed in the coal-scuttle, the fire implements, and other patient listeners of a like character.

It may be well to state that these bosom friends and comrades of half a hundred years had quarrelled at seven o'clock that evening over a very important matter—the accuracy of individual timepieces. The watch of Mr Danbury Dawes had said it was five minutes before seven; that of Mr Joseph Riggs three minutes after. Since then neither had spoken to the other, but each slyly had set his watch by the big clock in the hall before going into dinner, and was prepared to meet any argument.

Twenty years ago these two old cronies had met James Brood in one of the blackest holes of Calcutta, a derelict being swept to perdition with the swiftness and sureness of a tide that knows no pause. They found him when the dregs were at his lips and the stupor of defeat in his brain. Without meaning to be considered Samaritans, good or bad, they dragged him from the depths and found that they had revived *a man*. Those were the days when James Brood's life meant nothing to him, days when he was tortured by the thought that it would be all too long for him to endure; yet he was not the kind to murder himself as men do who lack the courage to go on living.

Weeks after the rescue in Calcutta, these two soldiers of fortune, and another John Desmond, learned from the lips of the man himself that he was not such as they, but rich in this world's goods, richer than the Solomon of their discreet imagination. Shaken, battered, but sobered, he related portions of his life's story to them, and they guessed the rest, being men who had lived by correctly guessing for half the years of their adventurous lives.

Like Brood they were Americans. But, unlike him, they had spent most of their lives in the deserts of time and had sown seeds which could never be reaped except in the form of narrative. Ever in pursuit of the elusive thing called luck, they had found it only in hairbreadth escapes from death, in the cunning avoidance of catastrophe, in devil-may-care leaps in the dark, in all the ways known to men who find the world too small.

Never had luck served them on a golden platter. For twenty-five years and more these three men, Dawes, Riggs, and poor John Desmond, had thrashed through the world in quest of the pot of gold at the foot of the rainbow, only to find that the rainbow was for ever lifting, for ever shifting; yet they complained not. They throve on misfortune, they courted it along with the other things in life, and they were unhappy only when ill luck singled one of them out and spared the others.

What Brood told them of his life brought the grim smile of appreciation to the lips of each. He had married a beautiful foreigner—an Austrian, they gathered—of excellent family, and had taken her to his home in New York City, a house in lower Fifth Avenue where his father and grandfather had lived before him. And that was the very house in which two of the wayfarers, after twenty years, now sat in rueful contemplation of a blue envelope.

A baby boy came to the Broods in the second year of their wedded life, but before that there had come a man—a music-master, dreamy-eyed, handsome, Latin; a man who played upon the harp as only the angels are believed to play. In his delirious ravings Brood cursed this man and the wife he had stolen away from him; he reviled the baby boy, even denying him; he laughed with blood-curdling glee over the manner in which he had cast out the woman who had broken his heart and crushed his pride; he wailed in anguish over the mistake he had made in allowing the man to live that he might gloat in triumph.

This much the three men who lifted him from hell were able to learn from lips that knew not what they said, and they were filled with pity. Later on, in a rational weakness, he told them more, and without curses. A deep, silent, steadfast bitterness succeeded the violent ravings. He became a wayfarer with them, quiet, dogged, fatal; where they went he also went; what they did so also did he.

Soon he led, and they followed. Into the dark places of the world they plunged. Perils meant little to him, death even less. They no longer knew days of privation, for he shared his wealth with them; but they knew no rest, no peace, no safety. Life had been a whirlwind before they came upon James Brood; it was a hurricane afterward.

Twice John Desmond, younger than Dawes and Riggs, saved the life of James Brood by acts of unparalleled heroism: once in a South African jungle when a lioness fought for her young, and again in upper India when, single-handed, he held off a horde of Hindus for days while his comrade lay wounded in a cavern. Dawes and Riggs, in the Himalayas, crept down the wall of a precipice, with five thousand feet between them and the bottom of the gorge, to drag him from a narrow ledge upon which he lay unconscious after a misstep in the night. More than once—aye, more than a dozen times—one or the other of these loyal friends stood between him and death, and times without number he, too, turned the grim reaper aside from them.

John Desmond, gay, handsome, and still young as men of his kind go, met the fate that brooks no intervention. He was the first to drop out of the ranks. In Cairo, during a curious period of inactivity some ten months after the advent of James Brood, he met the woman who conquered his venturesome spirit; a slim, clean, pretty English governess in the employ of a British admiral's family. They were married inside of a fortnight. After the quiet little ceremony, from which the sinister presence of James Brood was missing, he shook the bronzed hands of his older comrades, and gave up the life he had led for the new one she promised. At the pier Brood appeared and wished him well, and he sailed away on a sea that bade fair to remain smooth to the end of time. He was taking her home to the little Maryland town that had not seen him in years.

Ten years passed before James Brood put his foot on the soil of his native land. Then he came back to the home of his fathers, to the home that had been desecrated, and with him came the two old men who now sat in his huge library before the crackling fire. He could go on with life, but they were no longer fit for its cruel hardships. His home became theirs. They were to die there when the time came.

Brood's son was fifteen years of age before he knew, even by sight, the man whom he called father. Up to the time of the death of his mother who died heart-broken in her father's home—he had been kept in seclusion.

There had been deliberate purpose in the methods of James Brood in so far as this unhappy child was concerned. When he cast out the mother he set his hand heavily upon her future.

Fearing, even feeling, the infernal certainty that this child was not his own, he planned with diabolical cruelty to hurt her to the limit of his powers and to the end of her days. He knew she would hunger for this baby boy of hers, that her heart could be broken through him, that her punishment could be made full and complete.

He sequestered the child in a place where he could not be found, and went his own way, grimly certain that he was making her pay! She died when Frederic was twelve years old, without having seen him again after that dreadful hour when, protesting her innocence, she had been turned out into the night and told to go whither she would, but never to return to the house she had disgraced. James Brood heard of her death when in the heart of China, and he was a haggard wreck for months thereafter.

He had worshipped this beautiful Viennese. He could not wreak vengeance upon a dead woman; he could not hate a dead woman. He had always loved her. It was after this that he stood on the firing-line of many a fiercely fought battle in the Orient, inviting the bullet that would rip through his heart.

It was not courage, but cowardice, that put him in spots where the bullets were thickest; it was not valour that sent him among the bayonets and sabres of a fanatical enemy. It was the thing at the bottom of his soul that told him she would come to him once more when the strife was ended, and that she was waiting for him somewhere beyond the border to hear his plea for pardon! Of such flimsy shreds is man's purpose made!

Five years after his return to New York he brought her son back to the house in lower Fifth Avenue and tried, with bitterness in his soul, to endure the word "father" as it fell from lips to which the term was almost strange.

The old men, they who sat by the fire on this wind-swept night and waited for the youth of twenty-two to whom the blue missive was addressed, knew the story of James Brood and his wife Matilde, and they knew that the former had no love in his heart for the youth who bore his name. Their lips were sealed. Garrulous on all other subjects, they were as silent as the grave on this.

They, too, were constrained to hate the lad. He made not the slightest pretence of appreciating their position in the household. To him they were pensioners, no more, no less; to him their deeds of valour were offset by the deeds of his father; there was nothing left over for a balance on that score. He was politely considerate; he was even kindly disposed toward their vagaries and whims; he endured them because there was nothing else left for him to do. But, for all that, he despised them; justifiably, no doubt, if one bears in mind the fact that they signified more to James Brood than did his long-neglected son.

The cold reserve that extended to the young man did not carry beyond him in relation to any other member of the household so far as James Brood was concerned. The unhappy boy, early in their acquaintance, came to realise that there was little in common between him and the man he called father. After a while the eager light died out of his own eyes and he no longer strove to encourage the intimate relations he had counted upon as a part of the recompense for so many years of separation and loneliness.

It required but little effort on his part to meet his father's indifference with a coldness quite as pronounced. He had never known the meaning of filial love; he had been taught by word of mouth to love the man he had never seen, and he had learned as one learns astronomy—by calculation. He hated the two old men because his father loved them.

In a measure, this condition may serve to show how far apart they stood from each other, James Brood and Frederic. Wanderlust and a certain feeling of unrest that went even deeper than the old habits kept James Brood away from his home many months out of the year. He was not an old man; in fact, he was under fifty, and possessed of the qualities that make for strength and virility even unto the age of fourscore years. While his old comrades, far up in the seventies, were content to sit by the fire in winter and in the shade in summer, he, not yet so old as they when their long stretch of intimacy began, was not resigned to the soft things of life. He was built of steel, and the steel within him called for the clash with flint. He loved the spark of fire that flashed in the contact.

It was a harsh December night when the two old men sat guard over the message from the sea, and it was on a warm June day that they had said good-bye to him at the outset of his most recent flight.

The patient butler, Jones, had made no less than four visits to the library since ten o'clock to awaken them and pack them off to bed. Each time he had been ordered away, once with the joint admonition to "mind his own business."

"But it is nearly midnight," protested Jones irritably, with a glance at the almost empty decanter.

"Jones," said Danbury Dawes with great dignity and an eye that deceived him to such a degree that he could not for the life of him understand why Jones was attending them in pairs, "Jones, you ought to be in—hic—bed, damn you both of you. Wha' you mean, sir, by coming in—hic—here thish time o' night dis-disturbing—"

"You infernal ingrate," broke in Mr Riggs fiercely, "don't you dare to touch that bottle, sir! Let it alone!"

"It's time you were in bed," pronounced Jones, taking Mr Dawes by the arm.

Mr Dawes sagged heavily in his chair and grinned triumphantly. He was a short, very fat old man.

"People who live in—hic—glass houses— — — —" he began amiably, and then suddenly was overtaken by the thought of the moment before. "Take your hand off of me, confoun' you! D' you sup-supposh I can go to bed with my bes' frien' out there—hic—in the mid-middle of Atlan'ic Oc-o-shum, sinking in four miles of wa-wa'er and cal ing f-far help?"

"Take him to bed, Jones," said Mr Riggs firmly. "He's drunk and-and utterly useless at a time like this. Take him along."

"Who the dev—hic—il are you, sir?" demanded Mr Dawes, regarding Mr Riggs as if he had never seen him before.

"You are both drunk," said Jones succinctly. Mr Riggs began to whimper.

"My bes' frien' is drawnin' by inches, and you come in here and tell me I'm drunk. It's most heartless thing I ever heard of. Isn't it, Danbury, ol' pal? Isn't it, damn you? Speak up!"

"Drawnin' by inches—hic—in four miles of wa-water," admitted Mr Dawes miserably. "My God, Jo-Jones, do you know how many—hic—inches there are in four miles?"

Moved by the same impulse, the two old men struggled to their feet and embraced each other, swayed by an emotion so honest that all sense of the ludicrous was removed. Even Jones, though he grinned, allowed a note of gentleness to creep into his voice.

"Come along, gentlemen, like good fellows. Let's go to bed. I'm sure the message to Mr Frederic is not as bad as you— —"

Mr Riggs, who was head and shoulders taller than Mr Dawes, made a gesture of despair with both arms, forgetting that they encircled his friend's neck, with the result that both of his bony elbows came in violent contact with Mr Dawes's ears, almost upsetting him.

"Don't argue, Jones," he interrupted dismally "I know it's bad news. So does Mr Dawes. Don't you, Danbury?"

"What d' you mean by—hic—knockin' my hat off?" demanded Mr Dawes furiously, shaking his fist at Mr Riggs from rather close quarters—so close, in fact, that Mr Riggs suddenly clapped his hands to his stomach and emitted a surprised groan.

Jones inserted his figure between them.

"Come, come, gentlemen; don't forget yourselves. What now, Mr Riggs?"

"I'm lookin' for the gentleman's hat, sir," said Mr Riggs impressively from a stooping posture.

"His hat is on the rack in the hall," said Jones sharply.

"Then I shan't ex-expect an—hic—'pology," said Mr Dawes magnanimously.

Mr Riggs opened his mouth to retort, but as he did so his eyes fell upon the blue envelope.

"Poor old Jim—poor old Jim Brood!" he groaned. "We mustn't lose a minute, Danbury. He needs us, old pal. We must start relief exp'ition' fore mornin'. Not a minute to be lost, Jones—not a — —"

The heavy front door closed with a bang at that instant, and the sound of footsteps, came from the hall—a quick, firm tread that had decision in it.

Jones cast a furtive, nervous glance over his shoulder.

"I'm sorry to have Mr Frederic see you like this," he said, biting his lip. "He hates it so."

The two old men made a commendable effort to stand erect, but no effort to stand alone. They linked arms and stood shoulder to shoulder.

"Show him in," said Mr Riggs magnificently.

"Now we'll fin' out wass in telegram off briny deep," said Mr Dawes, straddling his legs a little farther apart in order to declare a staunch front.

"It's worth waiting up for," said Mr Riggs.

"Abs'lutely," said his staunch friend.

Frederic Brood appeared in the door, stopping short just inside the heavy curtains. There was a momentary picture, such as a stage-director would have arranged. He was still wearing his silk hat and top-coat, and one glove had been halted in the process of removal. Young Brood stared at the group of three, a frank stare of amazement. A crooked smile came to his lips.

"Somewhat later than usual, I see," he said, and the glove came off with a jerk. "What's the matter, Jones? Rebellion?"

"No, sir. It's the wireless, sir."

"Wireless?"

"Briny deep," said Mr Dawes, vaguely pointing.

"Oh," said young Brood, crossing slowly to the table. He picked up the envelope and looked at the inscription. "Oh," said he again in quite a different tone on seeing that it was addressed to him. "From father, I dare say," he went on, a fine line appearing between his eyebrows.

The old men leaned forward, fixing their blear eyes upon the missive.

"Le's hear the worst, Freddy," said Mr Riggs.

The young man ran his finger under the flap and deliberately drew out the message. There ensued another picture. As he read, his eyes widened and then contracted; his firm young jaw became set and rigid. Suddenly a short, bitter execration fell from his lips and the paper crumpled in his hand. Without another word he strode to the fireplace and tossed it upon the coals. It flared for a second and was wafted up the chimney, a charred, feathery thing.

Without deigning to notice the two old men who had sat up half the night to learn the contents of that wonderful thing from the sea, he whirled on his heel and left the room. One might have noticed that his lips were drawn in a mirthless, sardonic smile, and that his eyes were angry.

"Oh, Lordy!" sighed Danbury Dawes, blinking, and was on the point of sitting down abruptly. The arm of Jones prevented.

"I never was so insulted in my——" began Joseph Riggs feebly.

"Steady, gentlemen," said Jones. "Lean on me, please."

CHAPTER II

James Brood's home was a remarkable one. That portion of the house which rightly may be described as "public" in order to distinguish it from other parts where privacy was enforced, was not unlike any of the richly furnished, old-fashioned places in the lower part of the city where there are still traces left of the Knickerbockers and their times. Dignified, stately, almost gloomy, it was a mansion in which memories dwelt, where the past strode unseen among sturdy things of mahogany and walnut and worn but priceless brocades and silks.

The crystal chandelier in the long drawing-room had shed light for the Broods since the beginning of the nineteenth century; the great old sideboard was still covered with the massive plate of a hundred years ago; the tables, the chairs, the high-boys, the chests of drawers, and the huge four-posters were like satin to the eye and touch; the rugs, while older perhaps than the city itself, alone were new to the house of Brood. They had been installed by the present master of the house.

Age, distinction, quality attended one the instant he set foot inside the sober portals. This was not the home of men who had been merely rich; it was not wealth alone that stood behind these stately investments.

At the top of the house were the rooms which no one entered except by the gracious will of the master. Here James Brood had stored the quaint, priceless treasures of his own peculiar fancy: exquisite, curious things from the mystic East, things that are not to be bought and sold, but come only to the hand of him who searches in lands where peril is the price.

Worlds separated the upper and lower regions of that fine old house; a single step took one from the sedate Occident into the very heart of the Orient; a narrow threshold was the line between the rugged West and the soft, languorous, seductive East. In this part of the house James Brood, when at home for one of his brief stays, spent many of his hours in seclusion, shut off from the rest of the establishment as completely as if he were the inhabitant of another world. Attended by his Hindu servant, a silent man named Ranjab, and on occasions by his secretary, he saw but little of the remaining members of his rather extensive household.

For several years he had been engaged in the task of writing his memoirs—so-called—in so far as they related to his experiences and researches of the past twenty years. It was not his intention to give this long and elaborate account of himself to the world at large, but to publish privately a very limited edition without regard for expense, copies of which were to find their way into exclusive collections and libraries given over to science and travel. This work progressed slowly because of his frequent and protracted absences. When at home, he laboured ardently and with a purpose that more than offset the periods of indifference.

His secretary and amanuensis was Lydia Desmond, the nineteen-year-old daughter of his one-time companion and friend, the late John Desmond, whose death occurred when the girl was barely ten years of age.

Brood, on hearing of his old comrade's decease, immediately made inquiries concerning the condition in which he had left his wife and child, with the result that Mrs Desmond was installed as housekeeper in the New York house and the daughter given every advantage in the way of an education.

Desmond had left nothing in the shape of riches except undiminished love for his wife and a diary kept during those perilous days before he met and married her. This diary was being incorporated in the history of James Brood's adventures, by consent of the widow, and was to speak for Brood in words he could not with modesty utter for himself.

In those pages John Desmond was to tell his own story in his own way, for Brood's love for his friend was broad enough even to admit of that. He was to share his life in retrospect with Desmond and the two old men, as he had shared it with them in reality.

Lydia's room, adjoining her mother's, was on the third floor at the foot of the small stairway leading up to the proscribed retreat at the top of the house. There was a small sitting-room off the two bed-chambers, given over entirely to Mrs Desmond and her daughter. In this little room Frederic Brood spent many a quiet, happy hour.

The Desmonds, mother and daughter, understood and pitied the lonely boy who came to the big house soon after they were themselves installed. His heart, which had many sores, expanded and glowed in the warmth of their kindness and affection; the plague of unfriendliness that was his by absorption gave way before this unexpected kindness, not immediately, it is true, but completely in the end.

By nature he was slow to respond to the advances of others; his life had been such that avarice accounted for all that he received from others in the shape of respect and consideration. He was prone to discount a friendly attitude, for the simple reason that in his experience all friendships were marred by the fact that their sincerity rested entirely upon the generosity of the man who paid for them—his father. No one had loved him for himself; no one had given him an unselfish thought in all the years of his boyhood.

The family with whom he had lived in a curious sort of retirement up to the time he was fifteen had no real feeling for him beyond the bounds of duty; his tutors had taken their pay in exchange for all they gave; his companions were men and women who dealt with him as one deals with a precious investment. He represented ease and prosperity to them—no more. As he grew older he understood all this. What warmth there may have been in his little heart was chilled by contact with these sordid influences.

At first he held himself aloof from the Desmonds; he was slow to surrender. He suspected them of the same motives that had been the basis of all previous attachments. When at last he realised that they were not like the others, his cup of joy, long an empty vessel, was filled to the brim and his happiness was without bounds.

They were amazed by the transformation. The rather sullen, unapproachable lad became at once so friendly, so dependent, that, had they not been acquainted with the causes behind the old state of reticence, his very joy might have made a nuisance of him. He followed Mrs Desmond about in very much the same spirit that inspires a hungry dog; he watched her with eager, half-famished eyes; he was on her heels four-fifths of the time.

As for Lydia, pretty little Lydia, he adored her. His heart began for the first time to sing with the joy of youth, and the sensation was a novel one. It had seemed to him that he could never be anything but an old man.

Not a day passed during his career at Harvard that he failed to write to one or other of these precious friends. His vacations were spent with them; his excursions were never carried out unless they found it possible to accompany him. He followed Mrs Desmond, met many women, but he thought of only two. They appeared to constitute all femininity so far as he was concerned. Through their awakening influence he came to find pleasure in the companionship of other young men, and, be it said for him, despite a certain unconquerable aloofness, he was one of the most popular men in his class.

It was his custom, on coming home for the night, no matter what the hour, to pause before Lydia's door on the way to his own room at the other end of the long hall. There was always a tender smile on his lips as he regarded the white panels before tapping gently with the tips of his fingers.

Then he would wait for the sleepy "Good night, Freddy," which invariably came from within, and he would sing out "Good night" as he made off to bed. Usually, however, he was at home long before her bedtime, and they spent the evenings together. That she was his father's secretary was of no moment. To him she was Lydia—his Lydia.

For the past three months or more he had been privileged to hold her close in his arms and to kiss her good night at parting. They were lovers now. The slow fuse of passion had reached its end and the flame was alive and shining with radiance that enveloped both of them.

On this night, however, he passed her door without knocking. His dark, handsome face was flushed and his teeth were set in sullen anger. With his hand on the knob of his own door, he suddenly remembered that he had failed Lydia for the first time, and stopped. A pang of shame shot through him. For a moment he hesitated and then started guiltily toward the forgotten door. Even as he raised his hand to sound the loving signal, the door was opened and Lydia, fully dressed, confronted him. For a moment they regarded each other in silence, she intently, he with astonishment not quite free from confusion.

"I'm—I'm sorry, dearest——" he began, his first desire being to account for his oversight.

"It *is* bad news?" she demanded, anxiously watching his face. "I was afraid, dear. I couldn't go to bed."

"You, too?" he exclaimed bitterly. "The old chaps—but it's a shame for you to have waited up, dear."

"Tell me what has happened. It can't be that your father is ill—or in danger. You are angry, Frederic; so it can't be that. What is it?"

He looked away sullenly.

"Oh, it's really nothing, I suppose. Just an unexpected jolt, that's all. I was angry for a moment——"

"You are still angry," she said, placing her hand on his arm. She was a tall, slender girl. Her eyes were almost on a level with his own. "Don't you want to tell me, dear?"

"He never gives me a thought," he said, compressing his lips. "He thinks of no one but himself. God, what a father!"

"Freddy, dear! You must not speak——"

"Haven't I some claim on his consideration? Is it fair that I should be ignored in everything, in every way? I won't put up with it, Lydia! I'm not a child. I'm a man and I am his son. But I might as well be a dog in the street for all the thought he gives to me!"

She put her finger to her lips, a scared look stealing into her dark eyes. Jones was conducting the two old men to their room on the floor below. A door closed softly. The voices died away.

"He is a strange man," she said. "He is a good man, Frederic."

"To everyone else, yes. But to me? Why, Lydia, I—I believe he hates me. You know what— —"

"Hush! A man does not hate his son. I've tried for years to drive that silly notion out of your mind. You— —"

"Oh, I know I'm a fool to speak of it, but I—I can't help feeling as I do. You've seen enough to know that I'm not to blame for it, either. And then— oh, what's the use whining about it? I've got to make the best of it, so I'll try to keep my mouth closed."

"Where is the message?"

"I threw it into the fire."

"What!"

"I was furious."

"Won't you tell me?"

"What do you think he has done? Can you guess what he has done to all of us?" She did not answer. "Well, I'll tell you just what he said in that wireless. It was from the *Lusitania*, twelve hundred miles off Sandy Hook— relayed, I suppose, so that the whole world might know—sent at four this afternoon. I remember every word of the cursed thing, although I merely glanced at it.

"'Send the car to meet Mrs Brood and me at the Cunard pier Thursday. Have Mrs Desmond put the house in order for its new mistress. By the way, you might inform her that I was married last Wednesday in Paris.' It was signed 'James Brood,' not even 'father.' What do you think of that for a thunderbolt?"

"Married?" she gasped. "Your father married?"

"'Put the house in order for its new mistress,'" he almost snarled. "'Inform her that I was married last Wednesday'! Of course he's married. Am I not to inform your mother? Isn't the car to meet Mrs Brood and him? Does he say anything about his son meeting him at the pier? No! Does he cable his son that he is married? No! Does he do anything that a real, human father would do? No! That message was a deliberate insult to me, Lydia, a nasty, rotten slap in the face. I mean the way it was worded. Just as if it wasn't enough that he had gone and married some cheap show-girl or a miserable foreigner or Heaven knows — — "

"Freddy! You forget yourself. Your father would not marry a cheap show-girl. You know that. And you must not forget that your mother was a foreigner."

"I'm sorry I said that," he exclaimed hoarsely. Then fiercely: "But can't you see what all this will come to? A new mistress of the house! It means your mother will have to go — that maybe you'll go. Nothing will be as it has been. All the sweetness gone — all the goodness! A woman in the house who will also treat me as if I didn't belong here! A woman who married him for his money, an adventuress. Oh, you can't tell me; I know! 'You might inform Mrs Desmond that I was married'! Good Lord!"

He began to pace the floor, striking one fist viciously in the palm of the other hand. Lydia, pale and trembling, seemed to have forgotten his presence. She was staring fixedly at the white surface of a door down the hall, and there was infinite pain in her wide eyes. Her lips moved once or twice; there was a single unspoken word upon them.

"Why couldn't he have wired me last week?" the young man was muttering. "What was his object in waiting until to-day? Wouldn't any other father in the world have telegraphed his only son if he were going to — to bring someone home like this? 'Have the car meet Mrs Brood and me'! If that isn't the quintessence of scorn! He orders me to do these things. He doesn't even honour me with a direct, personal message. He doesn't tell *me* he is married. He asks me to inform someone else."

Lydia, leaning rather heavily against the door, spoke to him in a low, cautious voice.

"Did you tell Mr Dawes and Mr Riggs?"

He stopped short.

"No! And they waited up to see if they could be of any assistance to him in an hour of peril! What a joke! Poor old beggars! I've never felt sorry for them before, but, on my soul, I do now. What will she do to the poor old chaps? I shudder to think of it. And she'll make short work of everything else she doesn't like around here, too. Your mother, Lydia — why, God help us, you know what will just have to happen in her case. It's — — "

"Don't speak so loudly, dear — please, please! She is asleep. Of course, we — we shan't stay on, Freddy. We'll have to go as soon as — — "

His eyes filled with tears. He seized her in his arms and held her close.

"It's a beastly, beastly shame, darling. Oh, Lord, what a fool a man can make of himself!"

"You must not say such things," she murmured, stroking his cheek with cold, trembling fingers.

"A fine trick to play on all of us!" he grated.

"Listen, Freddy darling: your father has a right to do as he chooses. He has a right to companionship, to love, to happiness. He has done everything for us that man could——"

"But why couldn't he have done the fine, sensible thing, Lydia? Why couldn't he have—have fallen in love with—with your mother? Why not have married her if he had to marry someone in——"

"Freddy!" she cried, putting her hand over his mouth.

He was not to be stopped. He gently removed her hand.

"Your mother is the finest woman in the world. Perhaps she wouldn't have him, but that's not the point. Good Lord, how I would have loved him for giving her to me as a mother. And here he comes, bringing some devil of a stranger into—oh, it's sickening!"

He had lowered his voice to a hoarse whisper, keeping his eyes fixed on the door down the hall. The girl lay very still in his arms. Suddenly a wild sob broke in her throat, and she buried her face on his shoulder.

"Why—why, don't cry, dearest! Don't!" he whispered miserably. "What a rotter I am! Inflicting you with my silly imaginings! Don't cry! I dare say everything will turn out all right. It's my beastly disposition. Kiss me!"

She kissed him swiftly. Her wet cheek lay for a second against his own, and then, with a stifled good night, she broke away from him. An instant later she was gone; her door was closed.

Somewhat sobered, and not a little perturbed by her outburst, he stood still for a moment, staring at the door. Then he turned and passed slowly into his own room.

A fire smouldered in the grate. In this huge, old-fashioned house there were grates in all of the spacious bedrooms, and not infrequently fires were started in them by the capable Jones. Frederic stood for he knew not how long above the half-dead coals, staring at them with a new and more bitter complaint at the back of his mind. Was there anything between Mrs Desmond and his father? What was back of that look of anguish in Lydia's eyes? He suddenly realised that he was muttering oaths, not of anger, but of pain.

The next morning he came down earlier than was his custom. His night had been a troubled one. Forgetting his own woes, or belittling them, he had thought only of what this news from the sea would mean to the dear woman he loved so well. No one was in the library, but a huge fire was blazing. A blizzard was raging.

Once upon a time, when he first came to the house, a piano had stood in the drawing-room. His joy at that time knew no bounds; he loved music. For his age he was no mean musician. But one evening his father, coming in unexpectedly, heard the player at the instrument. For a moment he stood transfixed in the doorway watching the eager, almost inspired face of the lad, and then, pale as a ghost, stole away without disturbing him. Strange to say, Frederic was playing a waltz of Ziehrer's, a Waltz that his mother had played when the honeymoon was in the full. The following day the piano was taken away by a storage company. The boy never knew why it was removed.

Frederic picked up the morning paper. His eye traversed the front page rapidly. There were reports of fearful weather at sea. Ships in touch with wireless stations flashed news of the riotous gales far out on the Atlantic, of tremendous seas that wreaked damage to the staunchest of vessels. The whole seaboard was strewn with the wreckage of small craft; a score of vessels were known to be ashore and in grave peril. The movement of passenger-vessels, at the bottom of the page, riveted his attention. The *Lusitania* was reported seven hundred miles out, and in the heart of the hurricane. She would be a day late.

The newspaper was slightly crumpled, as if someone else had read it before him. He found himself wondering how he would feel if the *Lusitania* never reached New York! He wondered what his sensations would be if a call for help came from the great vessel, if the dreadful news came that she was sinking with all on board!

He looked up from the paper with what actually seemed to him to be a guilty feeling. Someone had entered the room. Mrs Desmond was coming toward him, a queer little smile on her lips. She was a tall, fair woman, an English type, and still extremely handsome. Hers was an honest beauty that had no fear of age.

"She is a staunch ship, Frederic," she said, without any other form of greeting. "She will be late, but there's really nothing to worry about."

"I'm not worrying," he said confusedly. "Lydia has told you the—the news?"

"Yes."

"Rather staggering, isn't it?" he said with a wry smile. In spite of himself he watched her face with curious intentness.

"Rather," she said briefly.

He was silent for a moment.

"I was instructed to inform you that he was married last Wednesday," he said, and his face hardened. "And to have the car meet them at the dock."

"It won't be necessary, Frederic. I have given Jones his instructions. You will not even have to carry out the orders."

"I suppose you don't approve of the way."

"I know just how you feel, poor boy. Don't try to explain. I know."

"You always understand," he said, lowering his eyes.

"Not always," she said quietly. There was something cryptic in the remark. He kept his eyes averted.

"Well, it's going to play hob with everything," he said, jamming his hands deep into his pockets. His shoulders seemed to hunch forward and to contract.

"I am especially sorry for Mr Dawes and Mr Riggs," she said. Her voice was steady and full of earnestness.

"Do they know?"

"They were up and about at daybreak, poor souls. Do you know, Freddy, they were starting off in this blizzard when I met them in the hall!"

"The deuce! I—I hope it wasn't on account of anything I may have said to them last night," he cried in contrition.

She smiled. "No. They had their own theory about the message. The storm strengthened it. They were positive that your father was in great peril. I don't like to tell you this, but they seemed to think that you couldn't be depended upon to take a hand in—in—well, in helping him. They were determined to charter a vessel of some sort and start off in all this blizzard to search the sea for Mr Brood. Oh, aren't they wonderful?"

He had no feeling of resentment toward the old men for their opinion of him. Instead, his eyes glowed with an honest admiration.

"By George, Mrs Desmond, they *are* great! They are *men*, bless their hearts. Seventy-five years old and still ready to face anything for a comrade! It *does* prove something, doesn't it?"

"It proves that your father has made no mistake in selecting his friends, my dear. My husband used to say that he would cheerfully die for James

Brood, and he knew that James Brood would have died for him just as readily. There is something in friendships of that sort that we can't understand. We never have been able to test our friends, much less ourselves. We— —"

"I would die for you, Mrs Desmond," cried Frederic, a deep flush overspreading his face. "For you and Lydia."

"You come by that naturally," she said, laying her hand upon his arm. "Blood will tell. Thank you, Frederic." She smiled. "I am sure it will not be necessary for you to die for me, however. As for Lydia, you must live, not die, for her."

"I'll do both," he cried impulsively.

"Before you go in to breakfast I want to say something else to you, Frederic," said she seriously. "Lydia has repeated everything you said to her last night. My dear boy, my husband has been dead for twelve years. I loved him, and he died loving me. I shall never marry another man. I am still the wife of John Desmond; I still consider myself bound to him. Can you understand?"

"I talked like a lunatic last night, I fear," he confessed. "I might have known. You, too, belong to the list of loyal ones Forgive me."

"There is nothing to forgive, dear," she said simply. "And now, one more word, Frederic. You must accept this new condition of affairs in the right spirit. Your father has married again, after all these years. It is not likely that he has done so without deliberation. Therefore, it is reasonable to assume that he is bringing home with him a wife of whom he at least is proud, and that should weigh considerably in your summing up of the situation. She will be beautiful, accomplished, refined, and good, Frederic. Of that you may be sure. Let me implore you to withhold judgment until a later day."

"I do not object to the situation, Mrs Desmond," said he, the angry light returning to his eyes, "so much as I resent the wording of that telegram. It is always just that way. He loses no chance to humiliate me. He— —"

"Hush! You are losing your temper again."

"Well, who wouldn't? And here's another thing, the very worst of all. How is this new condition going to affect you, Mrs Desmond?" She was silent for a moment.

"Of course, I shan't stay on here, Frederic. I shall not be needed now. As soon as Mrs Brood is settled here I shall go."

"And you expect me to be cheerful and contented!" he cried bitterly.

"You are a man, Frederic. It is for you to say yea and nay; women must say one or the other. A man may make his own bed, but he doesn't always have to lie in it."

"Sounds rather like Solomon," he said ruefully. "I suppose you mean that if I'm not contented here I ought to get out and look for happiness elsewhere, reserving the right to come back if I fail?"

"Something of the sort," she said.

"My father objects to my going into business or taking up a profession. I am dependent on him for everything. But why go into that? We've talked it over a thousand times. I don't understand, but perhaps you do. It's a dog's way of living."

"Your father is making a man of you."

"Oh, he is, eh?" with great scorn.

"Yes. He will make you see some day that the kind of life you lead is not the kind you want. Your pride, your ambition will rebel. Then you will make something out of life for yourself."

"I don't think that is in his mind, if you'll pardon me. I sometimes believe he actually wants me to stay as I am, always a dependent. Why, how can he expect me to marry and— —" He stopped short, his face paling.

"Go on, please."

"Well, it looks to me as if he means to make it impossible for me to marry, Mrs Desmond. I've thought of it a good deal."

"And is it impossible?"

"No. I shall marry Lydia, even though I have to dig in the streets for her. It isn't that, however. There's some other reason back of his attitude, but for the life of me I can't get at it."

"I wouldn't try to get at it, my dear," she said. "Wait and see. Come, you must have your coffee. I am glad you came down early. The old gentlemen are at breakfast now. Come in."

He followed her dejectedly, a droop to his shoulders.

Mr Dawes and Mr Riggs were seated at the table. Lydia, a trifle pale and distrait, was pouring their third cup of coffee. The old men showed no sign of their midnight experience. They were very wideawake, clear-eyed, and alert, as old men will be who do not count the years of life left in the span appointed for them.

"Good morning, Freddy," said they, almost in one voice.

As he passed behind their chairs on his way to Lydia's side, he slapped each of them cordially on the back. They seemed to swell with relief and gratitude. He was not in the habit of slapping them on the back.

"Good morning, gentlemen," said he. Then he lifted Lydia's slim fingers to his lips. "Good morning, dear."

She squeezed his fingers tightly and smiled. A look of relief leaped into her eyes; she drew a long breath. She poured his coffee for him every morning. Her hand shook a little as she lifted the tiny cream-pitcher.

"I didn't sleep very well," she explained in a low voice.

His hand rested on her shoulder for a moment in a gentle caress. Then he sat down in the chair Jones had drawn out for him.

"Well, gentlemen, when does the relief boat start?" he asked, with a forced attempt at humour.

Mr Dawes regarded him with great solemnity.

"Freddy, it's too late. A man can be saved from the scourge, tigers, elephants, lions, snakes, and almost everything else in God's world, but, blast me, he can't be protected against women! They are deadly. They can overpower the strongest of men, sir. Your poor father is lost for ever. I never was so sorry for anyone in my life."

"If he had only called for help a week or so ago, we could have saved him," lamented Mr Riggs. "But he never even peeped. Lordy, Lordy, and just think of it, he yelled like an Indian when that lion leaped on him at Nairobi!"

"Poor old Jim!" sighed Mr Dawes. "He'll probably have to ask us to pull out, too. I imagine she'll insist on making a spare bedroom out of our room, so's she can entertain all of her infernal relations. Jones, will you give me some more bacon and another egg?"

"And I thought it was nothing but a shipwreck," murmured Mr Riggs plaintively.

Frederic hurried through breakfast. Lydia followed him into the library.

"Are you going out, dear?" she asked anxiously.

"Yes. I've got to do something. I can't sit still and think of what's going to happen. I'll be back for luncheon."

Half an hour later he was in the small bachelor apartment of two college friends, a few blocks farther up-town, and he was doing the thing he did nearly every day of his life in a surreptitious way. He sat at the cheap upright piano in their disordered living-room and, unhampered by the presence of young men who preferred music as it is rendered for the masses, played as if his very soul was in his fingers.

CHAPTER III

The next three or four days passed slowly for those who waited. A spirit of uneasiness pervaded the household. Among the servants, from Jones down, there was dismay. It was not even remotely probable that Mrs Desmond would remain, and they confessed to a certain affection for her, strange as it may appear to those who know the traits of servants who have been well treated by those above them.

Frederic flatly refused to meet the steamer when she docked. As if swayed by his decision, Dawes and Riggs likewise abandoned a plan to greet the returning master and his bride as they came down the gangplank. But for the almost peremptory counsel of Mrs Desmond, Brood's son would have absented himself from the house on the day of their arrival. Jones and a footman went to the pier with the chauffeur.

It was half-past two in the afternoon when the automobile drew up in front of the house and the fur-coated footman nimbly hopped down and threw open the door.

James Brood, a tall, distinguished-looking man of fifty, stepped out of the limousine. For an instant, before turning to assist his wife from the car, he allowed his keen eyes to sweep the windows on the lower floor. In one of them stood his son, holding the lace curtains apart and smiling a welcome that seemed sincere. He waved his hand to the man on the side-walk. Brood responded with a swift, almost perfunctory gesture, and then held out his hand to the woman who was descending.

Frederic's intense gaze was fixed on the stranger who was coming into his life. At a word from Brood she glanced up at the window. The smile still lingered on the young man's lips, but his eyes were charged with an expression of acute wonder. She smiled, but he was scarcely aware of the fact. He watched them cross the side-walk and mount the steps.

He had never looked upon a more beautiful creature in all his life. A kind of stupefaction held him motionless until he heard the door close behind them. In that brief interval a picture had been impressed upon his senses that was to last for ever.

She was slightly above the medium height, slender and graceful even in the long, thick coat that enveloped her. She did not wear a veil. He had a swift but enduring glimpse of dark, lustrous eyes; of long lashes that drooped; of a curiously pallid, perfectly modelled face; of red lips and very white teeth; of jet-black hair parted above a broad, clear brow to curtain the temple and ear; of a firm, sensitive chin. Somehow he received the extraordinary impression that the slim, lithe body was never cold; that she expressed in some indefinable way the unvarying temperature of youth.

He hurried into the hall, driven by the spur of duty. They were crossing the vestibule. Jones, who had preceded them in a taxicab, was holding open the great hall door. Dawes and Higgs, shivering quite as much with excitement as from the chilly blast that swept in through the storm-doors, occupied a point of vantage directly behind the butler. They suggested a reception committee. Frederic was obliged to remain in the background.

He heard his father's warm, almost gay response to the greetings of the old men, whose hands he wrung with fervour that was unmistakable. He heard him present them to the new Mrs Brood as "the best old boys in all the world," and they were both saying, with spasmodic cackles of pleasure, that she "mustn't believe a word the young rascal said."

He was struck by the calm, serene manner in which she accepted these jocular contributions to the occasion. Her smile was friendly, her handshake cordial, and yet there was an unmistakable air of tolerance, as of one who is accustomed to tribute. The rather noisy acclamations of the old adventurers brought no flush of embarrassment to her cheek; not the flicker of an eyelid, nor a protesting word or frown. She merely smiled and thanked them in simple, commonplace phrases.

Frederic, who was given to forming swift impressions, most of which sprang from his own varying moods and were seldom permanent, formed an instant and rather startling opinion of the newcomer. She was either a remarkable actress or a woman whose previous station in life had been far more exalted than the one she now approached. He had an absurd notion that he might be looking upon a person of noble birth.

Her voice was low-pitched and marked by huskiness that was peculiar in that it was musical, not throaty. Frederic, on first seeing her, had leaped to the conclusion that her English would not be perfect. He was somewhat surprised to discover that she had but the faintest trace of an accent.

The exchange of greetings at the door seemed to him unnecessarily prolonged. He stood somewhat apart from the little circle, uncomfortable and distinctly annoyed with the old men who, in their garrulous gallantry, blocked the way in both directions. He awoke suddenly, however, to the realisation that he had been looking into his new stepmother's eyes for a long time and that she was returning his gaze with some intensity.

"And this?" she said, abruptly breaking in upon one of Danbury's hasty reminiscences, effectually ending it. "This is Frederic?"

She came directly toward the young man, her small, gloved hand extended. Her eyes were looking into his with an intentness that disconcerted him. There was no smile on her lips. It was as if she regarded this moment as a pronounced crisis.

Frederic mumbled something fatuous about being glad to see her, and felt his face burn under her steady gaze. His father came forward.

"Yes; this is Frederic, my dear," he said, without a trace of warmth in his voice. As she withdrew her hand from Frederic's clasp James Brood extended his. "How are you, Frederic?"

"Quite well, sir."

They shook hands in the most perfunctory manner.

"I need not ask how you are, father," said the son, after an instant's hesitation. "You never looked better, sir."

"Thank you. I *am* well. Ah, Mrs Desmond! It is good to be home again with you all. My dear, permit me to introduce Mrs John Desmond. You have heard me speak of my old comrade and — —"

"I have heard you speak of Mr Desmond a thousand times," said his wife. There may have been a shade of emphasis on the prefix, but it was so slight that no one remarked it save the widow of John Desmond, who had joined the group.

"The best pal a man ever had," said Mr Dawes with conviction. "Wasn't he, Riggs?"

"He was," said Mr Riggs loudly, as if expecting someone to dispute it.

"Will you go to your room at once, Mrs Brood?" asked Mrs Desmond.

The new mistress of the house had not offered to shake hands with her, as James Brood had done. She had moved closer to Frederic and was smiling in a rather shy, pleading way, in direct contrast to her manner of the moment before. The smile was for her stepson. She barely glanced at Mrs Desmond.

"Thank you, no. I see a nice big fire, and—oh, I have been so cold!" She shivered very prettily.

"Come!" cried her husband. "That's just the thing." No one spoke as they moved toward the library. "We must try to thaw out," he added dryly, with a faint smile on his lips.

His wife laid her hand on Frederic's arm. "It is cold outside, Frederic," she said; "very cold. I am not accustomed to the cold."

If anyone had told him beforehand that his convictions, or his prejudices, could be overthrown in the twinkling of an eye, he would have laughed him to scorn. He was prepared to dislike her. He was determined that his hand should be against her in the conflict that was bound to come.

And now, in a flash, his incomprehensible heart proved treacherous. She had touched some secret spring in the bottom of it, and a strange, new emotion rushed up within him, like the flood which finds a new channel and will not be denied by mortal ingenuity. A queer, wistful note of sympathy in her voice had done the trick. Something in the touch of her fingers on his arm completed the mystery. He was conscious of a mighty surge of relief. The horizon cleared for him.

"We shall do our best to keep you warm," he said quite gaily, and was somewhat astonished at himself.

They had preceded the others into the library. James Brood was divesting himself of his coat in the hall, attended by the leechlike old men. Mrs Desmond stood in the doorway, a detached figure.

"You must love me, Frederic. You must be very, very fond of me, not for your father's sake, but for mine. Then we shall be great friends, not antagonists."

He was helping her with her coat.

"I confess I looked forward to you with a good deal of animosity," he said.

"It was quite natural," she said simply. "A stepmother is not of one's own choosing, as a rule."

"She's usually resented," said he.

"But I shall not be a stepmother," she said quickly. Her eyes were serious for an instant, then filled with a luminous smile. "I shall be Yvonne to you, and you Frederic to me. Let it be a good beginning."

"You are splendid," he cried. "It's not going to be at all bad."

"I am sure you will like me," she said composedly.

Brood joined them at the fireside.

"My dear, Mrs Desmond will show you over the house when you are ready. You will be interested in seeing the old place. Later on I shall take you up to my secret hiding-place, as they say in books. Ranjab will have the rooms in order by this evening. Where is your daughter, Mrs Desmond?"

"She is at work on the catalogue, Mr Brood, in the jade room. In your last letter you instructed her to finish that — —"

"But this is a holiday, Mrs Desmond," said he, frowning. "Jones, will you ask Miss Lydia to join us for tea at half-past four?"

"You will adore Lydia," said Frederic to Mrs Brood.

Apparently she did not hear him, for she gave no sign. She was looking about the room with eyes that seemed to take in everything. For the moment her interest appeared to be centred on the inanimate, to the complete exclusion of all other objects. Frederic had the odd notion that she was appraising her new home with the most calculating of minds.

Even as he watched her he was struck by the subtle change that came into her dark eyes. It lingered for the briefest moment, but the impression he got was lasting. There was something like dread in the far-away look that settled for a few seconds and then lifted. She caught him looking at her, and smiled once more, but nervously. Then her glance went swiftly to the face of James Brood, who was listening to something that Mrs Desmond was saying. It rested there for a short but intense scrutiny, and the smile began to die.

"I am sure I shall be very happy in this dear old house," she said quietly. "Your own mother must have loved it, Frederic."

James Brood started. Unnoticed by the others, his fingers tightened on the gloves he carried in his hand.

"I never knew my mother," said the young man. "She died when I was a baby."

"But of course this was her home, was it not?"

"I don't know," said Frederic uncomfortably. "I suppose so. I—I came here a few years ago, and — —"

"But even though you never knew her, there must still be something here that—that—how shall I say it? I mean, you must feel that she and you were here together years and years ago. One may never have seen his mother, yet he can always feel her. There is something—shall I say spiritual, in — —"

Her husband broke in upon these unwelcome reflections. His voice was curiously harsh.

"Mrs Desmond is waiting, Yvonne."

She drew herself up.

"Are you in such great haste, Mrs Desmond?" she asked in a voice that cut like a knife. Instinctively she glanced at Frederic's face. She saw the muscles of the jaw harden and an angry light leap into his eyes. Instantly her arrogance fell away. "I beg your pardon, Mrs Desmond. I have many bad habits. Now will you kindly show me to my room? I prefer that you and not one of the servants should be my guide. *Au revoir*, Frederic. Till tea-time, James."

Her eyes were sparkling, her husky voice once more full of the appealing quality that could not be denied. The flush of injured pride faded from Mrs Desmond's brow and a faint look of surprise crept into her eyes. She was surprised at her own inclination to overlook the affront, and not by the change in Mrs Brood's manner. She smiled an unspoken pardon and stood aside for the new mistress to pass in front of her. To her further amazement the younger woman laid a hand upon her arm and gave it a gentle, friendly pressure.

The men watched them in silence as they left the room side by side. A moment later they heard the soft laughter of the two women as they mounted the stairs.

Frederic drew a long breath.

"She's splendid, father," he said impulsively.

Brood's face was still clouded. He did not respond to the eager tribute.

Mr Dawes cleared his throat and cast a significant glance toward the dining-room.

"What do you say to a drink to the bride, Jim?" he said, somewhat explosively. He had been silent for a longer period than usual. It wasn't natural for him to be voiceless, even when quite alone.

"Good idea," added Mr Riggs. "I was just thinking of it myself. A health to the bride, my boy, and good luck to you both."

"A glass to prosperty," said Mr Dawes, with a wave of his hand.

"And two for posterity," added Mr Riggs in an ecstasy of triumph.

A flush mounted to Brood's cheek. Young Frederic abruptly turned away.

"Thank you, my friends," said Brood, after a moment. "I'll leave the bumpers to you, if you don't mind. It isn't meet that the groom should drink to himself, and that's what you are suggesting. Go and have your drinks, gentlemen, but leave me out."

They looked disappointed, aggrieved.

"I said posterity," expostulated Mr Riggs. "No harm in your drinking to *that*, is there?"

"Shut up, Riggs," hissed Mr Dawes, nudging him with some violence.

"Oh!" said his friend, with a quick look at Frederic. Then, as if inspired: "Come on, Freddy. Join us. Come and drink to the—to your—er—stepmother." He floundered miserably. "My God!" he gasped under his breath.

"Thank you, Mr Riggs. I'm not drinking," said Frederic.

Dawes conducted Riggs to the dining-room door. There he turned and remarked:

"Stick to that resolution, Freddy. See what old man Riggs has come to! If it wasn't for me and your father he'd be in the gutter."

"That's right, Freddy," agreed Mr Riggs with rare amiability. He felt that he owed something to Frederic in the way of apology.

Father and son faced each other after the old men had disappeared. They were a striking pair, each in his way an example of fine, clean manhood. The father was taller by two inches than the son, and yet Frederic was nearly six feet in his stockings. Both were spare men, erect and gracefully proportioned.

Brood gave out the impression of great strength, of steel sinews, of invincible power; Frederic did not suggest physical strength, and yet he was a clean-limbed, well-built fellow. He had a fine head, a slim body whose every movement proclaimed nervous energy, and a face that denoted temperament of the most pronounced character. His hair was black and straight, growing thickly above the forehead and ears; his eyes were of a deep gray, changeable at the dictates of his emotions. A not unhealthy pallor lay on the surface of his skin, readily submissive to the sensations which produce colour at the slightest provocation. His eyebrows were rather thick, but delicately arched, and the lashes were long. It was not a strong face, nor was it weak; it represented character without force.

On the other hand, James Brood's lean, handsome face was full of power. His gray eyes were keen, steady, compelling, and seldom alight with warmth. His jaw was firm, square, resolute, and the lines that sank heavily into the flesh in his cheeks were put there not by age but by the very vigour of manhood. His hair was quite gray.

Frederic waited for his father to speak. He had ventured a remark before the departure of the old men and it had been ignored. But James Brood had nothing to say.

"She is very attractive, father," said the young man at last, almost wistfully. He did not realise it, but he was groping for sympathy. Brood had been in the house for a quarter of an hour, after an absence of nearly a year, and yet he might have been away no longer than a day for all that he revealed in his attitude toward his son. His greeting had been cold, casual, matter-of-fact. Frederic expected little more than that; still he felt in a vague way that now, if never again, the ice of reserve might be broken between them, if only for a moment. He was ready and willing to do his part.

Brood was studying the young man's face with an intensity that for the moment disconcerted him. He seemed bent on fixing certain features in his mind's eye, as if his memory had once played him false and should not do so again. It was a habit of Brood's, after prolonged separations, to look for something in the boy's face that he wanted to see and yet dreaded, something that might have escaped him when in daily contact with him. Now, at the end of the rather offensive scrutiny, he seemed to shake his head slightly, although one could not have been sure.

"And as charming as she is attractive, Frederic," he said, with a faint flush of the enthusiasm he suppressed.

"Who is she?" asked his son, without realising the bluntness of his question.

"Who *is* she?" repeated his father, raising his eyebrows slightly. "She is Mrs James Brood."

"I—I beg your pardon," stammered Frederic. "I didn't mean to put it in that way. Who was she? Where did you meet her, and—oh, I want to know all there is to tell, father. I've heard nothing. I am naturally curious."

Brood stopped him with a gesture.

"She was Yvonne Lestrange before we were married, Mlle Lestrange; we met some time ago at the house of a mutual friend in Paris. I assure you her references are all that could be desired." His tone was sarcastic.

Frederic flushed.

"I'm sorry I asked the questions, sir," he said stiffly.

Brood suddenly laughed, a quiet laugh that had some trace of humour and a touch of compunction in it.

"I beg your pardon, Frederic. Come up to my room and smoke a cigar with me while I'm changing. I'll tell you about her. She is wonderful."

To his own surprise, and to Frederic's astonishment, he linked his arm in the young man's and started toward the hall. Afterward he was to wonder even more than he wondered then what it was that created the sudden desire to atone for the hurt look he had brought into the eyes of Matilde's son and the odd longing to touch his arm gently.

CHAPTER IV

Lydia met Brood and Frederic at the top of the stairs. She had received the message through Jones and was on her way to dress for tea. The master of the house greeted her most cordially. He was very fond of this lovely, gentle daughter of John Desmond.

Into their association had stolen an intimate note that softened the cold reserve of the man to a marked degree. There was something brave and joyous in this girl that had always appealed to James Brood. He seldom failed to experience a sense of complete relaxation when with her; his hard eyes softened, his stern mouth took on the quiet smile of contentment.

His chief joy was to chat with her over the work he was doing, and to listen to her frank, honest opinions. There was no suggestion of constraint in her manner. She was not afraid of him. That was the thing about her, perhaps, that warmed his stone-cold heart, although he hardly would have admitted it to be the case.

She regarded herself as his secretary, or his amanuensis, in the strict way of speaking, but he considered her to be a friend as well, and treated her with a freedom that was not extended to others.

A faint gleam of astonishment lurked in the girl's eyes as she stood before the two men. Never, in her experience, had there been such an exhibition of friendliness between father and son. A curious throb of joy rushed up from her heart and lodged in her throat. For the first time she found it difficult to respond with composure to Brood's lively comments. Tears were lying close to the surface of her eyes; tears of relief and gratitude. The buoyant expression in Frederic's told a new story. Her heart rejoiced.

"Nonsense!" said Brood, when she announced that she was going in to change her gown. "You never looked so pretty, my dear, as you do at this instant. I want Mrs Brood to see you for the first time just as you are. You are a shirt-waist girl, Lydia. You couldn't be lovelier than you are now. Isn't that true, Frederic?"

"You'll spoil her, father," said Frederic, his face glowing.

Her prettiest frown opposed them.

"But you, after all, you are not women," she said. "Women don't look at each other through masculine eyes. They look at a girl not to see how pretty she is, but to see what it is that makes her pretty."

"But this is to be a family tea-party," protested Brood. "It isn't a function, as the society reporter would say. Come just as you are to please me."

"A tea-party and an autopsy are very much alike, Mr Brood," said she. "One can learn a lot at either. Still, if you'd like to have Mrs Brood see me as I really am, I'll appear *sans* plumage."

"I'd like it," said he promptly. "I am sure you will like each other, Lydia."

"I am glad you did not say we would admire each other," said she quaintly. "You look very happy, Mr Brood," she went on, her eyes bright.

"I believe I *am* happy," said he.

"Then we shall all be happy," was her rejoinder.

She returned to the jade room on the upper floor, where she had been at work on the catalogue. Brood had a very large and valuable collection of rare jade. A catalogue, she knew, would have but little significance, in view of the fact that the collection was not likely to be exhibited to public view. Still it was his whim, and she had found considerable pleasure in carrying out his belated orders.

The jade room, so called, was little more than a large closet off the remarkable room which James Brood was pleased to call his "hiding-place," or, on occasions, his "retreat." No one ventured into either of these rooms except by special permission.

Ranjab, his Indian servant, slept in an adjoining room, and it was whispered about the house that not even James Brood had viewed its interior. This silent, unapproachable man from the mysterious heart of India locked his door when he entered the room and locked it when he came out. No one, not even the master, thought of entering. Mr Dawes in his cups, or out of them, was responsible for the impression that the man kept deadly serpents there. As a matter of fact, Ranjab was a peaceable fellow and desperately afraid of snakes.

Lydia loved the feel of the cold, oily lumps of jade. There were a few pieces of porcelain of extreme rarity and beauty as well, and several priceless bits of cloisonné, but it was the jade she loved. There were two or three hundred objects of various sizes and colours, and all were what might be called museum pieces. To each was attached a tag disclosing certain facts concerning its origin, its history, and the date of its admission to the Brood collection. It appeared to be Lydia's task to set down these dates and facts in chronological order. Her imagination built quaint little stories about each of the ancient figures. She believed in fairies.

She had been at work for half an hour or longer when a noise in the outer room attracted her attention. She had the odd feeling that someone was looking at her through the open door, and swiftly turned.

Except when occupied by Brood, the room was darkened by means of heavy window-hangings; the effect was that produced by the gloaming just before the stars appeared. Objects were shadowy, indistinct, mysterious. The light from the jade room door threw a diverging ray across the full length of the room. In the very centre of this bright strip sat a placid effigy of Buddha that Brood had found in a remote corner of Siam, serenely stolid on top of its thick base of bronze and lacquer, with a shining shrine for a background.

In the dim edge of the shadow, near the door at the far end of the room, Lydia made out the motionless, indistinct figure of a woman. The faint outlines of the face were discernible, but not so the features. For a moment the girl stared at the watcher and then advanced to the door.

"Who is it?" she inquired, peering.

A low, husky voice replied, with a suggestion of laughter in the tones.

"I am exploring the house."

Lydia came forward at once.

"Oh, it is Mrs Brood. I beg your pardon. Shall I switch on the lights?"

"Are there such awful things as electric lights in this wonderful room?" cried the other, disappointed. "I can't believe it of my husband. He couldn't permit anything so bizarre as that."

"They are emergency lights," laughed Lydia. "He never uses them, of course. They are for the servants."

"You are Lydia?"

"Yes, Mrs Brood."

"I have been prowling everywhere. Your good mother deserted me when my maid arrived with Ranjab a short time ago. Isn't this the dread *Bluebeard room?* Shall I lose my head if I am discovered by the ogre?"

The girl felt the spell stealing over her. The low voice of the woman in the shadow was like a sensuous caress. She experienced a sudden longing to be closer to the speaker, to listen for the very intake of her breath.

"You have already been discovered by the ogre, Mrs Brood," said Lydia gaily, "and your head appears to be quite safe."

"Thank you," rather curtly, as if repelling familiarity. It was like a dash of cold water to Lydia's spirits. "You may turn on the lights. I should like to see *you*, Miss Desmond."

The girl crossed the room, passing close to the stranger in the house. The fragrance of a perfume hitherto unknown to her separated itself from the odour of sandalwood that always filled the place; it was soft, delicate, refreshing. It was like a breath of cool, sweet air filtering into a close, stuffy enclosure. One could not help drawing in a long, full breath, as if the lungs demanded its revivifying qualities.

A soft, red glow began to fill the room as Lydia pulled the cord near the door. There was no clicking sound, no sharp contact of currents; the light came up gradually, steadily, until the whole space was drenched with its refulgence. There were no shadows. Every nook and corner seemed to fill with the warm, pleasant hue of the setting sun and yet no visible means appeared.

As the light grew brighter and brighter the eyes of the stranger swept the room with undisguised wonder in their depths.

"How extraordinary!" she murmured, and then turned swiftly toward the girl. "Where does it come from? I can see no lights. And see! There are no shadows, not even beneath the table yonder. It—it is uncanny—but, oh, how lovely!"

Lydia was staring at her with wide-open eyes, frankly astonished. The eager, excited gleam vanished from Mrs Brood's lovely eyes. They narrowed slightly.

"Why do you stare at me?" she demanded.

"I beg your pardon," cried the girl, blushing.

"I—I couldn't help it, Mrs Brood. Why, you are young!" The exclamation burst from her lips.

"Young?" queried the other, frowning.

"I—I expected——" began Lydia, and stopped in pretty confusion.

"I see. You expected a middle-aged lady? And why, pray, should James Brood marry a middle-aged person?"

"I—I don't know. I'm sorry if I have offended you."

Mrs Brood smiled, a gay, pleased little smile that revealed her small, even teeth.

"You haven't offended me, my dear," she said. "You offend my husband by thinking so ill of him, that's all." She took the girl in from head to foot with critical eyes. "He said you were very pretty and very lovable. You are lovely. Isn't it a horrid word? Pretty! No one wants to be pretty. Yes, you are just what I expected."

Lydia was the taller of the two women—a matter of two inches perhaps—and yet she had the curious feeling that she was looking upward as she gazed into the other's eyes. It was the way Mrs Brood held herself.

"He has known me since I was a little girl," she said, as if to account for Brood's favourable estimate.

"And he knew your mother before you were born," said the other. "She, too, is—shall I say pretty?"

"My mother isn't pretty, Mrs Brood," said Lydia, conscious of a sudden feeling of resentment.

"She is handsome," said Mrs Brood with finality. Sending a swift glance around the room, she went on: "My husband delights in having beautiful things about him. He doesn't like the ugly things of this world."

Lydia flinched, she knew not why. There was a sting to the words, despite the languidness with which they were uttered.

Risking more than she suspected, she said:

"He never considers the cost of a thing, Mrs Brood, if its beauty appeals to him." Mrs Brood gave her a quizzical, half-puzzled look. "You have only to look about you for the proof. This one room represents a fortune." The last was spoken hastily.

"How old are you, Miss Desmond?" The question came abruptly.

"I am nineteen."

"You were surprised to find me so young. Will it add to your surprise if I tell you that I am ten years older than you?"

"I should have said not more than three or four years."

"I am twenty-nine—seven years older than my husband's son."

"It doesn't seem credible."

"Are you wondering why I tell you my age?"

"Yes," said Lydia bluntly.

"In order that you may realise that I am ten years wiser than you, and that you may not again make the mistake of under-estimating my intelligence."

The colour faded from Lydia's face. She grew cold from head to foot. Involuntarily she moved back a pace. The next instant, to her unbounded surprise, Mrs Brood's hands were outstretched in a gesture of appeal, and a quick, wistful smile took the place of the imperious stare.

"There! I am a nasty, horrid thing. Forgive me. Come! Don't be stubborn. Shake hands with me and say that you're sorry I said what I did."

It was a quaint way of putting it, and her voice was so genuinely appealing that Lydia, after a moment's hesitation, extended her hands. Mrs Brood grasped them in hers and gripped them tightly.

"I think I should like to know that you are my friend, Lydia. Has it occurred to you that I am utterly without friends in this great city of yours? I have my husband, that is all. Among all these millions of people there is not one who knows that I exist. Isn't it appalling? Can you imagine such a condition? There is not one to whom I can give an honest smile. Nor am I likely to have many friends here. Indeed, I shall not lift my finger to gain them. You will know me better one day, Lydia, and you will understand. But now—to-day, to-morrow—now—I must have someone to whom I may offer my friendship and have something to hope for in return."

Lydia could hardly credit her ears.

"I am sure you will have many friends, Mrs Brood," she began, vaguely uncomfortable.

"I don't want them," cried the other sharply. "Poof! Are friends to be made in a day? No! Admirers, yes. Enemies, yes. But friends, no. I shall have no real friends here. It isn't possible. I am not like your people. I cannot become like them. I shall know people and like them, no doubt, but—poof! I shall not have them for friends."

"I can't understand why you want me for a friend," said Lydia stiffly. "My position here is not what——"

Mrs Brood had not released the girl's hands. She interrupted her now by dropping them as if they were of fire.

"You don't want to be my friend?"

"Yes, yes—of course——"

"You are my husband's friend?"

"Certainly, Mrs Brood. He is *my* friend."

"What is *your* position here?"

Lydia's face was flaming.

"I thought you knew. I am his secretary, if I may be allowed to dignify my——"

"And you are Frederic's friend?"

"Yes."

"Despite your position?"

"I don't understand you, Mrs Brood."

Once more the warm, enchanting smile broke over the face of the other.

"Isn't it perfectly obvious, Lydia?"

The girl could no more withstand the electric charm of the woman than she could have fought off the sunshine. She was bewildered and completely fascinated.

"It's—it is very good of you," she murmured, her own eyes softening as they looked into the deep velvety ones that would not be denied. Even as she wondered whether she could ever really like this magnetic creature, she felt herself surrendering to the spell of her. "But perhaps you will not like me when you know me better."

"Perhaps," said Mrs Brood calmly, almost indifferently, and dismissed the subject. "What an amazing room! One can almost feel the presence of the genii that created it at the wish of the man with the enchanted lamp. As a rule, Oriental rooms are abominations, but this—ah, this is not an Oriental room after all. It is a part of the East itself—of the real East. I have sat in emperors' houses out there, my dear, and I have slept in the palaces of kings. I have seen just such things as these, and I know that they could not have been transported to this room except by magic. My husband is a magician."

"These came from the palaces of kings, Mrs Brood," said Lydia enthusiastically. "Kings in the days when kings were real. This rug——"

"I know," interrupted the other. "It was woven by five generations of royal weavers. Each of these borders represents the work of a lifetime. It is the carpet of rubies, and a war was prolonged for years because an emperor would not give it up to the foe who coveted it above all other riches. His heart's blood stains it to this day. His empire was wiped out by the relentless foe, his very name effaced, but the heart's blood still is there, Lydia. That can never be wiped out. My husband told me the story. It must have cost him a fortune."

"It is worth a fortune," said Lydia.

A calculating squint had come into Mrs Brood's eyes while she was speaking. To Lydia it appeared as if she were trying to fix upon the value of the wonderful carpet.

"A collector has offered him—how much? A hundred thousand dollars, is not that it? Ah, how rich he must be!"

"The collector you refer to— —"

"I was referring to my husband," said Mrs Brood, unabashed. "He is very rich, isn't he?"

Lydia managed to conceal her annoyance. "I think not, as American fortunes are rated."

"It doesn't matter," said the other carelessly. "I have my own fortune. And it is not my face," she added with her quick smile. "Now let us look farther. I must see all of these wonderful things. We will not be missed, and it is still half an hour till tea-time. My husband is now telling his son all there is to be told about me—who and what I am, and how he came to marry me. Not, mind you, how I came to marry him, but—the other way round. It's the way with men past middle age."

Lydia hesitated before speaking.

"Mr Brood does not confide in Frederic. I am afraid they have but little in common. Oh, I shouldn't have said that!"

Mrs Brood regarded her with narrowing eyes.

"He doesn't confide in Frederic?" she repeated in the form of a question. Her voice seemed lower than before.

"I'm sorry I spoke as I did, Mrs Brood," said the girl, annoyed with herself.

"Is there a reason why he should dislike his son?" asked the other, regarding her fixedly.

"Of course not," cried poor Lydia.

There was a moment of silence.

"Some day, Lydia, you will tell me about Mr Brood's other wife."

"She died many years ago," said the girl evasively.

"I know," said Mrs Brood. "Still, I should like to hear more of the woman he could not forget in all those years—until he met me."

She grew silent and preoccupied, a slight frown marking her forehead as she resumed her examination of the room and its contents.

It is quite impossible adequately to describe the place in which the two women met for the first time. Suffice to say, it was long, narrow, and, being next below the roof, low-ceilinged. The walls were hung with rich, unusual tapestries whose subdued tones seemed to lure one back to the undimmed glory of Solomon's days, to the even more remote realms of those gods and goddesses on whom our fancy thrives despite the myths they were.

Silks of a weight and lustre that taxed credulity; golden threads interweaving gems of the purest ray; fringe and galloons with the solemn waste of ages in their thin, lovely sheen; over all the soft radiance of an *Arabian Night* and the gentle touch of a *Scheherazade*. Here hung transported the fabulous splendours of Ind, the shimmering treasures of Ming, and the loot of the *Forty Thieves*.

The ceiling, for want of a better name, was no less than a canopy constructed out of a single rug of enormous dimensions and incalculable value, gleaming with the soft colours of the rainbow, shedding a serene iridescence over the entire room to shame the light of day.

The furniture, the trappings, the ornaments throughout were of a most unusual character. A distinctly regal atmosphere prevailed. No article there but had come from the palace of a ruler in the East, from the massive gold and lacquered table to the tiniest piece of bronze or the lowliest hassock. Chairs that had served as thrones, chests that had contained the treasures of potentates, robes that had covered the bodies of kings and queens, couches on which had nestled the favourites of sultans, screens and mirrors that had reflected the jewels of an empire—*all* were here to feed the senses with dreams imperial.

Great lanterns hung suspended beside the shrine at the end of the room, but were now unlighted. On the table at which Brood professed to work stood a huge lamp with a lacelike screen of gold. When lighted, a soft, mellow glow oozed through the shade to create a circle of golden brilliance over a radius that extended but little beyond the edge of the table, yet reached to the benign countenance of Buddha close by.

Over all this fairylike splendour reigned the serene, melting influence of the god to whom James Brood was wont to confess himself. The spell of the golden image dominated everything.

In the midst of this magnificence moved the two women—one absurdly out of touch with her surroundings, yet a thing of beauty; the other blending intimately with the warm tones that enveloped her. She was lithe, sinuous, with the grace of the most seductive of dancers. Her dark eyes reflected the mysteries of the Orient; her pale, smooth skin shone with the clearness of alabaster; the crimson in her lips was like the fresh stain of blood; the very fragrance of her person seemed to steal out of the unknown. She was a part of the marvellous setting, a gem among gems.

She had attired herself in a dull Indian-red afternoon gown of chiffon. The very fabric seemed to cling to her supple body with a sensuous joy of contact. Even Lydia, who watched her with appraising eyes, experienced a swift, unaccountable desire to hold this intoxicating creature close to her own body.

There were two windows in the room, broad openings that ran from near the floor almost to the edge of the canopy. They were so heavily curtained that the light of day failed to penetrate to the interior of the apartment. Mrs Brood approached one of these windows. Drawing the curtains apart, she let in an ugly gray light from the outside world. The illusion was spoiled at once.

"How cold and pallid the world really is!" she cried, a shiver passing over her slim body.

The sky above the housetops was bleak and drab in the waning light of late afternoon. Over the summits of loft-buildings to the south and west hung the smoke from the river beyond, smudgy clouds that neither drifted nor settled.

She looked down into a sort of courtyard and garden that might have been transplanted from distant Araby. Uttering an exclamation of wonder, she turned to Lydia.

"Is this New York or am I bewitched?"

"Mr Brood transformed the old carriage yard into a—I think Mr Dawes calls it a Persian garden. It is rather bleak in winter-time, Mrs Brood, but in the summer it is really enchanting. See, across the court on the second floor, where the windows are lighted, those are your rooms. It is an enormous house, you'll find. Do you see the little balcony outside your windows, and the vines creeping up to it? You can't imagine how sweet it is of a summer night with the moon and stars——"

"But how desolate it looks to-day, with the dead vines and the colourless stones! Ugh!"

She dropped the curtains. The soft, warm glow of the room came back, and she sighed with relief.

"I hate things that are dead," she said.

At the sound of a soft tread and the gentle rustle of draperies, they turned. Ranjab, the Hindu, was crossing the room toward the small door which gave entrance to his closet. He paused for an instant before the image of Buddha, but did not drop to his knees, as all devout Buddhists do. Mrs

Brood's hand fell lightly upon Lydia's arm. The man turned toward them a second or two later.

His dark, handsome face was hard set and emotionless as he bowed low to the new mistress of the house. The fingers closed tightly on Lydia's arm. Then he smiled upon the girl, a glad smile of devotion. His swarthy face was transfigured. A moment later he unlocked his door and passed into the other room. The key turned in the lock with a slight rasp.

"I do not like that man," said Mrs Brood. Her voice was low and her eyes were fixed steadily on the closed door.

CHAPTER V

The ensuing fortnight brought the expected changes in the household. James Brood, to the surprise of not only himself, but others, lapsed into a curious state of adolescence. His infatuation was complete. The once dominant influence of the man seemed to slink away from him as the passing days brought up the new problems of life. Where he had lived to command he now was content to serve.

His friends, his son, his servants viewed the transformation with wonder, not to say apprehension. It was not difficult to understand his infatuation for the—shall we say enchantress? He was not the only one there to fall under the spell. But it was almost unbelievable that he should submit to thraldom with the complacency of a weakling.

Love, which had been lying bruised and unconscious within him for twenty years and more, arose from its stupor and became a thing to play with, as one would play with a child. The old, ugly vistas melted into dreamy, adolescent contemplations of a paradise in which he could walk hand-in-hand with the future and find that the ghosts of the past no longer attended him along the once weary way.

It would not be true to say that the remarkable personality of the man had suffered. He was still the man of steel, but re-tempered. The rigid broadsword was made over into the fine, flexible blade of Toledo. He could be bent but not broken.

It pleased him to submit to Yvonne's commands,

Not that they were arduous or peremptory; on the contrary, they were suggestions in which his own comfort and pleasure appeared to be the inspiration. He found something like delight in being rather amiably convinced of his own shortcomings; in learning from her that his life up to this hour had been a sadly mismanaged affair; that there were soft, fertile spots in his heart where things would grow in spite of him. He enjoyed the unique spectacle of himself in the process of being made over to fit ideals that he would have scorned a few months before.

She was too wise to demand, too clever to resort to cajolery. She was a Latin. Diplomacy was hers as a birthright. Complaints, appeals, sulks would have gained nothing from James Brood. It would not have occurred to her to employ these methods. From the day she entered the house she was its mistress. She was sure of her ground, sure of herself, fettered by no sense of doubt as to her position there, bound by no feminine notion of gratitude to man, as many women are who find themselves married. It might almost be said of her that she ruled without making a business of it.

To begin with, she miraculously transferred the sleeping quarters of Messrs Dawes and Riggs from the second floor front to the third floor back without arousing the slightest sign of antagonism on the part of the crusty old gentlemen who had occupied one of the choice rooms in the house with uninterrupted security for a matter of nine or ten years. This was a feat that James Brood himself would never have tried to accomplish. They had selected this room at the first instant of occupation, because it provided something of a view up and down the street from the big bow window, and they wouldn't evacuate.

Mrs Brood explained the situation to them so graciously, so convincingly, that they even assisted the servants in moving their heterogeneous belongings to the small, remote room on the third floor, and applauded her plan to make a large sitting-room of the chamber they were deserting. It did not occur to them for at least three days that they had been imposed upon, cheated, maltreated, insulted, and then it was too late. The decorators were in the big room on the second floor.

Perhaps they would not have arrived at a sense of realisation even then if it had not come out in the course of conversation that it was not to be a *general* sitting-room, but one with reservations. The discovery of what they secretly were pleased to call duplicity brought an abrupt end to the period of abstemiousness that had lasted since the day of her arrival, when, out of courtesy to the bride, they had turned their backs upon the tipple.

Now, however, the situation was desperate. She had tricked them with her wily politeness. They had been betrayed by the wife of their bosom friend. Is it small cause for wonder, then, that the poor gentlemen as manfully turned back to the tipple and got gloriously, garrulously drunk in the middle of the afternoon and also in the middle of the library, where tea was to have been served to a few friends asked in to meet the bride?

The next morning a fresh edict was issued. It came from James Brood, and it was so staggering that the poor gentlemen were loath to believe their ears. As a result of this new command they began to speak of Mrs Brood in the privacy of their own room as "that woman." Of course, it was entirely due to her mischievous, malevolent influence that a spineless husband put forth the order that they were to have nothing more to drink while they remained in his house.

This command was modified to a slight extent later on. Brood felt sorry for the victims. He loved them, and he knew that their pride was injured a great deal more than their appetite. In its modified form the edict allowed them a small drink in the morning and another at bedtime, but the doses (as they sarcastically called them) were to be administered by Jones the butler, who held the key to the situation and—the sideboard.

"Is this a dispensary?" wailed Mr Dawes in weak horror. "Are we to stand in line and solicit the common necessities of life? Answer me, Riggs! Confound you, don't stand there like a wax figure! Say something!"

Mr Riggs shook his head bleakly.

"Poor Jim," was all that he said, and rolled his eyes heavenward.

Mr Dawes reflected. After many minutes the tears started down his rubicund cheeks. "Poor old Jim," he sighed. And after that they looked upon Mrs Brood as the common enemy of all three.

The case of Mrs John Desmond was disposed of in a summary but tactful manner.

"If Mrs Desmond is willing to remain, James, as housekeeper instead of friend, all well and good," said Mrs Brood, discussing the matter in the seclusion of her boudoir. "I doubt, however, whether she can descend to that. You have spoiled her, my dear."

Brood was manifestly pained and uncomfortable.

"She was the wife of my best friend, Yvonne. I have never permitted her to feel——"

"Ah," she interrupted, "the wives of best friends! Nearly every man has the wife of a best friend somewhere in his life's history." She shook her head at him with mock mournfulness.

He flushed. "I trust you do not mean to imply that——"

"I know what you would say. No, I do not mean anything of the sort. Still, you now have a wife of your own. Is it advisable to have also the wife of a best friend?"

"Really, Yvonne, all this sounds very suspicious and—unpleasant. Mrs Desmond is the soul of——"

"My dear man, why should you defend her? I am not accusing her. I am merely going into the ethics of the situation. If you can forget that Mrs Desmond is the wife of your friend and come to regard her as a servant in your establishment, no one will be more happy than I to have her about the place. She is fine, she is competent, she is a lady. But she is not my equal here. Can't you understand?"

He was thoughtful for a moment.

"I dare say you are right. The conditions are peculiar. I can't go to her and say that she must consider herself as—oh, no, that would be impossible."

"I should like to have Mrs Desmond as my friend, not as my housekeeper," said his wife simply.

"By Jove, and that's just what I should like," he cried.

"There is but one way, you know."

"She must be one or the other, eh?"

"Precisely," she said with firmness. "In my country, James, the wives of best friends haven't the same moral standing that they appear to have in yours. Oh, don't scowl so! Shall I tell you again that I do not mean to reflect on Mrs Desmond's virtue—or discretion? Far from it. If she is to be my friend, she cannot be your housekeeper. That's the point. Has she any means of her own? Can she——"

"She has a small income, and an annuity which I took out for her soon after her poor husband's death. We were the closest of friends——"

"I understand, James. You are very generous and very loyal. I quite understand. Losing her position here, then, will not be a hardship?"

"No," said he soberly.

"I am quite competent, James," she said brightly. "You will not miss her, I am sure."

"It isn't that, Yvonne," he sighed. "Mrs Desmond and Lydia have been factors in my life for so long that—— But, of course, that is neither here nor there. I will explain the situation to her to-morrow. She will understand."

"Thank you, James. You are really quite reasonable."

"Are you laughing at me, darling?"

She gave him one of her searching, unfathomable glances, and she smiled with roguish mirth.

"Isn't it your mission in life to amuse and entertain me?"

"I love you, Yvonne. Good God, how I love you!" he cried abruptly.

His eyes burned with a sudden flame of passion as he bent over her. His face quivered; his whole being tingled with the fierce spasm of an uncontrollable desire to crush the warm, adorable body to his breast in the supreme ecstasy of possession.

She surrendered herself to his passionate embrace. A little later she withdrew herself from his arms, her lips still quivering with the fierceness of his kisses. Her eyes, dark with wonder and perplexity, regarded his transfigured face for a long, tense moment.

"Is this love, James?" she whispered. "Is this the real, true love?"

"What else, in Heaven's name, can it be?" he cried. He was sitting upon the arm of her chair, looking down at the strangely pallid face.

"But should love have the power to frighten me?"

"Frighten, my darling?"

"Oh, it is not you who are frightened," she cried. "You are the man. But I—ah, I am only the woman."

He stared. "What an odd way to put it, dear."

Then he drew back, struck by the curious gleam of mockery in her eyes.

"Was it like this twenty-five years ago?" she asked.

"Yvonne!"

"Did you love her—like this?"

He managed to smile. "Are you jealous?"

"Tell me about her."

His face hardened. "Some other time, not now."

"But you loved her, didn't you?"

"Don't be silly, dear."

"And she loved you. If you loved her as you love me, she could not have helped——"

"Please, please, Yvonne!" he exclaimed, a dull red setting in his cheek.

"You have never told me her name——"

He faced her, his eyes as cold as steel. "I may as well tell you now, Yvonne, that her name is never mentioned in this house."

She seemed to shrink down farther in the chair.

"Why?" she asked, an insistent note in her voice.

"It isn't necessary to explain." He walked away from her to the window and stood looking out over the bleak little courtyard. Neither spoke for many minutes, and yet he knew that her questioning gaze was upon him and that when he turned to her again she would ask still another question. He tried to think of something to say that would turn her away from this hated subject.

"Isn't it time for you to dress, dearest? The Gunnings live pretty far up north and the going will be bad with Fifth Avenue piled up with snow——"

"Doesn't Frederic ever mention his mother's name?" came the question that he feared before it was uttered.

"I am not certain that he knows her name," said he levelly. The knuckles of his hands, clenched tightly behind his back, were white. "He has never heard me utter it."

She looked at him darkly. There was something in her eyes that caused him to shift his own steady gaze uncomfortably. He could not have explained what it was, but it gave him a curiously uneasy feeling, as of impending peril. It was not unlike the queer, inexplicable, though definite, sensing of danger that more than once he had experienced in the silent, tranquil depths of great forests.

"But you loved her just the same, James, up to the time you met me. Is not that true?"

"No!" he exclaimed loudly. "It is not true."

"I wonder what could have happened to make you so bitter toward her," she went on, still watching him through half-closed eyes. "Was she unfaithful to you? Was——"

"Good God, Yvonne!" he cried, an angry light jumping into his eyes— the eyes that so recently had been ablaze with love.

"Don't be angry, dearest," she cried plaintively. "We Europeans speak of such things as if they were mere incidents. I forget that you Americans take them seriously, as tragedies."

He controlled himself with an effort. The pallor in his face would have alarmed anyone but her.

"We must never speak of—of that again, Yvonne," he said, a queer note of hoarseness in his voice. "Never, do you understand?" He was very much shaken.

"Forgive me," she pleaded, stretching out her hand to him. "I am foolish, but I did not dream that I was being cruel or unkind. Perhaps, dear, it is because I am—jealous."

"There is no one—nothing to be jealous of," he said, passing a hand over his moist brow. Then he drew nearer and took her hand in his. It was as cold as ice.

"Your hand is cold, darling," he cried.

"And yours, too," she said, looking down at their clasped hands, a faint smile on her lips. Suddenly she withdrew her fingers from his strong grip. A slight shiver ran over her frame. "Ugh! I don't like cold hands!"

He laughed rather desolately. "Suppose that I were to say the same to you?"

"I am temperamental; you are not," she replied coolly. "Sit down, dear. Let us be warm again."

"Shall I have the fire replenished — —"

"No," she said with her slow smile, "you don't understand."

He lounged again on the arm of her chair. She leaned back and sighed contentedly, the smile on her red lips growing sweeter with each breath that she took. He felt his blood warming once more.

For a long time they sat thus, looking into each other's eyes without speaking. He was trying to fathom the mystery that lurked at the bottom of those smiling wells; she, on the other hand, deluded herself with the idea that she was reading his innermost thought.

"I have been considering the advisability of sending Frederic abroad for a year or two," said he at last.

She started. She had been far from right in her reading.

"Now? This winter?"

"Yes. He has never been abroad."

"Indeed? And he is half European, too. It seems — forgive me, James. Really, you know, I cannot always keep my thoughts from slipping out. You shouldn't expect it, dear."

"How did you know that his — his mother was a European?" he inquired abruptly.

"Dear me! What manner of woman do you think I am? Without curiosity? I should be a freak. I have inquired of Mrs Desmond. There was no harm in that."

"What did she tell you? But no! It doesn't matter. We shan't discuss it. We — —"

"She told me little or nothing," she broke in quickly. "You may rest quite easy, James."

"Upon my word, Yvonne, I don't understand — —"

"Let us speak of Frederic."

"I suppose it is only natural that you should inquire," he said resignedly.

"Of my servants," she added pointedly.

He flushed slightly. "I dare say I deserve the rebuke. It will not be necessary to pursue that line of inquiry, however. I shall tell you the story myself some day, Yvonne. Will you not bear with me?"

She met the earnest appeal in his eyes with a slight frown of annoyance.

"Who is to tell me the wife's side of the story?"

The question was like a blow to him. He stared at her as if he had not heard aright. Before he could speak she went on coolly.

"I dare say there are two sides to it, James. It's usually the case."

He winced. "There is but one side to this one," he said, a harsh note in his voice.

"That is why I began my inquiries with Mrs Desmond," she said enigmatically. "But I shan't pursue them any farther. You love *me*; that is all I care to know—or that I require."

"I *do* love you," he said, almost imploringly. She stroked his gaunt cheek. "Then we may let the other woman—go hang, eh?"

He felt the cold sweat start on his brow. Her callous remark slashed his finer sensibilities like the thrust of a dagger. He tried to laugh, but only succeeded in producing a painful grimace.

"And now," she went on, as if the matter were fully disposed of, "we will discuss something tangible, eh? Frederic."

"Yes," said he, rather dazedly. "Frederic."

"I am very, very fond of your son, James," she said. "How proud you must be to have such a son."

He eyed her narrowly. How much of the horrid story did she know? How much of it had John Desmond told to his wife?

"I am surprised at your liking him, Yvonne. He is what I'd call a difficult young man."

"I haven't found him difficult."

"Morbid and unresponsive."

"Not by nature, however. There is a joyousness, a light-heartedness in his character that has never got beyond the surface until now, James."

"Until now?"

"Yes. And you talk of sending him away. Why?"

"He has wanted to go abroad for years. This is a convenient time for him to go."

"But I am quite sure he will not care to go at present—not for a while, at least."

"And why not, may I ask?"

"Because he is in love."

"In love!" he exclaimed, his jaw setting hard.

"He is in love with Lydia."

"I'll put a stop to that!"

"And why, may I ask?" she mimicked.

"Because—why——" he burst out, but instantly collected himself. "He is not in a position to marry, that's all."

"Financially?"

He swallowed hard. "Yes."

"Poof!" she exclaimed, dismissing the obstacle with a wave of her slim hand. "A cigarette, please. There is another reason why he shouldn't go—an excellent one."

"The reason you've already given is sufficient to convince me that he ought to go at once. What is the other one, pray?"

She lighted a cigarette from the match he held. "What would you say if I were to tell you that I object to his going away—at present?"

"I should ask the very obvious question."

"Because I like him, I want him to like me, and I shall be very lonely without him," she answered calmly.

"You are frank, to say the least," said he, laughing.

"And serious. I don't want him to go away at present. Later on, yes; but not now. I shall need him, James."

"You will be lonely, you say."

"Certainly. You forget that I am young."

"I see," said he, a sudden pain in his heart. "Perhaps it would be more to the point if you were to say that I forget that I am old."

She laughed. It was a soft, musical laugh that strangely stilled the tumult in his breast.

"You are younger than Frederic," she said. "Unless we do something to prevent it, your son will be an old man before he is thirty. Don't send him away now, James. Let me have him for a while. I mean it, dear. He is a lonely boy, and I know what it is to be lonely."

"You?" he cried. "Why, you've never known anything but— —"

"One can be lonely even in the heart of a throng," she said cryptically. "No, James, I will not have him sent away."

He resented the imputation. "Why do you say that I am sending him away?"

"Because you are," she replied boldly.

He was silent for a moment. "We will leave it to Frederic," he said.

Her face brightened. "That is all I ask. He will stay."

There was another pause. "You two have become very good friends, Yvonne."

"He is devoted to me."

"Don't spoil him in making him over," he said dryly.

She blew cigarette—smoke in his face and laughed. There was a knock at the door.

"Come in!" she called.

Frederic entered.

CHAPTER VI

Acertain element of gaiety invaded the staid old house in these days. The new mistress was full of life and the joy of living. She was accustomed to adulation, she was used to the tumult of society. Her life, since she left the convent school, evidently had been one in which rest, except physical, was unknown.

Yvonne Lestrange, in a way, had been born to purple and fine linen. She had never known deprivation of any description. Neither money, position, nor love had been denied her during the few years in which her charm and beauty had flashed across the great European capitals, penetrating even to the recesses of royal courts.

It is doubtful if James Brood knew very much concerning her family when he proposed marriage to her, but it is certain that he did not care. He first saw her at the home of a British nobleman, but did not meet her. Something in the vivid, brilliant face of the woman made a deep and lasting impression on him. There was an instant when their eyes met through an opening in the throng which separated them. He was not only conscious of the fact that he was staring at her, but that she was looking at him in a curiously penetrating way.

There was a mocking smile on her lips at the time. He saw it fade away, even as the crowd came between. He knew that the smile had not been intended for him, but for someone of the eager cavaliers who surrounded her, and yet there was something singularly direct in the look she gave him.

Later on he made inquiries of his host, with whom he had hunted big game in Africa, and learned that she was a guest in the home of the Russian ambassador. He did not see her again until they met in the south of France a few months later. On this occasion they were guests at the same house, and he took her into dinner. He had not forgotten her, and it gratified him immensely to discover that she remembered him.

That single glance in the duke's house proved to be a fatal one for both. They were married inside of a month. The virile, confident American had conquered where countless suppliants of a more or less noble character had gone down to defeat.

He asked but one question of her; she asked none of him. The fact that she was the intimate friend and associate of the woman in whose home he met her was sufficient proof of her standing in society, although that would have counted for little so far as Brood was concerned.

She was the daughter of a baron; she had spent much of her life in Paris, coming from St Petersburg when a young girl; and she was an orphan with an independent fortune of her own.

Her home in Paris, where she had lived with some degree of permanence for the past four or five years, was shared with an estimable, though impoverished, lady of rank, the Countess de Rochambert, of middle age and undeniable qualifications as a chaperon, even among those who are prone to laugh at locksmiths. Such common details as these came to Brood in the natural way and were not derived from any effort on his part to secure information concerning Mlle Lestrange. Like the burned child, he asked a question which harked back to an unforgotten pain.

"Have you ever loved a man deeply, devotedly, Yvonne—so deeply that there is pain in the thought of him?"

She replied without hesitation.

"There is no such man, James. You may be sure of that."

"I am confident that I can hold your love against the future, but no man is vital enough to compete with the past. Love doesn't really die, you know. If a man cannot hold a woman's love against all new-comers, he deserves to lose it. It doesn't follow, however, that he can protect himself against the man who appears out of the past and claims his own."

"You speak as though the past had played you an evil trick," she said.

He did not mince words.

"Years ago a man came out of the past and took from me the woman I loved and cherished."

"Your—your wife?" she asked in a voice suddenly lowered.

"Yes," he said quietly.

She was silent for a long time.

"I wonder at your courage in taking the risk again," she said.

"I think I wonder at it myself," said he. "No, I am not afraid," he went on, as if convincing himself that there was no risk. "I shall make you love me to the end, Yvonne. I am not afraid. But why do you not ask me for all the wretched story?"

"It is not unlike all stories of its kind, my dear," she said with an indifference that amazed him. "They are all alike. Why should I ask? The wife takes up with an old lover; she deceives her husband; the world either does or does not find out about it; the home is wrecked; the husband takes to drink; the wife pretends she is happy; the lover takes to women; and the world goes on just the same in spite of them. Sometimes the husband kills. It is of no moment. Sometimes the wife destroys herself. It is a trifle. The whole business is like the magazine story that is for ever being continued in our next. No, I do not ask you for your story, James. Some time you may tell me, but not to-day. I shouldn't mind hearing it if it were an original tale, but God knows it isn't. It's as old as the Nile. But you may tell me more about your son. Is he like you, or like his mother?"

Brood's lips were compressed.

"I can't say that he is like either of us," he said shortly.

She raised her eyebrows slightly.

"Ah," she said. "That makes quite a difference. Perhaps, after all, I shall be interested in the story." Her manner was so casual, so serenely, matter-of-fact, that he could hardly restrain the sharp exclamation of annoyance that rose to his lips.

He bit his lip and allowed the frank insinuation to go unanswered. He consoled himself with the thought that she must have spoken in jest without intention. He had the uncomfortable feeling that she would make light of his story, too, when the time came for revelations. A curious doubt took root in his mind: Would he ever be able to understand the nature of this woman whom he loved and who appeared to love him so unreservedly? As time went on the doubt became a conviction. She proved to be utterly beyond Brood's comprehension.

The charm and beauty of the new mistress of James Brood's heart and home was to become the talk of the town. Already, in the first month of her reign, she had drawn to the old house the attention not only of the parasites who feed on novelty, but of families that had long since given up Brood as a representative figure in the circle into which he had been born.

He had dropped out of their lives so completely in the passing years that no one took the trouble to interest himself in the man's affairs. His self-effacement had been complete. The story of his ill-fated marriage was an almost forgotten page in the history of the town.

Old friends now cudgelled their brains to recall the details of the break between him and the first Mrs Brood, who, they were bound to remember, was also beautiful, fascinating, and an adornment to the rather exclusive circle in which they moved. No one could point to the real cause of the separation, however, for the excellent reason that the true conditions were never revealed to anyone outside the four walls of the house from which she was banished.

Memory merely brought to mind the fact that the young husband became a wanderer on the face of the earth, and that his once joyous face was an almost forgotten object.

Brood, in the full pride of possession, awoke to the astounding realisation that he wanted people to envy him this wonderful creature. He wanted men to covet her! He longed to have the world see her at his side, and to feel that the world was saying: "She belongs to James Brood."

It was not the cheap, ordinary New York society, the insufferably rich and vulgar of the metropolis that he sought to conquer, but the fine old families with whom rests the real verdict. He knew that those families were not many in these days of haste and waste, but he also knew that the rush of frivolity had not weakened their position. Their word was still the law. Serenely confident, he revealed his wife to the few, and waited.

It cannot be said that she conquered, for that would be to imply design on her part. Possibly she considered the game unworthy of the effort. For, in truth, Yvonne Brood despised Americans. She made small pretence of liking them. The rather closely knit circle of Parisian aristocracy which she affected is known to tolerate, but not to invite, the society of even the best of Americans.

She was no larger than her environment. Her views upon and her attitude toward the Americans were not created by her but for her. The fact that James Brood had reached the inner shrine of French self-worship no doubt put him in a class apart from all other Americans, so far as she was concerned. At least it may account for an apparent inconsistency, in that she married him without much hesitation.

She welcomed the admiration and attention of the friends he brought to the house by one means or another during the first few weeks. If she was surprised to find them cultured, clever, agreeable specimens, she failed to mention the discovery to him. They amused her and therefore served a purpose. She charmed them in exchange for the tribute they paid to her.

Those whom she liked the least she took no pains to please; in fact, she endured them so politely that while they may have secretly resented her indifference, they could do no less than openly profess admiration for her. She offended no one, yet she managed with amazing adroitness to rid herself of the bores. It happened, however, that the so-called bores were the very people that Brood particularly wanted her to cultivate. She found them stupid, but respectable.

They were for ever telling her that she would like New York when she got used to it.

Her warmest friend and admirer—one might almost say slave—was Frederic Brood. She had transformed him. He was no longer the silent, moody youth of other days, but an eager, impetuous playmate, whose principal object in life was to amuse her. If anyone had tried to convince him that he could have regarded Mrs Desmond's dethronement and departure with equanimity he would have protested with all the force at his command. But that would have been a month ago!

When the time came for his old friend to leave the house over which she had presided for ten of the gentlest years of his life, his heart was sore and his throat was tight with pain, but he accepted the inevitable with a resignation that once would have been impossible.

From the outset he realised that Mrs Desmond would have to go. At first he rebelled within himself against the unspoken edict. Afterward he was surprised to find that he regarded himself as selfish in even wishing that she might stay, when it was so palpably evident that the situation could not long remain pleasant for either Mrs Desmond or Mrs Brood. He saw Lydia and her mother leave without the slightest doubt in his mind that it was all for the best.

The Desmonds took a small apartment just around the corner from Brood's home, in a side street, and in the same block. Their windows looked down into the courtyard in the rear of Brood's home. Frederic assisted them in putting their new home in order. It was great fun for Lydia and him, this building of what they were pleased to call "a nest."

Lydia may have seen the cloud in their sky, but he did not. To him the world was bright and gladsome, without a shadow to mar its new beauty. He was enthusiastic, eager, excited. She fell in with his spirit, but her pleasure was shorn of some of its keenness by the odd notion that it was not to endure.

He even dragged Yvonne around to the little flat to expatiate upon its cosiness with visual proof to support his somewhat exaggerated claims. Her lazy eyes took in the apartment at a glance and she was done with it.

"It is very charming," she said with her soft drawl. "Have you no cigarettes, Lydia?"

The girl flushed and looked to Frederic for relief. He promptly produced his own cigarettes. Yvonne lighted one and then stretched herself in the Morris chair.

"You should learn to smoke," she went on.

"Mother wouldn't like me to smoke," said Lydia rather bluntly.

A faint frown appeared on Frederic's brow, only to disappear with Yvonne's low, infectious laugh.

"And Freddy doesn't like you to smoke either, *aïe?*" she said.

"He may have changed his mind recently, Mrs Brood," said the girl, smiling so frankly that the edge was taken off of a rather direct implication.

"I don't mind women smoking," put in Frederic hastily. "In fact, I rather like it, the way Yvonne does it. It's a very graceful accomplishment."

"But I am too clumsy to——" began Lydia.

"My dear," interrupted the Parisienne, carelessly flicking the ash into a *jardinière* at her elbow, "it is very naughty to smoke, and clumsy women never should be naughty. If you really feel clumsy, don't, for my sake, ever try to do anything wicked. There is nothing so distressing as an awkward woman trying to be devilish."

"Oh, Lydia couldn't be devilish if she tried!" cried Frederic, with a quick glance at the girl's half-averted face.

"Don't say that, Frederic," she cried. "That's as much as to say that I *am* clumsy and awkward."

"And you are not," said Yvonne decisively. "You are very pretty and graceful and adorable, and I am sure you could be very wicked if you set about to do it."

"Thank you," said Lydia dryly.

"By the way, this window looks almost directly down into our courtyard," said Yvonne abruptly. She was leaning on her elbow, looking out upon the housetops below. "There is my balcony, Freddy. And one can almost look into your father's lair from where I sit."

She drew back from the window suddenly, a passing look of fear in her eyes. It was gone in a second, and would have passed unnoticed but for the fact that Frederic was, as usual, watching her face with rapt interest. He caught the curious transition and involuntarily glanced below.

The heavy curtains in the window of his father's retreat were drawn apart, and the dark face of Ranjab, the Hindu, was plainly distinguishable.

He was looking up at the window in which Mrs Brood was sitting. Although Frederic was far above, he could see the gleaming white of the man's eyes. The curtains fell quickly together and the gaunt, brown face was gone.

An odd feeling of uneasiness came over the young man. It was the feeling of one who suddenly realises that he is being spied upon. He could not account for the faint chill that ran through his body, leaving him strangely cold and drear.

What was the meaning of that intense scrutiny from his father's window? Was Ranjab alone in the room? How did he happen to expose himself at the very instant Yvonne appeared in the window above? These and other questions raced through Frederic's puzzled brain. Out of them grew a queer, almost uncanny feeling that the Hindu had called to her in the still, mysterious voice of the East, and, although no sound had been uttered, she had heard as plainly as if he actually had shouted to her across the intervening space.

He recalled the tales of the old men, in which they spoke of the unaccountable swiftness with which news leaped across the unpopulated deserts, far in advance of any material means of transmission. Along the reaches of the Nile and in the jungles of India, weird instances of the astonishing projection of thought across vast spaces were constantly being reported. There was magic in the air. News travelled faster than the swiftest steed, even faster than the engines of man, into the most remote places, and yet there was no visible, tangible force behind the remarkable achievement.

His father had said more than once that the Hindu and the Egyptian possessed the power to be in two distinct places at the same time. He was wont to establish his theory by reciting the single instance of a sick dragoman who had been left behind in a village on the edge of the desert, with no means of crossing the vast stretch. And yet, when the caravan reached its destination after a long but record-breaking march, the man himself met them on the outskirts of the town with the astonishing report that he was quite well and strong after a two weeks' rest in his own house just inside of the city gates.

How he had passed them on the desert, and how he had reached his home a fortnight ahead of them, was one of the greatest mysteries James Brood had ever sought to unravel. The man's presence there created no surprise among the native members of the caravan. To them it was a most ordinary thing.

Again, in the depths of an Indian jungle Brood expressed the wish that he had brought with him a certain rifle he had left at home. Not a man left the camp, and yet at the end of the week a strange Hindu appeared with the rifle, having traversed several hundred miles of practically unexplored country in the time that would have been required to get the message to Lahore by horse alone.

James Brood, a sensible man, was a firm believer in magic.

This much Frederic knew of Ranjab: if James Brood needed him, no matter what the hour or the conditions, the man appeared before him as if out of nowhere and in response to no audible summons.

Was there, then, between these two, the beautiful Yvonne and the silent Hindu, a voiceless pact that defied the will or understanding of either?

He had not failed to note a tendency on her part to avoid the Hindu as much as possible. She even confessed to an uncanny dread of the man, but could not explain the feeling. Once she requested her husband to dismiss the faithful fellow. When he demanded the reason, however, she could only reply that she did not like the man and would feel happier if he were sent away. Brood refused, and from that hour her fear of the Hindu increased.

Now she was speaking in a nervous hurried manner to Lydia, her back toward the window. In the middle of a sentence she suddenly got up from the chair and moved swiftly to the opposite side of the room, where she sat down again as far as possible from the window.

Frederic found himself watching her face with curious interest. All the time she was speaking her eyes were fixed on the window. It was as if she expected something to appear there. There was no mistaking the expression. After studying her face in silence for a few minutes, Frederic himself experienced an irresistible impulse to turn toward the window. He half expected to see the Hindu's face there, looking in upon them, a perfectly absurd notion when he remembered that they were at least one hundred feet above the ground.

Presently she arose to go. No, she could not wait for Mrs Desmond's return.

"It is charming here, Lydia," she said, surveying the little sitting-room with eyes that sought the window again and again in furtive darts. "Frederic must bring me here often. We shall have cosy times here, we three. It is so convenient, too, for you, my dear. You have only to walk around the corner, and there you are—at your place of business, as the men would say."

Lydia was to continue as Brood's amanuensis. He would not listen to any other arrangement.

"Oh, I do hope you will come, Mrs Brood!" cried the girl earnestly. "My piano will be here to-morrow, and you shall hear Frederic play. He is really wonderful."

"I'm the rankest duffer going, Yvonne," broke in Frederic, but his eyes were alight with pleasure.

"You play?" asked Mrs Brood, regarding him rather fixedly.

"He disappears for hours at a time," said Lydia, speaking for him, "and comes home humming fragments from—oh, but I am not supposed to tell! Forgive me, Frederic. Dear me! What have I done?" She was plainly distressed.

"No harm in telling Yvonne," said he, but uneasily. "You see, it's this way: father doesn't like the idea of my going in for music. He is really very much opposed to it. So I've been sort of stealing a march on him—going up to a chum's apartment and banging away to my heart's content. It's rather fun, too, doing it on the sly. Of course, if father heard of it he'd—he'd—well, he'd be nasty about it, that's all."

"Nasty?"

"He got rid of our own piano a long time ago, just because he doesn't like music."

"But he does like music," said Yvonne, her voice a little huskier than usual. "In Paris we attended the opera, the concerts. I am sure he likes music."

"I fancy it must have been my fault, then," said Frederic wryly. "I was pretty bad at it in those days."

"He will not let you have a piano in the house?"

"I should say not!"

She gave them a queer little smile. "We shall see," she said, and that was all.

"I say, it would be great if you could get him to——"

"I am sure he would like Frederic's music now, Mrs Brood," Lydia broke in eagerly.

"What do you play—what do you like best, Frederic?" inquired Yvonne.

"Oh, those wonderful little Hungarian things most of all; the plaintive little melodies— —"

He stopped as she began to hum lightly the strains of one of Ziehrer's jaunty waltzes.

"By Jove, how did you guess? Why, it's my favourite. I love it, Yvonne!"

"You shall play it for me—to-morrow, Lydia?"

"Yes. The piano will be here in the morning."

"But how did you guess— —"

"Never mind! I am a witch, aïe? Come! I must be off now, Frederic. There are people coming to have tea with me."

As they descended in the elevator Frederic, unable to contain himself, burst out rapturously:

"By Jove, Yvonne, it will be fun, coming over here every day or so for a little music, won't it? I can't tell you how happy I shall be."

"It is time you were happy," said she, looking straight ahead, and many days passed before he had an inkling of all that lay behind her remark.

As they entered the house Jones met them in the hall.

"Mr Brood telephoned that he would be late, madam. He is at the customs office about the boxes."

She paused at the foot of the stairs.

"How long has he been out, Jones?"

"Since two o'clock, madam. It is now half-past four."

"There will be five or six in for tea, Jones. You may serve it in Mr Brood's study."

"Yes, madam."

A look of surprise flitted across the butler's impassive face. For a moment he had doubted his hearing.

"And ask Ranjab to put away Mr Brood's writing materials and reference-books."

"I shall attend to it myself, madam. Ranjab went out with Mr Brood."

"Went out!" exclaimed Yvonne.

Frederic turned upon the butler.

"You must be mistaken, Jones," he said sharply.

"I think not, sir. They went away together in the automobile. He has not returned."

A long look of wonder and perplexity passed between young Brood and his stepmother.

She laughed suddenly and unnaturally. Without a word she started up the stairs. He followed more slowly, his puzzled eyes fixed on the graceful figure ahead. At the upper landing she stopped. Her hand grasped the railing with rigid intensity.

Ranjab emerged from the shadows at the end of the hall. He bowed very deeply.

"The master's books and papers 'ave been removed, madam. The study is in order."

CHAPTER VII

The two old men, long since relegated to a somewhat self-imposed oblivion, on a certain night discussed, as usual, the affairs of the household in the privacy of their room on the third floor. Not, however, without first convincing themselves that the shadowy Ranjab was nowhere within range of their croaking undertones. From the proscribed regions downstairs came the faint sounds of a piano and the intermittent chatter of many voices. Someone was playing "La Paloma."

These new days were not like the old ones. Once they had enjoyed, even commanded, the full freedom of the house. It had been their privilege, their prerogative, to enter into every social undertaking that was planned. They had come to regard themselves as hosts, or, at the very least, guests of honour on such occasions.

Not that the occasions were many where guests came to be entertained by James Brood of old, but it seemed to be an accepted and quite agreeable duty of theirs to convince the infrequent visitors that Brood's house was really quite a jolly place, and that it would pay them to drop in oftener. They had a joyous way of lifting the responsibility of conversation from everyone else; and, be it said to their credit, there was no subject on which they couldn't talk with decision and fluency, whether they knew anything about it or not.

And nowadays it was different. They were not permitted to appear when guests were in the house. The sumptuous dinners, of which they heard something from the servants, were no longer graced by their presence. They were amazed, and not a little irritated, to learn, by listening at the head of the stairs, that the unfortunate guests, whoever they were, always seemed to be enjoying themselves. They couldn't understand how such a condition was possible.

They dined, to dignify the function somewhat, at least an hour before the guests arrived, and then shuffled off to their little back room, where they affected cribbage but indulged in something a great deal more acrimonious. They said many harsh things about the new mistress of the house. They could not understand what had come over James Brood. There was a time, said they, when no one could have led him around by the nose, and now he was as spineless as an angleworm.

On nights when guests were expected they were not permitted to have a drop of anything to drink, Mrs Brood declaring that she could not afford to run the risk of having them appear in the drawing-room despite the edict. They also had a habit of singing rather boisterously when intoxicated, something about a girl in Bombay; or, when especially happy, about a couple of ladies in Hottentot land who didn't mind the heat.

It was a matter of discretion, therefore, to lock up the spirits, and, after a fashion, to lock up the old gentlemen as well.

As a concession they were at liberty to invade the "retreat," and to make themselves at home among the relics. Guests were seldom, if ever, taken up to Brood's room. Only the most intimate of friends were admitted. Even the jade room, with all of its priceless treasures, was closed to "outsiders," for Brood had the idea that people as a rule did not possess a great amount of intelligence. So it was usually quite safe to allow Mr Dawes and Mr Riggs to run loose in the study, with the understanding, of course, that they were not to venture beyond the top of the stairs, and were not to smoke pipes.

Brood had been working rather steadily at his journal during the past two or three weeks. He had reached a point in the history where his own memory was somewhat vague, and had been obliged to call upon his old comrades to supply the facts. For several nights they had sat with him, going over the scenes connected with their earliest acquaintance; those black days in Calcutta.

Lydia had brought over her father's notes and certain transcripts of letters he had written to her mother before their marriage. The four of them were putting these notes and narratives into chronological order. Brood, after three months of married life and frivolity, suddenly had decided to devote himself almost entirely to the completion of the journal.

He denied himself the theatre, the opera, and kindred features of the passing show, and, as he preferred to entertain rather than to be entertained, seldom found it necessary to go into the homes of other people. Yvonne made no protest. She merely pressed Frederic into service as an escort when she desired to go about, and thought nothing of it. Whatever James Brood's views of this arrangement were, he appeared to accept it good-naturedly.

But the lines had returned to the corners of his mouth and the old, hard look to his eyes. And there were times when he spoke harshly to his son; times when he purposely humbled him in the presence of others without apparent reason.

On this particular night Yvonne had asked a few people in for dinner. They were people whom Brood liked especially well, but who did not appeal to her at all. As a matter of fact, they bored her. Yet she was happy in pleasing him. When she told him that they were coming he favoured her with a dry, rather impersonal smile and asked, with whimsical good humour, why she chose to punish herself for the sins of *his* youth.

She laid her cheek against his and purred. For a moment he held his breath. Then the fire in his blood leaped into flame. He clasped the slim, adorable body in his strong arms and crushed her against his breast. She kissed him, and he was again the fierce, eager, unsated lover. It was one of their wonderful, imperishable moments, moments that brought oblivion.

Then, as he frequently did of late, he held her off at arm's length and searched her velvety eyes with a gaze that seemed to drag the very secrets out of her soul. She went deathly white and shivered. He took his hands from her shoulders and smiled. She came back into his arms like a dumb thing seeking protection, and continued to tremble as if frightened.

When company was being entertained downstairs Mr Dawes and Mr Riggs, with a fidelity to convention that was almost pitiful, invariably donned their evening clothes. They considered themselves remotely connected with the festivities, and, that being the case, the least they could do was to "dress up."

Moreover, they dressed with great care and deliberation. There was always the chance that they might be asked to come down; or, what was even more important, Mrs Brood might happen to encounter them in the upper hall, and in that event it was imperative that she should be made to realise how stupid she had been.

Usually at nine o'clock they strolled into the study and smoked one of Brood's cigars with the gusto of real guests. It was their habit to saunter about the room, inspecting the treasures with critical, appraising eyes, very much as if they had never seen them before. They even handled some of the familiar objects with an air of bewilderment that would have done credit to a Cook's tourist.

It was also a habit of theirs to try the doors of a large teakwood cabinet in one corner of the room. The doors were always locked, and they sighed with patient doggedness. Some time, they told themselves, Ranjab would forget to lock those doors, and then— —

"Joe," said Mr Dawes, after he had tried the doors on this particular occasion, "I made a terrible mistake in letting poor Jim get married again. I'll never forgive myself." He had said this at least a hundred times during the past three months. Sometimes he cried over it.

"Danbury, old pal, you must not take all the blame for that. I am as much at fault as you, blast you!" Mr Riggs always ended his confession with an explosion that fairly withered his friend and gave the lie to his attempt at humility.

"That's right," snapped Mr Dawes; "curse me for it!"

"Don't make so much noise."

"If you were ten years younger I'd—I'd——" blustered Dawes.

"I wish Jack Desmond had lived," mused the other, paying no attention to the belligerent. "He would have put a stop to this fool marriage."

They sat down and pondered.

"If Jim had to marry someone, why didn't he marry right here at home?" demanded Dawes, turning fiercely on his friend.

"Because." said Riggs, with significant solemnity, "he is in the habit of marrying away from home. Look at the first one. He married her, didn't he? And see what came of it. He ought to have had more sense the second time. But marrying men never do get any sense. They just marry, that's all."

"Jim's getting mighty cranky of late," ruminated Dawes, puffing away at his unlighted cigar. "It's a caution the way he snaps Freddy off these days. He—he hates that boy, Joe."

"Sh—h! Not so loud!"

"Confound you, don't you know a whisper when you hear it?" demanded Dawes, who, in truth, had whispered.

Another potential silence.

"Freddy goes about with her a good deal more than he ought to," said Riggs at last. "They're together two-thirds of the time. Why—why, he heels her like a trained dog. Playing the pianner morning, noon, and night, and out driving, and going to the theatre, and——"

"I've a notion to tell Jim he ought to put a stop to it," said the other. "It makes me sick."

"Jim'll do it without being told one o' these days, so you keep out of it. Say, have you noticed how piqued Lydia's looking these times? She's not the same girl, Dan; not the same girl. Something's wrong." He shook his head gloomily.

"It's that dog-goned woman," announced Dawes explosively, and then looked over his shoulder with apprehension. A sigh of relief escaped him.

"She's got no business coming in between Lydia and Freddy," said Riggs. "Looks as though she's just set on busting it up. What can she possibly have against poor little Lydia? She's good enough for Freddy. Too good, by hokey! 'Specially when you stop to think."

"Now don't begin gossiping," warned Dawes, glaring at him. "You're as bad as an old woman."

"Thinking ain't gossiping, confound you! If I wanted to gossip I'd up and say flatly that Jim Brood knows down in his soul that Freddy is no son of his. He— —"

"You've never heard him say so, Joe."

"No; but I can put two and two together. I'm no fool."

"I'd advise you to shut up."

"Oh, you would, would you?" with vast scorn. "I'd like to know who it was that talked to Mrs Desmond about it. Who put it into her head that Jim doubts— —"

"Well, didn't she say I was a lying old busybody?" snapped Danbury triumphantly. "Didn't she call me down, eh? I'd like to know what more you could expect than that. Didn't she make me take back everything I said?"

"She did," said Riggs with conviction. "And I believe she would have thrashed you if she'd been a man, just as she said she would. And didn't I advise her to do it, anyway, on the ground that you're an old woman and— —"

"That's got nothing to do with the present case," interrupted Dawes hastily. "What we ought to be thinking about now is how to get rid of this woman that's come in here to wreck our home. She's an interloper. She's a foreigner. She— —"

"You must admit she treats us very politely," said Riggs weakly.

"Certainly she does. She has to. If she tried to come any of her high-and-mighty—ahem! Yes, Joseph, I consider Mrs Brood the loveliest, most charming— —"

"It was the wind blowing the curtain, Danbury," said Riggs, reassuringly.

"As I was saying," resumed his friend, "I'd tell her what I thought of her almighty quick if she got uppish with me. The trouble is, she's so darned careful what she says to my face. I've never seen anybody as sweet as she is when she's with a feller. That all goes to prove that she's sly and unnatural. No woman ever lived who could be sweet all the time and still be as God made her. Why, she even comes up here and tries to be sweet on that 'Great Gawd Budd' thing over there. I heard her ask Ranjab one day why he never prostrated himself before the image."

"Well?" demanded Riggs, as the other paused.

"She didn't have sense enough to know that Ranjab is a Brahmin, a worshipper of Vishnu and Shiva. I also heard her say that you had been so drunk up here one night that a lady fainted when she saw you sprawled out on the couch. She thought you were dead."

"I haven't been drunk in ten years! What's more, I don't remember ever having seen a strange woman in this room since I came here to visit Jim Brood, twelve years ago. She must be crazy."

"She didn't say you saw the woman. She said the woman saw you," said Dawes witheringly.

"No one ever thought of locking that cupboard until she came," said Riggs, abruptly altering the trend of speech but not of thought. His gaze shifted to the cabinet. "Jim is like wax in her hands."

"He has no right to forget those days in Calcutta, when we shared our grog with him. No, Joe, we're not good enough for him in these days. She has bewitched him, poor devil. I've stuck to him like a brother for twenty years—both of us have for that matter——"

"Like twin brothers," amended Joseph.

"Exactly. We don't forget those old days in Tibet, Turkestan, the Congo, the Sahara——"

"I should say we don't! Who is really writing this book of his? Who supplies all the most important facts? Who—who—well, that's all. Who?"

"We do, old chap. But you'll find that we shan't have our names on the title-page. She'll see to that. She'll have us shunted off like a couple of deck-hands. Lydia can tell you how much of the material I have supplied. She knows, bless her heart. You furnished a lot, too, Joe, and John Desmond the rest."

"Oh, Jim has done his share."

"I'll admit he has done all of the writing. I don't pose as a literary man."

"Seems to me he's sticking closer to the work than ever before," mused Riggs. "We ought to finish it by spring, the way we're going now."

"I still say, however, that he ought to put a stop to it."

"Stop to what?"

"Her running around with Freddy. What else?"

"No harm in it, is there?"

"No; I suppose not," the other reflected. "Still they're pretty young, you know. Besides, she's French."

"So was Joan of Arc," said his friend in rebuttal.

Mr Dawes leaned a little closer.

"I wonder how Mrs Desmond likes having her over there playing the piano every afternoon with Freddy, while Lydia's over here copying things for Jim and working her poor little head off. Ever stop to think about that?"

"I think about it all the time. And, by thunder, I'm not the only one who does, either. Jim thinks a good deal, and so does Lydia. It's a darned — —"

Mr Riggs happened to look up at that instant. Ranjab was standing in front of him, his arms folded across his breast, in the habitual pose of the Hindu who waits. The man was dressed in the costume of a high-caste Brahmin; the commonplace garments of the Occident had been laid aside, and in their place were the vivid, dazzling colours of Ind, from the bejewelled sandals to the turban which crowned his swarthy brow and gleamed with rubies and sapphires uncounted.

Mr Riggs's mouth remained open as he stared blankly at this ghost of another day. Not since the old days in India had he seen Ranjab in native garb, and even then he was far from being the resplendent creature of to-night, for Ranjab in his home land was a poor man and without distinction.

"Am I awake?" exclaimed Mr Riggs in such an awful voice that Mr Dawes gave over staring at the cabinet and favoured him with an impatient kick on the ankle.

"I guess that'll wake you up if — —" and then he saw the Hindu. "The Ranjab!"

Ranjab was smiling, and when he smiled his dark face was a joy to behold. His white teeth gleamed and his sometime unfeeling eyes sparkled with delight. He liked the two old men. They had stood, with Brood, between him and grave peril far back in the old days when even the faintest gleam of hope apparently had been blotted out.

"Behold!" he cried, magnificently spreading his arms. "I am made glorious! See before you the prince of magic! See!"

With a swift, deft movement he snatched the half-smoked cigar from the limp fingers of Mr Riggs and, first holding it before their blinking eyes, tossed it into the air. It disappeared!

"Well, of all the — —" began Mr Riggs, sitting up very straight. His eyes were following the rapid actions of the Hindu. Unlocking a drawer in the big table, the latter peered into it and then beckoned the old men to his side. There lay the cigar and beside it a much-needed match.

"I don't want to smoke it," said Mr Riggs, vigorously declining his property. "The darned thing's bewitched." Whereupon Ranjab took it out of the drawer and again threw it into the air. Then he calmly reached above his head and plucked a fresh cigar out of space, obsequiously tendering it to the amazed old man, who accepted it with a sheepish grin.

"You haven't lost any of your old skill," said Mr Dawes, involuntarily glancing at his own cigar to make sure that he had it firmly gripped in his stubby fingers. "You ought to be in a sideshow, Ranjab."

Ranjab paused, before responding, to extract a couple of billiard balls and a small paper-knife from the lapel of Dawes's coat.

"I am to perform to-night, *sahib*, for the mistress's guests. It is to be— what you call him? A side-show? Ranjab is to do his tricks for her, as the dog performs for his master."

The smile had disappeared. His face was an impenetrable mask once more. Had their eyes been young and keen, however, they might have caught the flash of anger in his.

"Going to do all the old tricks?" cried Mr Riggs eagerly. "By George, I'd like to see 'em again; wouldn't you, Dan? I'm glad we've got our good clothes on. Now you see what comes of always being prepared for——"

"Sorry, *sahib*, but the master has request me to entertain you before the guests come up. Coffee is to be served here."

"That means we'll have to clear out?" said Riggs slowly.

"But see!" cried Ranjab, genuinely sorry for them. He became enthusiastic once more. "See! I shall do them all—and better, too, for you."

For ten minutes he astonished the old men with the mysterious feats of the Indian fakir. They waxed enthusiastic. He grinned over the pleasure he was giving them. Suddenly he whipped out a short, thin sword from its scabbard in his sash. The amazing, incomprehensible sword-swallowing act followed.

"You see, Ranjab has not forgot," he cried in triumph. "He have not lost the touch of the wizard, *aih*."

"You'll lose your gizzard some day, doing that," said Dawes grimly. "It gives me the shivers."

Then, before their startled, horror-struck eyes, the Hindu coolly plunged the glittering blade into his breast, driving it in to the hilt!

"Good Lord!" shouted the two old men.

Ranjab serenely replaced the sword in its scabbard.

"It is not always the knife that finds the heart," said he, so slowly, so full of meaning, that even the old men grasped the significance of the cryptic remark.

"A feller can be fooled, no matter how closely he watches," said Mr Dawes, and he was not referring to the amazing sword trick.

"No, sir," said Mr Riggs, with gloomy irrelevance, "I don't like that woman."

The old spell of the Orient had fallen upon the ancients. They were hearing the vague whisperings of voices that came from nowhere, as they had heard them years ago in the mystic silences of the East.

"*Sh—h!* One comes," said Ranjab softly. "It will be the master's son."

An instant later his closet door closed noiselessly behind him and the old men were alone, blinking at each other. There was no sound from the hall. They waited, watching the curtained door. At last they heard footsteps on the stairs, quick footsteps of the young.

Frederic strode rapidly into the room.

CHAPTER VIII

His face was livid with rage. For a moment he glowered upon the two old men, his fingers working spasmodically, his chest heaving with the volcanic emotions he was trying so hard to subdue. Then he whirled about to glare into the hall.

"In God's name, Freddy, what's happened?" cried Mr Riggs, all a-tremble.

They had never seen him in a rage before. There had been occasions when they had secretly criticised James Brood's treatment of the unhappy boy, but from the youth himself there had come no complaint, only the hurt, puzzled look of one who endures because an alternative does not suggest itself. Intuitively the old men knew that his present condition was due to something his father had said or done, and that it must have been unusually severe to have provoked the wrath that he made no effort to conceal.

It was not in their honest old hearts to hold grievance against the lad, notwithstanding his frequent periods of impatience where they were concerned, periods when they were admittedly as much at fault as he, by the way. Usually he made up for these lapses by a protracted season of sweetness and consideration that won back not only their sympathy, but the affection they had felt for him since his lonely boyhood days.

Some minutes passed before he could trust himself to speak. Ugly veins stood out on his pale temples as he paced the floor in front of them. Eventually Mr Dawes ventured the vital question in a somewhat hushed voice:

"Have you—quarrelled with your father, Freddy?"

The young man threw up his arms in a gesture of despair. There was a wail of misery in his voice as he answered:

"In the name of God, why should he hate me as he does? What have I done? Am I not a good son to him?"

"Hush!" implored Mr Dawes nervously. "He'll hear you."

"Hear me!" cried Frederic, and laughed aloud in his recklessness. "Why shouldn't he hear me? I'll not stand it a day longer. He wouldn't think of treating a dog as he treats me. I—I—why, he is actually forcing me to hate him. I *do* hate him! I swear to Heaven it was in my heart to kill him down there just now. I— — —" He could not go on. He choked up and the tears rushed to his eyes. Abruptly turning away, he threw himself upon the couch and buried his face on his arms, sobbing like a little child.

The old men, distressed beyond the power of speech, mumbled incoherent words of comfort as they slowly edged toward the door. They tiptoed into the hall, and neither spoke until their bedroom door was closed behind them. Mr Dawes even tried it to see that it was safely latched.

"It's got to come," said Mr Riggs, wiping his eyes but neglecting to blow his nose—recollecting in good time the vociferous noise that always attended the performance. "Yes, sir; it's bound to come. There's going to be a smash, mark my words. It can't go on." He sat down heavily and stared rather pathetically at his friend, who was the picture of lugubrious concern.

"Yes, sir," said Mr Dawes bleakly, "as sure as you're alive, Joey. That boy's spunk is going to assert itself some day, and then—good Lord, what then? He'll curse Jim to his teeth and—and Jim'll up and tell him the truth. I—I don't know what will happen then."

Riggs swallowed hard—a gulping sound.

"Freddy's the kind of a feller who'll kill himself, Danny. He's as high strung as a harp. Something will snap. I hate to think of it. Poor lad! It—it ain't his fault that things are not as they ought to be."

"If Jim Brood ever tells him he's no son of his, he'll break the boy's heart."

"I'm not so sure of that," said Riggs sagely. "Sometimes I think Freddy would be darned glad to know it."

The curtains parted and Yvonne looked in upon the wretched Frederic. There was a look of mingled pain and commiseration in her wide-open eyes. For a moment she stood there regarding him in silence. Then she swiftly crossed the room to the couch in the corner, where he sat huddled up, his shoulders still shaking with the misery that racked him.

Her eyes darkened into the hungry, yearning look of one who would gladly share or assume all of the suffering of another whose happiness was dear to her—the look of a gentle mother. The mocking, seductive gleam was gone, and in its place was the glow of infinite pity. Her hand went out to touch the tousled hair, but stopped before contact. Slowly she drew back, with a glance of apprehension toward the door of the Hindu's closet. An odd expression of alarm crept into her eyes.

"Frederic," she said softly, almost timorously.

He lifted his head quickly and then sprang to his feet. His eyes were wet and his lips were drawn. Shame possessed him. He tried to smile, but it was a pitiful failure.

"Oh, I'm so ashamed of—of— —" he began in a choked voice.

"Ashamed because you have cried?" she said quickly. "But no! It is good to cry; it is good for men to cry. But when a strong man breaks down and sheds tears, I am—oh, I am heartbroken. A woman's tears mean nothing, but a man's? Oh, they are terrible! But come! You must compose yourself. The others will be here in a few minutes. I ran away from them on the pretext that I—but it is of no consequence. It is enough that I am here. You must go to your room and bathe your face. Go at once. Your father must not know that you have cried. He— — —"

"Curse him!" came from between Frederic's clenched teeth.

"Hush!" she cried, with another glance at Ranjab's door. She would have given much to know whether the Hindu was there or still below-stairs. "You must not say such— —"

"I will say it, Yvonne—I'll say it to his face! I don't care if the others do see that I have been crying. I want them to know how he hurts me, and I want them to hate him for it."

"For my sake, Frederic, calm yourself. I implore you to go to your room. Come back later, but go now."

He was struck by the seriousness in her voice and manner. An ugly, crooked smile writhed about the corners of his mouth.

"I suppose you're trying to smooth it over so that they won't consider him a brute. Is that it?"

"Hush! Please, please! You know that my heart aches for you, *mon ami*. It was cruel of him, it was cowardly—yes, cowardly! Now I have said it!" She drew herself up and turned deliberately toward the little door across the room.

His eyes brightened. The crooked sneer turned into an imploring smile.

"Forgive me, Yvonne! You must see that I'm beside myself. I—I— — —"

"But you must be sensible. Remember he is your father. He is a strange man. There has been a great deal of bitterness in his life. He— — —"

"Have I been the cause of a moment's bitterness to him?" cried Frederic. "Why should he hate me? Why— — —"

"You are losing control of yourself again, Frederic."

"But I can't go on the way things are now. He's getting to be worse than ever. I never have a kind word from him, seldom a word of any description. Never a kind look. Can't you understand how it goads me to———"

"Yes, yes! You've said all this before, and I have listened to you when I should have reminded you that he is my husband," she said impatiently.

"By Heaven, I don't see how you can love him!" he cried boldly. "Sometimes I wonder if you do love him. He is as selfish, as unfeeling as oh, there's no word for it. Why, in the name of God, did you ever marry such a man? You couldn't have loved him." Something in her expression brought him up sharply. Her eyes had narrowed; they had the look of a wary, hunted thing that has been driven into a corner. He stared. "Forgive me, Yvonne. I—I———"

"You don't know what you are saying," she panted. "Are you accusing me?"

"No, no! What a coward, what a dog I am!" he cried abjectly.

A queer little smile stole into her face. It was even more baffling than the expression it displaced.

"I am your friend," she said slowly. "Is this the way to reward me?"

He dropped to his knees and covered her hands with kisses, mumbling his plea for forgiveness.

"I am so terribly unhappy," he said over and over again. "I'd leave this house to-night if it were not that I can't bear the thought of leaving you, Yvonne. I adore you. You are everything in the world to me. I———"

"Get up!" she cried out sharply. He lifted his eyes in dumb wonder and adoration, but not in time to catch the look of triumph that swept across her face.

"You will forgive me?" he cried, coming to his feet. "I—I couldn't help saying it. It was wrong—wrong! But you *will* forgive me, Yvonne?"

She turned away, walking slowly toward the door. He remained rooted to the spot, blushing with shame and dismay.

"Where are you going? To tell *him?*" he gasped.

She did not reply at once, but drew the *portières* apart and peered down the stairs beyond, her attitude one of tense anxiety. As she faced him a smile of security was on her lips. She leaned gracefully against the jamb of the door, her arms dropping to her sides.

"Yes, I will forgive you," she said calmly, and he realised in a flash that the verdict would have been different if there had been the remotest chance that his declaration was overheard. She would have denied him.

"I adore you, Yvonne," he cried in low tones, striding swiftly toward her, only to halt as he caught the smile of derision in her eyes. "I don't mean it in the way you think. You are so good to me. You have given me so much joy and happiness, and—and you understand me so well. I could die for you, Yvonne. I *would* die for you. It's not the kind of love you are in the habit of commanding, you who are so glorious and so beautiful. It's the love of a dog for his master."

She waited an instant, and then came toward him. He never could have explained the unaccountable impulse that forced him to fall back a few steps as she approached. Her eyes were gazing steadily into his, and her red lips were parted.

"That is as it should be," she was saying, but he was never sure that he heard the words. His knees grew weak. He was in the toils! "Now you must pull yourself together," she went on, in such a matter-of-fact tone that he straightened up involuntarily. "Come! Wipe the tear-stains from your cheeks."

He obeyed, but his lip still quivered with the rage that had been checked by the ascendancy of another and even more devastating emotion. She was standing quite close to him now, her slender figure swaying slightly as if moved by some strange, rhythmic melody to which the heart beat time.

Her eyes were soft and velvety again, her smile tender and appealing. The vivid white of her arms and shoulders seemed to shed a soft light about her, so radiant was the sheen of the satin skin. Her gown was of black velvet, cut very low, and with scarcely any ornamentation save the great cluster of rubies at the top of her corsage. They gleamed like coals of fire against the skin, which appeared to absorb and reflect their warmth.

There was a full red rose in her dark hair. She wore no ear-rings, no finger-rings except the narrow gold band on her left hand. A wide, exquisitely designed gold bracelet fitted tightly about her right forearm, as if it had been welded to the soft white flesh. Yvonne's ears were lovely; she knew better than to disfigure them. Her hands were incomparably beautiful; she knew their full value unadorned.

She moved closer to him and with deft fingers applied her tiny lace handkerchief to his flushed cheeks and eyes, laughing audibly as she did so; a low gurgle of infinite sweetness and concern.

He stood like a statue, scarcely breathing, the veins in his throat throbbing violently.

"There!" she said, and deliberately touched the *mouchoir* to her own smiling lips before replacing it in her bodice next to the warm, soft skin. "Lydia must not see that her big baby sweetheart has been crying," she went on, and if there was mockery in her voice it was lost on him. He could only stare as if bereft of all his senses.

"I have been thinking, Frederic," she said, suddenly serious, "perhaps it would be better if we were not alone when the others come up. Go at once and fetch the two old men. Tell them I expect them here to witness the magic. It appears to be a family party, so why exclude them? Be quick!"

He dashed off to obey her command. She lighted a cigarette at the table, her unsmiling eyes fixed on the door to the Hindu's closet. Then, with a little sigh, she sank down on the broad couch and stretched her supple body in the ecstasy of complete relaxation.

The scene at the dinner-table had been most distressing. Up to the instant of the outburst her husband had been in singularly gay spirits, a circumstance so unusual that the whole party wondered not a little. If the others were vaguely puzzled by his high humour, not so Yvonne. She understood him better than anyone else in the world; she read his mind as she would have read an open book.

There was riot, not joy, in the heart of the brilliant talker at the head of the table. He was talking against the savagery that strained so hard at its leash.

At her right sat Frederic, at her left the renowned Dr Hodder, whose feats at the operating table were vastly more successful than his efforts at the dinner-table. He was a very wonderful surgeon, but equally famous as a bore of the first rank. Yvonne could not endure him. His jokes were antediluvian, and his laughter over them an abomination.

He had an impression, as many famous men have, that the sole duty of a dinner guest is to be funny in the loudest voice possible, drowning out all competition, and to talk glowingly about the soup, as if nothing else was required to convince the hostess that he considered her dinner irreproachable and her cook a jewel. Still, it was agreed Dr Hodder was a wonderful surgeon.

Mrs Desmond and Lydia were there. (This was an excellent opportunity to entertain them on an occasion of more or less magnitude.) There were also present Bertie Gunning and his pretty wife, Maisie, both of whom Yvonne liked; and the Followed sisters, with two middle-aged gentlemen from one of the clubs.

Miss Followed was forty, and proved it by cheerfully discussing events that happened at least that far back in her life. Her sister Janey was much younger, quite pretty, and acutely ingenuous. The middle-aged gentlemen ate very little. They were going to a supper at the Knickerbocker later on for someone whose name was Lilly. Occasionally it was Lil. It rather gratified them to be chided about the lady.

Frederic, deceived by his father's sprightly mood, entered rather recklessly into the lively discussion. He seldom took his eyes from the face of his beautiful stepmother, and many of his remarks were uttered *sotto voce* for her ear alone.

Suddenly James Brood called out his name in a sharp, commanding tone. Frederic, at the moment engaged in a low exchange of words with Yvonne, did not hear him. Brood spoke again, loudly, harshly. There was dead silence at the table.

"We will excuse you, Frederic," said he, a deadly calm in his voice. The puzzled expression in the young man's face slowly gave way to a steady glare of fury. He could not trust himself to speak. "I regret exceedingly that you cannot take wine in moderation. A breath of fresh air will be of benefit to you. You may join us upstairs later on."

"I haven't drunk a full glass of champagne," began the young man in amazed protest.

Brood smiled indulgently, but there was a sinister gleam in his gray eyes. "I think you had better take my advice," he said.

"Very well, sir," said Frederic in a low, suppressed voice, his face paling. Without another word he got up from the table and walked out of the room.

He spoke the truth later on when he told Yvonne that he could not understand. But she understood. She knew that James Brood had endured the situation as long as it was in his power to endure, and she knew that it was her fault entirely that poor Frederic had been exposed to this crowning bit of humiliation.

As she sat in the dim study awaiting her stepson's reappearance with the two old men, her active, far-seeing mind was striving to estimate the cost of that tragic clash. Not the cost to herself or to Frederic, but to James Brood!

The Messrs Dawes and Riggs, inordinately pleased over the rehabilitation, were barely through delivering themselves of their protestations of undying fealty when the sound of voices came up from the lower hall. Frederic started to leave the room, not caring to face those who had witnessed his unwarranted degradation. Yvonne hurried to his side.

"Where are you going?" she cried sharply.

"You cannot expect me to stay here— —"

"But certainly!" she exclaimed. "Listen! I will tell you what to do."

Her voice sank to an imperative whisper. He listened in sheer amazement, his face growing dark with rebellion as she proceeded to unfold her plan for a present victory over his father.

"No, no! I can't do that! Never, Yvonne," he protested.

"For my sake, Freddy. Don't forget that you owe something to me. I command you to do as I tell you. It is the only way. Make haste! Open the window, get the breath of air he prescribed, and when they are all here, *apologise for your condition!*"

When Dr Hodder and Mrs Gunning entered the room a few minutes later young Brood was standing in the open window, drinking in the cold night air, and she was blithely regaling the blinking old men with an account of her stepson's unhappy efforts to drink all the wine in sight! As she told it, it was a most amusing experiment.

James Brood was the last to enter, with Miss Followed. He took in the situation at a glance. Was it relief that sprang into his eyes as he saw the two old men?

Frederic came down from the window, somewhat too swiftly for one who is moved by shame and contrition, and faced the group with a well-assumed look of mortification in his pale, twitching face. He spoke in low, repressed tones, but not once did he permit his gaze to encounter that of his father.

"I'm awfully sorry to have made a nuisance of myself. It does go to my head, and I—I dare say the heat of the room helped to do the work. I'm all right now, however. The fresh air did me a lot of good. Hope you'll all overlook my foolish attempt to be a devil of a fellow." He hesitated a moment and then went on, more clearly. "I'm all right now, father. It shall not happen again, I can promise you that."

A close observer might have seen the muscles of his jaw harden as he uttered the final sentence. He intended that his father should take it as a threat, not as an apology.

Brood was watching him closely, a puzzled expression in his eyes; gradually it developed into something like admiration. In the clamour of voices that ensued the older man detected the presence of an underlying note of censure for his own behaviour. For the first time in many years he experienced a feeling of shame.

Someone was speaking at his elbow. Janey, in her young, enthusiastic voice, shrilled something into his ear that caused him to look at her in utter amazement. It was so astounding that he could not believe he heard aright. He mumbled in a questioning tone, "I beg your pardon," and she repeated her remark.

"How wonderfully like you Frederic is, Mr Brood." Then she added: "Do you know, I've never noticed it until to-night? It's really remarkable."

"Indeed," Brood responded somewhat icily.

"Don't you think so, Mr Brood?"

"No, I do not, Miss Janey," said he distinctly.

"Maisie Gunning was speaking of it just a few minutes ago," went on the girl, unimpressed. "She says you are very much alike when you are—are———" here she foundered in sudden confusion.

"Intoxicated?" he inquired, without a smile.

She blushed painfully. "No, no! When you are angry. There, I suppose I shouldn't have said it, but———"

"It is a most gratifying discovery," said he, and turned to speak to Mrs Desmond. He did not take his gaze from Frederic's white, set face, however; and, despite the fact that he knew the girl had uttered an idle commonplace, he was annoyed to find himself studying the features of Matilde's boy with an interest that seemed almost laughable when he considered it later on.

His guests found much to talk about in the room. He was soon being dragged from one object to another and ordered to reveal the history, the use, and the nature of countless things that obviously were intended to be just what they seemed; such as rugs, shields, lamps, and so forth. He was ably assisted by Messrs Riggs and Dawes, who lied prodigiously in a frenzy of rivalry.

"What a perfectly delightful Buddha!" cried Miss Janey, stopping in front of the idol. "How perfectly lovely he is—or is it a she, Mr Brood?"

He did not reply at once. His eyes were on Frederic and Yvonne, who had come together at last and were conversing earnestly apart from the rest of the group. He observed that Lydia was standing quite alone near the table, idly handling a magazine. To the best of his recollection, Frederic had scarcely spoken to the girl during the evening.

"This is where I work and play and dream, Miss Janey, and practise the ogre's art. It is a forbidden chamber, my sanctuary," —with a glance at the idol—"and here is where I sometimes chop off pretty young women's heads and hang them from the window-ledge as a warning to all other birds of prey."

Miss Janey laughed gleefully, attracting Yvonne's attention. Then she sang out across the room:

"Your husband says he is an ogre. Is he?"

Yvonne came languidly toward them.

"My husband manages to keep me in his enchanted castle without chains and padlocks, and that is saying a great deal in this day and age, my dear. Would you call him an ogre after that?"

"Perhaps it is the old story of the fairy queen and the ogre."

"You may be sure I'd be an ogre if there was no other way of keeping you, my dear," said Brood. There was something in his voice that caused her to look up into his face quickly.

Dr Hodder, being a wonderful surgeon, managed to cut his finger with a razor-edged kris at that instant, drawing a little shriek from Miss Followed, to whom he was jocularly explaining that scientific Malays used the thing in removing one another's appendices, the surgeon being the one who survived the operation.

During the excitement incident to the bloodletting the middle-aged gentlemen glanced furtively at their watches and indulged in a mental calculation from which they emerged somewhat easier in their minds. It still wanted an hour before the theatres were out.

"Dreadful bore," yawned one of them behind his hand.

"Stupidest woman I ever sat next to," said the other,

Then both looked at their watches again.

Frederic joined Lydia at the table.

"A delicious scene, wasn't it?" he asked bitterly in lowered tones.

Her fingers touched his.

"What did he mean, Freddy? Oh, I felt so sorry for you. It was dreadful."

"Don't take it so seriously, Lyddy," he said, squeezing her hand gently. Both of them realised that it was the nearest thing to a caress that had passed between them in a fortnight or longer. A wave of shame swept through him. "Dear old girl—my dear old girl," he whispered brokenly.

Her eyes radiated joy, her lips parted in a wan, tremulous smile of surprise, and a soft sigh escaped them.

"My dear, dear boy," she murmured, and was happier than she had been in weeks.

"See here, old chap," said one of the middle-aged gentlemen, again consulting his watch as he loudly addressed his host, "can't you hurry this performance of yours along a bit? It is after ten, you know."

"A quarter after," said the other middle-aged gentleman.

"I will summon the magician," said Brood. "Be prepared, ladies and gentlemen, to meet the devil. Ranjab is the prince of darkness."

He lifted his hand to strike the gong that stood near the edge of the table.

Involuntarily four pairs of eyes fastened their gaze upon the door to the Hindu's closet. Three mellow, softly reverberating "booms" filled the room. Almost instantly the voice of the Hindu was heard.

"*Aih, sahib!*"

He came swiftly into the room from the hall, and not from his closet. The look of relief in Yvonne's eyes was short-lived. She saw amazement in the faces of the two old men—and knew!

"After we have had the feats of magic," Brood was saying, "Miss Desmond will read to you, ladies and gentlemen, that chapter of our journal——"

"My word!" groaned both of the middle-aged gentlemen, looking at their watches.

"Relating to——"

"You'll have to excuse me, Brood, really, you know. Important engagement up-town——"

"Sit down, Cruger," exclaimed Hodder. "The lady won't miss you."

"Relating to our first encounter with the great and only Ranjab," pursued Brood oracularly. "We found him in a little village far up in the mountains. He was under the sentence of death for murder. By the way, Yvonne, the kris you have in your hand is the very weapon the good fellow used in the commission of his crime. He was in prison and was to die within a fortnight after our arrival in the town. I heard of his unhappy plight and all that had led up to it. His case interested me tremendously. One night, a week before the proposed execution, my friends and I stormed the little prison and rescued him. We were just getting over the cholera and needed excitement. That was fifteen years ago. He has been my trusted body-servant ever since. I am sure you will be interested in what I have written about that thrilling adventure."

Yvonne had dropped the ugly knife upon the table as if it were a thing that scorched her fingers.

"Did he—really kill a man?" whispered Miss Janey with horror in her eyes.

"He killed a woman. His wife, Miss Janey. She had been faithless, you see. He cut her heart out. And now, Ranjab, are you ready?"

The Hindu salaamed.

"Ranjab is always ready, *sahib*," said he.

CHAPTER IX

The next day, after a sleepless night, Frederic announced to his stepmother that he could no longer remain under his father's roof. He would find something to do in order to support himself. It was impossible to go on pretending that he loved or respected his father, and the sooner the farce was ended the better it would be for both of them.

She, too, had passed a restless night. She slept but little. It was a night filled with waking dreams as well as those which came in sleep. There was always an ugly, wriggly kris in those dreams of hers, and a brown hand that was for ever fascinating her with its uncanny deftness.

Twice in the night she had clutched her husband's shoulder in the terror of a dream, and he had soothed her with the comfort of his strong arms. She crept close to him and slept again, secure for the moment against the sorcery that haunted her. He had been surprised, even gratified, when she came into his room long after midnight, to creep shivering into his bed. She was like a little child "afraid of the dark."

Her influence alone prevented the young man from carrying out his threat. At first he was as firm as a rock in his determination. He was getting his few possessions together in his room when she tapped on his door. After a while he abandoned the task and followed her rather dazedly to the boudoir, promising to listen to reason. For an hour she argued and pleaded with him, and in the end he agreed to give up what she was pleased to call his preposterous plan.

"Now, that being settled," she said with a sigh of relief, "let us go and talk it all over with Lydia."

"I'd—I'd rather not, Yvonne," he said, starting guiltily. "There's no use worrying her with the thing now. As a matter of fact, I'd prefer that she—well, somehow I don't like the idea of explaining matters to her."

"There's nothing to explain."

He looked away. He realised that he could not explain the thing even to himself.

"Well, then, I don't want her to know that I thought of leaving," he supplemented. "She wouldn't understand."

"No?"

"She's so open and above-board about everything," he explained nervously.

"It has seemed to me of late, Frederic, that you and Lydia are not quite so—what shall I say?—so enamoured of each other. What has happened?" she inquired so innocently, so naïvely, that he looked at her in astonishment. She was watching him narrowly. "I am sure you fairly live at her house. You are there nearly every day, and yet—well, I can feel rather than see the change in both of you. I hope———"

"I've been behaving like an infernal sneak, Yvonne!" cried he, conscience-stricken. "She's the finest, noblest girl in all this world, and I've been treating her shamefully."

"Dear me! In what way, may I inquire?"

"Why, we used to—oh, but why go into all that? It would only amuse you. You'd laugh at us for silly fools. But I can't help saying this much: she doesn't deserve to be treated as I'm treating her now, Yvonne. It's hurting her dreadfully, and——"

"What have you been doing that she should be so dreadfully afflicted?" she cried ironically.

"I've been neglecting her, ignoring her, humiliating her, if you will force me to say it," he said firmly. "Good Lord, if anyone had told me three months ago that I'd ever be guilty of giving Lydia an instant's pain, I'd—I'd———"

"You would do what?"

"Don't laugh at me, Yvonne," he cried miserably.

She became serious at once. "Do you still love her?"

"Yes! Yes!" he shouted, as if there was some necessity for convincing himself as well as his listener.

"And she loves you?"

"I—I—certainly! At least I think she does," he floundered. His forehead was moist and cold.

"Then why this sudden misgiving, this feeling of doubt, this self-abasement?"

"I don't understand it myself," he said rather bleakly. "I—I give you my word, I don't know what has come over me. I'm not as I used to be. I'm———"

"We have been married a scant four months," she said gently. "Would you expect a woman to shed her mystery in so short a time as that?"

"There is something in your eyes———" he began, and shook his head in utter perplexity. "You startle me once in a while. There are times when you seem to be looking at me through eyes that are not your own. It's—it's—quite uncanny. If you———"

"I assure you my eyes are all my own," she cried flippantly, and yet there was a slight trace of nervousness in her manner. "Do you intend to be nice and good and reasonable, James? I mean about poor Frederic."

His face clouded again.

"Do you know what you are doing to that boy?" he asked bluntly.

"Quite as well as I know what you are doing to him," she replied quickly.

He stiffened. "Can't you see what it is coming to?"

"Yes. He was on the point of leaving your house, never to come back to it again. That's what it is coming to," she said.

"Do you mean to say———"

"He was packing his things to go away to-day———"

"Why—why, he'd starve!" cried the man, shaken in spite of himself. "He has never done a day's labour; he doesn't know how to earn a living. He———"

"And who is to blame? You, James; you! You have tied his hands, you have penned him up in———"

"We will not go into that," he interrupted coldly.

"Very well. As you please. I said that he was going away, perhaps to starve, but he has changed his mind. He has taken my advice."

"Your advice?"

"I have advised him to bide his time."

"It sounds rather ominous."

"If he waits long enough you may discover that you love him and his going would give you infinite pain. Then is the time for him to go."

"Good Heaven!" he cried in astonishment. "What a remarkable notion of the fitness———"

"That will be his chance to repay you for all that you have done for him, James," said she, as calm as a May morning.

"Have I ever said that I do not love him?" he demanded shortly.

"For that matter, have you ever said that you do not hate him?"

"By Jove, you are a puzzle to me!" he exclaimed, and a fine moisture came out on his forehead.

"Let the boy alone, James," she went on earnestly. "He is— — —"

"See here, Yvonne," he broke in sternly, "that is a matter we can't discuss. You do not understand, and I cannot explain certain things to you. I came here just now to ask you to be fair to him, even though I may not appear to be. You are— — —"

"That is also a matter we cannot discuss," said she calmly.

"But it is a thing we are going to discuss, just the same," said he. "Sit down, my dear, and listen to what I have to say. Sit down!"

For a moment she faced him defiantly. He was no longer angry, and therein lay the strength that opposed her. She could have held her own with him if he had maintained the angry attitude that marked the beginning of their interview. As it was, her eyes fell after a brief struggle against the dominant power in his, and she obeyed, but not without a significant tribute to his superiority in the shape of an indignant shrug.

"No one has ever lectured me before, James," she said, affecting a yawn. "It will be a new and interesting experience."

"And I trust a profitable one," said he rather grimly. "I shouldn't call it a lecture, however. A warning is better."

"That should be more thrilling, in any event."

He took one of her hands in his and stroked it gently, even patiently.

"I will come straight to the point. Frederic is falling in love with you. Wait! I do not blame him. He cannot help himself. No more could I, for that matter, and he has youth, which is a spur that I have lost. I have watched him, Yvonne. He is—to put it cold-bloodedly—losing his head. Leaving me out of the question altogether, if you choose, do you think you are quite fair to him? I am not disturbed on your account or my own, but—well, can't you see what a cruel position we are likely to find ourselves— — —"

"Just a moment, James," she interrupted, sitting up very straight in the chair and meeting his gaze steadfastly. "Will you spare me the conjectures and come straight to the point as you have said? The warning, if you please."

He turned a shade paler.

"Well," he began deliberately, "it comes to this, my dear: one or the other of you will have to leave my house if this thing goes on."

She shot a glance of incredulity at his set face. Her body became rigid.

"Do you know what you are saying?"

"Yes."

"You would serve me as you served his real mother more than twenty years ago?"

"The cases are not parallel," said he, wincing.

"You drove her out of your house, James."

"I have said that we cannot discuss———"

"But I choose to discuss it," she said firmly. "The truth, please. You drove her out?"

"She made her bed, Yvonne," said he huskily.

"Did you warn her beforehand?"

"It—it wasn't necessary."

"What was her crime?"

"Good God, Yvonne! I can't allow———"

"Was it as great as mine?" she persisted.

"Oh, this is ridiculous. I———"

"Did she leave you cheerfully, gladly, as I would go if I loved another, or did she plead with you—oh, I know it hurts! Did she plead with you to give her a chance to explain? Did she?"

"She was on her knees to me," he said, the veins standing out on his temples.

"On her knees to you? Begging? For what? Forgiveness?"

"No! She was like all of her kind. She was innocent! Ha, ha!"

Yvonne arose. She stood over him like an accusing angel.

"And to this day, James Brood, to this very hour, you are not certain that you did right in casting her off!"

"Oh, I say!" He sprang to his feet.

"You have never really convinced yourself that she was untrue to you, in spite of all that you said and did at the time."

"You are going too far! I———"

"All these years you have been trying to close your ears to the voice of that wretched woman, and all these years you have been wondering— wondering—wondering! You have been mortally afraid, my husband."

"I tell you, I was certain—I was sure of———"

"Then why do you still love her?"

He stared at her open-mouthed, speechless.

"Why do you still love her?"

"Are you mad?" he gasped. "Good God, woman, how can you ask that question of me, knowing that I love you with all my heart and soul? How———"

"With all your heart, yes! But with your soul? No! That other woman has your soul. I have heard your soul speak, and it speaks of her—yes, to her!"

"In God's name, what———"

"Night after night, in your sleep, James Brood, you have cried out to 'Matilde.' You have sobbed out your love for her, as you have been doing for twenty years or more. In your sleep your soul has been with her. With me at your side, you have cried on 'Matilde'! You have passed your hand over my face and murmured 'Matilde'! Not once have you uttered the word 'Yvonne'! And now you come to me and say: 'We will come straight to the point'! Well, now you may come straight to the point. But do not forget, in blaming me, that you love another woman!"

He was petrified. Not a drop of blood remained in his face.

"Is this true, this that you are telling me?" he cried, dazed and shaken.

"You need not ask. Call upon your dreams for the answer, if you must have one."

"It is some horrible, ghastly delusion. It cannot be true. Her name has not passed my lips in twenty years. It is not mentioned in my presence. I have not uttered that woman's name———"

"Then how should I know her name? Her own son does not know it, I firmly believe. No one appears to know it except the man who says he despises it."

"Dreams! Dreams!" he cried scornfully. "Shall I be held responsible for the unthinkable things that happen in dreams?"

"No," she replied significantly; "you should not be held accountable. She must be held accountable. You drove out her body, James, but not her spirit. It stands beside you every instant of the day and night. By day you do not see her; by night—ah, you tremble! Well, she is dead, they say. If she were still alive I myself might tremble, and with cause."

"Before God, I love you, Yvonne. I implore you to think nothing of my maunderings in sleep. They—they may come from a disordered brain. God knows there was a time when I felt that I was mad, raving mad. These dreams are——"

To his surprise she laid her hand gently on his arm.

"I pity you sometimes, James. My heart aches for you. You are a man—a strong, brave man, and yet you shrink and cringe when a voice whispers to you in the night. You sleep with your doubts awake. Yes, yes, I believe you when you say that you love me. I am sure that you do; but let me tell you what it is that I have divined. It is Matilde that you are loving through me. When you kiss me there is in the back of your mind somewhere the thought of kisses that were given long ago. When you hold me close to you it is the body of Matilde that you feel, it is her breath that warms your cheeks. I am Matilde, not Yvonne, to you. I am the flesh on which that starved love of yours feeds; I represent the memory of all that you have lost; I am the bodily instrument."

"This is—madness!" he exclaimed, and it was not only wonder that filled his eyes. There was a strange fear in them, too.

"I do not expect you to admit that all this is true, James," she went on patiently. "You will confess one day that I am right, however; to yourself, if not to me. If the time should ever come when I give to you a child———" She shivered and turned her eyes away from his.

He laid an unsteady hand upon the dark head. "There, there," he murmured brokenly.

"It would be Matilde's child to you," she concluded, facing him again without so much as a quaver in her voice, she spoke calmly, as if the statement were the most commonplace remark in the world.

"Good Heaven, Yvonne!" he exclaimed, drawing back in utter dismay. "You must compose yourself. This is———"

"I am quite myself, James," she said coolly. "Can you deny that you think of her when you hold me in your arms? Can you———"

"Yes!" he almost shouted. "I can and do deny!"

"Then you are lying to yourself, my husband," she said quietly.

He fairly gasped.

"Good God! What manner of woman are you?" he cried hoarsely. "A sorceress? A—but no, it is not true!"

She smiled. "All women are sorceresses. They feel. Men only think. Poor Frederic! You try to hate him, James, but I have watched you when you were not aware. You search his face intently, almost in agony—for what? For the look that was his mother's—for the expression you loved in———"

He burst out violently.

"No! By Heaven, you are wrong there! I am not looking for Matilde in Frederic's face."

"For his father, then?" she inquired slowly.

The perspiration stood out on his brow. He made no response. His lips were compressed.

"You have uttered her name at last," she said wonderingly, after a long wait for him to speak.

Brood started. "I—I—oh, this is torture!"

"We must mend our ways, James. It may please you to know that I shall overlook your mental faithlessness to me. You may go on loving Matilde. She is dead. I am alive. I have the better of her there, *aïe?* The day will come when she will be dead in every sense of the word. In the meantime, I am content to enjoy life. Frederic is quite safe with me, James; very much safer than he is with you. And now let us have peace. Will you ring for tea?"

He sat down abruptly, staring at her with heavy eyes. She waited for a moment and then crossed over to pull the old-fashioned bell-cord.

"We will ask Lydia and Frederic to join us, too," she said. "It shall be a family party, the five of us."

"Five?" he muttered.

"Yes," she said, without a smile.

CHAPTER X

Afortnight passed. Yvonne held the destiry of three persons in her hand. They were like figures on a chess-board, and she moved them with the sureness, the unerring instinct of any skilled disciple of the philosopher's game. They were puppets; she ranged them about her stage in swift-changing pictures, and applauded her own effectiveness. There were no rehearsals. The play was going on all the time, whether tragedy, comedy, or chess.

Brood's uneasiness increased. His moody eyes were seldom lifted to meet the question that he knew lurked in hers. She had given him a tremendous shock. There was seldom a moment in which he was not making strange inquiries of himself.

Was it possible that she had spoken the truth about him? Could such a condition of mind exist without his knowledge? Was this love he professed to feel for her but the flame springing into life from those despised embers of long ago? Was it true that his inner self, his subconscious being, recognised no other claim to his love than the one held so insecurely by its original possessor? Was it true that his soul went back to her the instant slumber came to close up the gap of years?

This strange, new wife of his had uttered amazing words; she had spoken without rancour; she had called his dreams to life; she had told him how he lived while asleep!

He arose in the mornings, haggard from lack of reposeful sleep. In a way, he slept with one ear open, constantly striving to catch himself with the dream-name on his lips. He would awake with a start many times in the night, and always there seemed to be the vague, ghostlike whisper of a name dying away in the stillness that greeted his return to wakefulness.

Now he confessed to himself that his dreams were of Matilde, as they had been during all the years. Heretofore they had been mere impressions upon his intelligence, and seldom remembered. They did not represent pictures or incidents in which she appeared as a potent factor, but brief monodies, with her name as the single note, her face a passing, yet impressive, vision. He had not realised how frequent, how real these dreams were until now.

He sometimes lay perfectly still after these awakenings, wondering if Yvonne was listening at his closed door, straining his ears for the sound of a creaking board that would betray her presence as she stole back to her own bed.

What surprised and puzzled him most was her serenity in the face of these involuntary revelations. She did not appear to be disturbed by the fact that his dreams, his most secret thoughts, were of another woman. There was nothing in her manner to indicate that she suffered any of the pangs of jealousy, humiliation, dismay, or doubt that might reasonably have been expected under the circumstances. She seemed to put the matter entirely out of her mind as trivial, unimportant, unvexing. He found himself wondering what his own state of mind would be if the conditions were reversed and it was she who cried out in her sleep.

Frederic was alert, shifty, secretive. He knew himself to be the link in the chain that would offer the least resistance of any if it came to the question of endurance. He realised that the slightest tug at the chain would cause it to snap, and that the break would never be repaired. His stepmother for the present fortified the weak spot in the chain; but would her strength be sufficient to support the strain that was to be imposed upon both links in the end?

He watched her like a hawk, ever on the lookout for the slightest signs of commendation, reproof, warning, encouragement. She alone stood between him and what appeared to be the inevitable. The truce was a mask that hid none of the real features of the situation. When would it be discarded?

After that illuminating hour in her boudoir he saw himself in a far from noble position. The situation was no longer indefinite. He had taken a step that could not be recalled. His loyalty to Lydia had been tested, and the sickening truth came out—he was a traitor! He knew in his soul that he loved the girl. His conscience told him so. But his conscience suddenly had become an elastic thing that stretched over a pretty wide scope of emotions. These he tried to analyse and, failing to do so with credit to himself, settled back into a state of apathy better described as sullen self-pity. He even went so far as to blame his father for the new blight that had been put upon him.

Of the three, Lydia alone faced the situation with courage. She was young, she was good, she was inexperienced, but she saw what was going on beneath the surface with a clarity of vision that would have surprised an older and more practised person; and, seeing, was favoured with the strength to endure pain that otherwise would have been insupportable.

She knew that Frederic was infatuated. She did not try to hide the truth from herself. The boy she loved was slipping away from her, and only chance could set his feet back in the old path from which he blindly strayed. Her woman's heart told her that it was not love he felt for Yvonne. The strange mentor that guides her sex out of the ignorance of youth into an understanding of hitherto unpresented questions revealed to her the nature of his feeling for this woman.

He would come back to her in time, she knew, chastened; the same instinct that revealed his frailties to her also defended his sense of honour. The unthinkable could never happen!

She judged Yvonne, too, in a spirit of fairness that was amazing, considering the lack of perspective that must have been hers to contend with. Despite a natural feeling of antagonism, present even before she saw the new wife of James Brood, and long before her influence affected Brood's son, Lydia found herself confronted by a curious faith in Yvonne's goodness of heart. It never entered the girl's mind to question the honour of this woman—no more than she would have questioned her own.

Vanity, love of admiration, the inherent fear of retrogression, greed for attention—any one of these might have been responsible for her conduct covering the past three months. There was certainly a reckless disregard for consequences on her part so far as . others—notably Frederic—were concerned. She could not be blind to his plight, and yet it was her pleasure to drag him out beyond his depth where he might struggle or drown while she, sirenlike, looked on for the moment and then turned calmly to the more serious business of combing her hair.

Her mother saw the suffering in the girl's eyes, but saw also the proud spirit that would have resented sympathy from one even so close as she. Down in the heart of that quiet, reserved mother smouldered a hatred for Yvonne Brood that would have stopped at nothing had it been in her power to inflict punishment for the wrong that was being done. She, too, saw tragedy ahead, but her vision was broader than Lydia's. It included the figure of James Brood.

Lydia worked steadily, almost doggedly, at the task she had undertaken to complete for the elder Brood. Every afternoon found her seated at the desk in the study opposite the stern-faced man who laboured with her over the seemingly endless story of his life. Something told her that there were secret chapters which she was not to write. She wrote those that were to endure; the others were to die with him.

He watched her as she wrote, and his eyes were often hard. He saw the growing haggardness in her gentle, girlish face; the wistful, puzzled expression in her dark eyes. A note of tenderness crept into his voice and remained there through all the hours they spent together. The old-time brusqueness disappeared from his speech; the sharp, authoritative tone was gone. He watched her with pity in his heart, for he knew it was ordained that one day he, too, was to hurt this loyal, pure-hearted creature even as the others were wounding her now.

He frequently went out of his way to perform quaint little acts of courtesy and kindness that would have surprised him only a short time before. He sent theatre and opera tickets to Lydia and her mother. He placed bouquets of flowers at the girl's end of the desk, obviously for her alone. He sent her home—just around the corner—in the automobile on rainy or blizzardy days.

But he never allowed her an instant's rest when it came to the work in hand, and therein lay the gentle shrewdness of the man. She was better off busy. There were times when he studied the face of Lydia's mother for signs that might show how her thoughts ran in relation to the conditions that were confronting all of them. But more often he searched the features of the boy who called him father.

Not one of them knew that there were solemn hours in all the days when Yvonne sat shivering in her room and stared, dry-eyed and bleak, at the walls which surrounded her, seeing not them, but something far beyond. Often she sat before her long cheval-glass, either with lowering eyes or in a sort of wistful wonder, never removing her steady gaze from the face reflected there. There were other times when she stood before the striking photograph of her husband on the dressing-table, studying the face through narrowed lids, as if she searched for something that baffled, yet impressed her.

Always, always there was music in the house. Behind the closed doors of his distant study James Brood listened in spite of himself to the persistent thrumming of the piano downstairs. Always were the airs light and seductive; the dreamy, plaintive compositions of Strauss, Ziehrer, and others of their kind and place.

Frederic, with uncanny fidelity to the preferences of the mother he had never seen, but whose influence directed him, affected the same general class of music that had appealed to her moods and temperament. Times there were, and often, when he played the very airs that she had loved, and then, despite his profound antipathy, James Brood's thoughts leaped back a quarter of a century and fixed themselves on love-scenes and love-times that would not be denied.

And again there were the wild, riotous airs that she had played with Feverelli, her soft-eyed music-master! Accursed airs—accursed and accusing!

He gave orders that these airs were not to be played, but failed to make his command convincing for the reason that he could not bring himself to the point of explaining why they were distasteful to him. When Frederic thoughtlessly whistled or hummed fragments of those proscribed airs he considered himself justified in commanding him to stop on the pretext that they were disturbing, but he could not use the same excuse for checking the song on the lips of his gay and impulsive wife. Sometimes he wondered why she persisted when she knew that he was annoyed. Her airy little apologies for her forgetfulness were of no consequence, for within the hour her memory was almost sure to be at fault again.

Mr Dawes fell ill. He ventured out one day when the winds of March were fierce and sharp, and, being an adventurer, caught the most dangerous sort of a cold. He came in shivering and considerably annoyed because Jones or Ranjab or some other incompetent servant had failed to advise him to wear an overcoat and galoshes. To his surprise Mrs Brood ordered a huge, hot drink of whisky and commanded him to drink it—"like a good boy." Then she had him stowed away in bed with loads of blankets about him.

Just before dinner she came up to see him. He was still shivering. So was Mr Riggs, for that matter, but Mr Riggs failed to shiver convincingly and did not receive the treatment he desired. Their unexpected visitor felt the pulse and forehead of the sick man, uttered a husky little cry of dismay, and announced that he had a fever. Whereupon Mr Dawes said, rather shamefacedly, that he would be all right in the morning and that it was nothing at all.

"We will have the doctor at once, Mr Dawes," said she, and instructed Mr Riggs to call Jones.

"I don't want a doctor," said Mr Dawes stoutly.

"I know you don't," said she, with her rarest smile; "but I *do*, you see."

"They're no good," said Mr Dawes.

"Better have one," advised Mr Riggs with sudden solemnity.

"Never had one in my life," said Mr Dawes. "Don't believe in 'em. I'll take a couple of stiff drinks before I go to bed and———"

"But you've gone to bed, you old dear," cried she, stroking his burning hand gently.

He was too astonished to say a word.

"Jumping Jees——" began Mr Riggs, completely staggered. "I mean, what doctor, Mrs Brood?"

"Jones will know. Now, Mr Dawes, you must do just as I tell you to do. You are nothing but a child, you know. If — — —"

"Hey, Joe!" called out the sick man desperately, but his comrade was gone. "Don't let him call a—doctor, Mrs Brood; please don't!" he implored.

She sat down on the edge of the bed, holding his hand between her soft, cool palms, and smiled at him so tenderly that he stared for a moment in utter bewilderment and then gulped mightily. "Hush!" she said.

"I—I don't want to be sick here, bothering you and upsetting everything— — —" he blubbered.

"We will have you up and about in a day or two," she said.

"But it's such an infernal nuisance. You oughtn't to be sitting here, either. It may be catching."

"Nonsense! I'm not afraid."

"It's—it's mighty good of you," he muttered, his eyes blinking.

"What are friends for, Mr Dawes, if they can't be depended upon in times of sickness?"

"Friends?" he gasped.

"Certainly. Am I not your friend?"

"I—I—well, by gosh!" he exploded. "I—I must tell this to Joe. He'll—I beg your pardon, I guess I'm a little flighty. Maybe I'm worse than I think. Delirious or something like that. Say, you don't think it's—it's serious, do you?"

"Of course not. A heavy cold, that's all. The doctor will break it up immediately."

"Maybe it's the grippe, eh?"

"Possibly."

"What's my temperature?"

"You mustn't worry, Mr Dawes. It's all right."

He was silent for a moment, steadfastly regarding the hand that stroked his wrinkled old paw so gently.

"If—if it should turn out to be pneumonia or lung fever, I wish you wouldn't let on to Joe," said he anxiously. "It would worry him almost to death. He's not very strong, you see. Nothing like me. I'm as strong as a bull. Never been sick in my— — —"

"I know," she said quietly. "He isn't half so strong as you, Mr Dawes. You are so strong you will be able to throw off this cold in a jiffy, as Jones would say. It won't amount to anything."

"If I get much worse you'd better send me to a hospital. Awful nuisance having a sick man about the place. Spoils everything. Don't hesitate about sending me off, Mrs Brood. I wouldn't be a trouble to you or Jim for— — —"

"You poor old dear! You shall stay right where you are, no matter what comes to pass, and I shall take charge of you myself."

"You?" She nodded her head briskly. "Well, by jiggers, I—I don't know what Joe'll say when I tell him this. Blast him; I'll bet my head he calls me a liar. If he does, blast him, I'll—oh, I beg your pardon! I don't seem to be able to get over the habit of— — —"

"Here is Mr Riggs—and my husband," she interrupted, as the door opened and the two men strode into the room. "Is Jones telephoning?"

"Yes," said Brood. "Why, what's gone wrong, old man?"

"It's all my fault," groaned Mr Riggs, sitting down heavily on the opposite side of the bed. "I let him go out without his overcoat. He's not a strong man, Jim. Least breath of air goes right through— —"

"See here, Riggs, you know better than that," roared the sick man wrathfully. "I can stand more— — —"

"There, there!" cried Mrs Brood reprovingly. "It isn't fair to quarrel with Mr Riggs. He can't very well abuse you in return, Mr Dawes, can he?"

"You may be on your death-bed," said Mr Riggs mournfully, as if that were reason enough for not abusing him.

"Nonsense," said Brood; but it was an anxious look that he shot at Yvonne. Mr Dawes's face was fiery hot.

"I shall come back to see you immediately after dinner, Mr Dawes," said she, and again stroked his hand.

The two old men stared after her rather blankly as she left the room. They couldn't believe their ears.

"She says she'll look after me herself," murmured Mr Dawes hazily. Mr Riggs tucked the covers about his chin. "Don't do that, Joe! Leave things alone, darn you. She fixed 'em as they ought to be." Mr Riggs obediently undid his work. "That's right. Now don't you do anything without askin' her, d'ye hear?"

"I was only trying to make you— — —"

"Well, don't do it. Leave everything to her." The upshot of it all was that Mr Dawes came near to dying. Pneumonia set in at once, and for many days he fought what appeared to be a losing fight. Then came the splendid days of convalescence, the happiest days of his life. The amazing Mrs Brood did "look after him." Nurses there were, of course, and doctors in consultation, but it was the much-berated mistress of the house who "pulled him through," as he afterward and always declared in acrimonious disputes with Mr Riggs who, while secretly blessing the wife of Brood, could not be driven into an open admission that she had done "anything more than anybody else would have done under the circumstances," —and not "half as much, for that matter, as he could have done had he been given a chance."

It may be well to observe here that Mr Riggs was of no earthly use whatever during the trying days. Indeed, he gave up hope the instant the doctor said "pneumonia," and went about the house saying "My God" to himself and everybody else in sepulchral whispers, all the while urging Heaven to "please do something." He was too pathetic for words.

A new and totally unsuspected element in Yvonne's make-up came to light at this troublous period. She forsook many pleasures, many comforts in her eagerness to help the suffering old man who, she must have known, in his heart had long despised her. She did not interfere with the nurses, yet made herself so indispensable to old Mr Dawes in the capacity of "visiting angel" that his heart overflowed with gratitude and love. Even when death hung directly above his almost sightless eyes he saw her smile of encouragement in the shadows, and his spirit responded with what might justly have been called the battle-cry of life.

To Brood this new side to Yvonne's far from understandable character was most gratifying. Seeing her in the rôle of good Samaritan was not so surprising to him as the real, unaffected sincerity with which she ministered to the wants of the querulous old man.

Even the nurses, habitually opposed to the good offices of "the family," were won over by this woman whose unparalleled sweetness levelled them into a condition of respect and love that surprised not only themselves but the doctors. They were quite docile from the start, and seldom, if ever, spoke of Mr Dawes as "the patient" or of his state as "the case." They got into the habit of alluding to him as the "dear old man," and somehow envied each other the hours "on duty." They were never sour.

And so, when it came time for Mr Dawes to thank the Lord for his escape, he refused to commit himself to anything so ridiculous! He even went so far as to declare that the doctor had nothing to do with it, a statement which rather staggered the nurses.

For hours Yvonne read to the blissful old chap. Sometimes she read to him in French, again in Russian, and occasionally in German. It was all one to him. He did not understand a word of it, but he was happy. He felt surprisingly young.

She gave up a month to him and he was prepared to give up his life to her. To his utter amazement, however, she did not exact anything so valuable as that. Indeed, when his recovery was quite complete, she calmly forgot his existence and he sank back into the oblivion from which calamity had dragged him; sank back to the unhappy level of Mr Riggs and all the others who failed to interest her; and there he dreamed of exalted days when she wanted him to live, contrasting them with these days in which he might just as well be dead for all she seemed to care! He was one of the "old men" again.

Mr Riggs, writhing with jealousy, repeatedly remarked, "I told you so," and somehow felt revenged for the insolent orders she had given to Jones, depriving him of the right to even approach the door of the room in which his lifelong friend was dying. It had been a hard week for Mr Riggs. He hated her as he had never hated anyone in his life before. And yet he thanked God for her, and would have died for her! Nothing, nothing in the world would have given him more pleasure than to be critically ill for her!

CHAPTER XI

"Is there anything wrong with my hair, Mr Brood?" asked Lydia, with a nervous little laugh.

They were in the study, and it was ten o'clock of a wet night in April. Of late he had required her to spend the evenings with him in a strenuous effort to complete the final chapters of the journal. The illness of Mr Dawes had interrupted the work, and he was now in a fever of impatience to make up for the lost time. He had declared his intention to go abroad with his wife as soon as the manuscript was completed. The editor of a magazine, a personal friend, had signified his willingness to edit the journal and to put it into shape for publication during the summer months, against Brood's return in the fall of the year.

The master of the house spared neither himself nor Lydia in these last few weeks. He wanted to clear up everything before he went away. Lydia's willingness to devote the extra hours to his enterprise would have pleased him vastly if he had not been afflicted by the same sense of unrest and uneasiness that made incessant labour a boon to her as well as to him.

Her query followed a long period of silence on his part. He had been suggesting alterations in her notes as she read them to him, and there were frequent lulls when she made the changes as directed. Without looking at him she felt, rather than knew, that he was regarding her fixedly from his position opposite. The scrutiny was disturbing to her. She hazarded the question for want of a better means of breaking the spell. Of late he had taken to watching her with moody interest. She knew that he was mentally commenting on the changes he could not help observing in her appearance and her manners. This intense, though perhaps unconscious, scrutiny annoyed her. Her face was flushed with embarrassment, her heart was beating with undue rapidity.

Brood started guiltily.

"Your hair?" he exclaimed. "Oh, I see. You women always feel that something is wrong with it. I was thinking of something else, however. Forgive my stupidity. We can't afford to waste time in thinking, you know, and I am a pretty bad offender. It's nearly half-past ten. We've been hard at it since eight o'clock. Time to knock off. I will walk around to your apartment with you, my dear. It looks like an all-night rain."

He went up to the window and pulled the curtains aside. Her eyes followed him.

"It's such a short distance, Mr Brood," she said. "I am not afraid to go alone."

He was staring down into the court, his fingers grasping the curtains in a rigid grip. He did not reply.

There was a light in the windows opening out upon Yvonne's balcony.

"I fancy Frederic has come in from the concert," he said slowly. "He will take you home, Lydia. You'd like that better, eh?"

He turned toward her, and she paused in the nervous collecting of her papers. His eyes were as hard as steel, his lips were set.

"Please don't ask Frederic to———" she began hurriedly.

"They must have left early," he muttered, glancing at his watch. Returning to the table he struck the big, melodious gong a couple of sharp blows. For the first time in her recollection it sounded a jangling, discordant note, as of impatience.

She felt her heart sink; an oppressing sense of alarm came over her.

"Good night, Mr Brood. Don't think of coming home with———"

"Wait, Frederic will go with you." It was a command. Ranjab appeared in the doorway. "Have Mrs Brood and Mr Frederic returned, Ranjab?"

"Yes, *sahib*. At ten o'clock."

"If Mr Frederic is in his room, send him to me."

"He is not in his room, *sahib*."

The two, master and man, looked at each other steadily for a moment. Something passed between them.

"Tell him that Miss Desmond is ready to go home."

"Yes, *sahib*." The curtains fell.

"I prefer to go home alone, Mr Brood," said Lydia, her eyes flashing. "Why did you send———"

"And why not?" he demanded harshly. She winced, and he was at once sorry. "Forgive me. I am tired and—a bit nervous. And you, too, are tired. You've been working too steadily at this miserable job, my dear child. Thank Heaven, it will soon be over. Pray sit down. Frederic will soon be here."

"I am not tired," she protested stubbornly. "I love the work. You don't know how proud I shall be when it comes out, and—and I realise that I helped in its making. No one has ever been in a position to tell the story of Tibet as you have told it, Mr Brood. Those chapters will make history. I———"

"Your poor father's share in those explorations is what really makes the work valuable, my dear. Without his notes and letters I should have been feeble indeed." He looked at his watch. "They were at the concert, you know—the Hungarian orchestra. A recent importation, 'Tzigane's' music. Gipsies." His sentences as well as his thoughts were staccato, disconnected.

Lydia turned very cold. She dreaded the scene that now seemed unavoidable. Frederic would come in response to his father's command, and then———

Someone began to play upon the piano downstairs. She knew, and he knew, that it was Frederic who played. For a long time they listened. The air, no doubt, was one he had heard during the evening, a soft, sensuous waltz that she had never heard before. The girl's eyes were upon Brood's face. It was like a graven image.

"God!" fell from his stiff lips. Suddenly he turned upon the girl. "Do you know what he is playing?"

"No," she said, scarcely above a whisper.

"It was played in this house by its composer before Frederic was born. It was played here on the night of his birth, as it had been played many times before. It was written by a man named Feverelli. Have you heard of him?"

"Never," she murmured, and shrank, frightened by the deathlike pallor in the man's face, by the strange calm in his voice. The gates were being opened at last! She saw the thing that was to stalk forth. She would have closed her ears against the revelations it carried. "Mother will be worried if I am not at home———"

"Guido Feverelli. An Italian born in Hungary. Budapest, that was his home, but he professed to be a gipsy. Yes, he wrote the devilish thing. He played it a thousand times in that room down——— And now Frederic plays it, after all these years. It is his heritage. God, how I hate the thing! Ranjab! Where is the fellow? He must stop the accursed thing. He———"

"Mr Brood! Mr Brood!" cried Lydia, appalled. She began to edge toward the door.

By a mighty effort Brood regained control of himself. He sank into a chair, motioning for her to remain. The music had ceased abruptly.

"He will be here in a moment," said Brood. "Don't go."

They waited, listening. Ranjab entered the room; so noiseless was his approach that neither heard his footsteps.

"Well?" demanded Brood, looking beyond.

"Master Frederic begs a few minutes' time, *sahib*. He is putting down on paper the music, so that he may not forget. He writes the notes, *sahib*. *Madame* assists."

Brood's shoulders sagged. His head was bent, but his gaze never left the face of the Hindu.

"You may go, Ranjab," he said slowly.

"Ten minutes he asks for, *sahib*, that is all." The curtains fell behind him once more.

"So that he may not forget!" fell from Brood's lips. He was looking at the girl, but did not address his words to her. "So that he may not forget! So that I, too, may not forget!"

Suddenly he arose and confronted the serene image of the Buddha. For a full minute he stood there with his hands clasped, his lips moving as if in prayer. No sound came from them.

The girl remained transfixed, powerless to move. Not until he turned toward her and spoke was the spell broken. Then she came quickly to his side. He had pronounced her name.

"You are about to tell me something, Mr Brood," she cried in great agitation. "I do not care to listen. I feel that it is something I should not know. Please let me go now. I— — —"

He laid his hands upon her shoulders, holding her off at arm's length.

"I am very fond of you, Lydia. I do not want to hurt you. Sooner would I have my tongue cut out than it should wound you by a single word. Yet I must speak. You love Frederic. Is not that true?"

She returned his gaze unwaveringly. Her face was very white.

"Yes, Mr Brood."

"I have known it for some time, although I was the last to see. You love him, and you are just beginning to realise that he is not worthy."

"Mr Brood!"

"Your eyes have been opened." She stared, speechless. "My poor girl, he was born to prove that honest love is the rarest thing in all this world."

"Oh, I beg of you, Mr Brood, don't— — —"

"It is better that we should talk it over. We have ten minutes. No doubt he has told you that he loves you. He is a lovable boy, he is the kind one *must* love. But it is not in his power to love nobly. He loves lightly as" — he hesitated, and then went on harshly — "as his father before him loved."

Anger dulled her understanding; she did not grasp the full meaning of his declaration. Her honest heart rose to the defence of Frederic.

"Mr Brood, I do care for Frederic," she flamed, standing very erect before him. "He is not himself, he has not been himself since she came here. Oh, I am fully aware of what I am saying. He is not to be blamed for this thing that has happened to him. No one is to blame. It had to be. I can wait, Mr Brood. Frederic loves me. I know he does. He will come back to me. You have no right to say that he loves lightly, ignobly. You do not know him as I know him. You have never tried to know him, never wanted to know him. You — oh, I beg your pardon, Mr Brood. I — I am forgetting myself."

"I am afraid you do not understand yourself, Lydia," said he levelly. "You are young, you are trusting. Your lesson will cost you a great deal, my dear."

"You are mistaken. I do understand myself," she said gravely. "May I speak plainly, Mr Brood?"

"Certainly. I intend to speak plainly to you."

"Frederic loves me. He does not love Yvonne. He is fascinated, as I also am fascinated by her, and you, too, Mr Brood. The spell has fallen over all of us. Let me go on, please. You say that Frederic loves like his father before him. That is true. He loves but one woman. You love but one woman, and she is dead. You will always love her. Frederic is like you. He loves Yvonne as you do — oh, I know it hurts! She cast her spell over you, why not over him? Is he stronger than you? Is it strange that she should attract him as she attracted you? You glory in her beauty, her charm, her perfect loveliness, and yet you love — yes, *love*, Mr Brood — the woman who was Frederic's mother. Do I make my meaning plain? Well, so it is that Frederic loves me. I am content to wait. I know he loves me."

Through all this Brood stared at her in sheer astonishment. He had no feeling of anger, no resentment, no thought of protest.

"You — you astound me, Lydia. Is this your own impression, or has it been suggested to you by — by another?"

"I am only agreeing with you when you say that he loves as his father loved before him — but not lightly. Ah, not lightly, Mr Brood."

"You don't know what you are saying," he muttered.

"Oh, yes, I do," she cried earnestly. "You invite my opinion; I trust you will accept it for what it is worth. Before you utter another word against Frederic, let me remind you that I have known both of you for a long, long time. In all the years I have been in this house I have never known you to grant him a tender, loving word. My heart has ached for him. There have been times when I almost hated you. He feels your neglect, your harshness, your—your cruelty. He— — —"

"Cruelty!"

"It is nothing less. You do not like him. I cannot understand why you should treat him as you do. He shrinks from you. Is it right, Mr Brood, that a son should shrink from his father as a dog cringes at the voice of an unkind master? I might be able to understand your attitude toward him if your unkindness was of recent origin, but— — —"

"Recent origin?" he demanded quickly.

"If it had begun with the advent of Mrs Brood," she explained frankly, undismayed by his scowl. "I do not understand all that has gone before. Is it surprising, Mr Brood, that your son finds it difficult to love you? Do you deserve— — —"

Brood stopped her with a gesture of his hand.

"The time has come for frankness on my part. You set me an example, Lydia. You have the courage of your father. For months I have had it in my mind to tell you the truth about Frederic, but my courage has always failed me. Perhaps I use the wrong word. It may be something very unlike cowardice that has held me back. I am going to put a direct question to you first of all, and I ask you to answer truthfully. Would you say that Frederic is like—that is, resembles his father?" He was leaning forward, his manner intense.

Lydia was surprised.

"What an odd thing to say! Of course he resembles his father. I have never seen a portrait of his mother, but— — —"

"You mean that he looks like me?" demanded Brood.

"Certainly. What do you mean?"

Brood laughed, a short, ugly laugh—and then fingered his chin nervously.

"He resembles his mother," he said.

"When he is angry he is very much like you, Mr Brood. I have often wondered why he is unlike you at other times. Now I know. He is like his mother. She must have been lovely, gentle, patient— — —"

"Wait! Suppose I were to tell you that Frederic is not my son?"

"I should not believe you, Mr Brood," she replied flatly. "What is it that you are trying to say to me?"

He turned away abruptly.

"I will not go on with it. The subject is closed. There is nothing to tell — at present."

She placed herself in front of him, resolute and determined.

"I insist, Mr Brood. The time *has* come for you to be frank. You must tell me what you meant by that remark."

"Has your mother never told you anything concerning my past life?" he demanded.

"What has my mother to do with your past life?" she inquired, suddenly afraid.

"I refer only to what she may have heard from your father. He knew more than any of them. I confided in him to a great extent. I had to unburden myself to someone. He was my best friend. It is not improbable that he repeated certain parts of my story to your mother."

"She has told me that you — you were not happy, Mr Brood."

"Is that all?"

"I — I think so."

"Is that all?" he insisted.

"When I was a little girl I heard my father say to her that your life had been ruined by — well, that your marriage had turned out badly," she confessed haltingly.

"What more did he say?"

"He said — I remember feeling terribly about it — he said you had driven your wife out of this very house."

"Did he speak of another man?"

"Yes. Her music-master."

"You were too young to know what that meant, eh?"

"I knew that you never saw her after — after she left this house."

"Will you understand how horrible it all was if I say to you now that — Frederic is not my son?"

Her eyes filled with horror.

"How can you say such a thing, Mr Brood? He is your son. How can you say———"

"His father is the man who wrote the accursed waltz he has just been playing! Could there be anything more devilish than the conviction it carries? After all these years, he———"

"Stop, Mr Brood!"

"I am sorry if I hurt you, Lydia. You have asked me why I hate him. Need I say anything more?"

"You have only made me love him more than ever before. You cannot hurt me through Frederic."

"I am sorry that it has come to such a pass as this. It is not right that you should be made to suffer, too."

"I do not believe all that you have told me. He *is* your son. He *is*, Mr Brood."

"I would to God I could believe that!" he cried in a voice of agony. "I would to God it were true!"

"You could believe it if you chose to believe your own eyes, your own heart." She lowered her voice to a half whisper. "Does—does Frederic know? Does he know that his mother—oh, I can't believe it!"

"He does not know."

"And you did drive her out of this house?" Brood did not answer. "You sent her away and and kept her boy, the boy who was nothing to you? Nothing!"

"I kept him," he said, with a queer smile on his lips.

"All these years? He never knew his mother?"

"He has never heard her name spoken."

"And she?"

"I only know that she is dead. She never saw him after—after that day."

"And now, Mr Brood, may I ask why you have always intended to tell me this dreadful thing?" she demanded, her eyes gleaming with a fierce, accusing light.

He stared. "Doesn't—doesn't it put a different light on your estimate of him? Doesn't it convince you that he is not worthy of———"

"No! A thousand times no!" she cried. "I love him. If he were to ask me to be his wife tonight I would rejoice—oh, I would rejoice! Someone is coming. Let me say this to you, Mr Brood: you have brought Frederic up as a butcher fattens the calves and swine he prepares for slaughter. You are waiting for the hour to come when you can kill his very soul with the weapon you have held over him for so long, waiting, waiting, waiting! In God's name, what has *he* done that you should want to strike him down after all these years? It is in my heart to curse you, but somehow I feel that you are a curse to yourself. I will not say that I cannot understand how you feel about everything. You have suffered. I know you have, and I—I am sorry for you. And knowing how bitter life has been for you, I implore you to be merciful to him who is innocent."

The man listened without the slightest change of expression. The lines seemed deeper about his eyes, that was all. But the eyes were bright and as hard as the steel they resembled.

"You would marry him?"

"Yes, yes!"

"Knowing that he is a scoundrel?"

"How dare you say that, Mr Brood?"

"Because," said he levelly, "he *thinks* he is my son." Voices were heard on the stairs, Frederic's and Yvonne's. "He is coming now, my dear," he went on, and then, after a pause fraught with significance, "and my wife is with him."

Lydia closed her eyes, as if in dire pain. A dry sob was in her throat.

A strange thing happened to Brood, the man of iron. Tears suddenly rushed to his eyes.

CHAPTER XII

Yvonne stopped in the doorway. Ranjab was holding the curtains aside for her to enter. The tall figure of Frederic loomed up behind her, his dark face glowing in the warm light that came from the room. She had changed her dress for an exquisite orchid-coloured tea-gown of chiffon under the rarest and most delicate of lace. For an instant her gaze rested on Lydia, and then went questioningly to Brood's face. The girl's confusion had not escaped her notice. Her husband's manner was but little less convicting. Her eyes narrowed.

"Ranjab said you were expecting us," she said slowly, with marked emphasis on the participle. She came forward haltingly, as if in doubt as to her welcome. "Are we interrupting?"

"Of course not," said Brood, a flush of annoyance on his cheek. "Lydia is tired. I sent Ranjab down to ask Frederic to— — "

Frederic interrupted, a trifle too eagerly. "I'll walk around with you, Lydia. It's raining, however. Shall I get the car out, father?"

"No, no!" cried Lydia, painfully conscious of the rather awkward situation. "And please don't bother, Freddy. I can go home alone. It's only a step." She moved toward the door, eager to be away.

"I'll go with you," said Frederic decisively. He stood between her and the door, an embarrassed smile on his lips. "I've got something to say to you, Lydia," he went on, lowering his voice.

"James dear," said Mrs Brood, shaking her finger at her husband, and with an exasperating smile on her lips, "you are working the poor girl too hard. See how late it is And how nervous she is. Why, you are trembling, Lydia! For shame, James."

"I am a little tired," stammered Lydia. "We are working so hard, you know, in order to finish the— — — "

Brood interrupted, his tone sharp and incisive.

"The end is in sight. We're a bit feverish over it, I suppose. You see, my dear, we have just escaped captivity in Thassa. It was a bit thrilling, I fancy. But we've stopped for the night."

"So I perceive," said Yvonne, a touch of insolence in her voice. "You stopped, I dare say, when you heard the tread of the vulgar world approaching the inner temple. That is what you broke into and desecrated, wasn't it?"

"The inner temple at Thassa," he said coldly.

"Certainly. The place you were escaping from when we came in."

It was clear to all of them that Yvonne was piqued, even angry. She deliberately crossed the room and threw herself upon the couch, an act so childish, so disdainful, that for a full minute no one spoke, but stared at her, each with a different emotion.

Lydia's eyes were flashing. Her lips parted, but she withheld the angry words that rose to them.

Brood's expression changed slowly from dull anger to one of incredulity, which swiftly gave way to positive joy. His wife was jealous!

Frederic was biting his lips nervously. He allowed Lydia to pass him on her way out, scarcely noticing her, so intently was his gaze fixed upon Yvonne. When Brood followed Lydia into the hall to remonstrate, the young man sprang eagerly to his stepmother's side.

"Good Lord, Yvonne!" he whispered, "that was a nasty thing to say. What will Lydia think? By gad, is it possible that you are jealous? Of Lydia?"

"Jealous?" cried she, struggling with her fury. "Jealous of that girl? Poof! Why should I be jealous of her? She hasn't the blood of a potato!"

"I can't understand you," he said in great perplexity. "You—you told me to-night that you are not sure that you really love him. You— — —"

She stopped him with a quick gesture. Her eyes were smouldering. "Where is he? Gone away with her? Go and look; do."

"They're in the hall. I shall take her home, never fear. I fancy he's trying to explain your insinuating— — —"

She turned on him furiously. "Are you lecturing me? What a tempest in a teapot!"

"Lydia's as good as gold. She— — —"

"Then take her home at once," sneered Yvonne. "This is no place for her."

Frederic paled. "You're not trying to say my father would—good Lord, Yvonne, you must be crazy! Why, that is impossible! If—if I thought— — —" He clenched his fists and glared over his shoulder, missing the queer little smile that flitted across her face.

"You do love her then," she said, her voice suddenly soft and caressing.

He stared at her in complete bewilderment.

"I—I—Lord, you gave me a shock!" He passed his hand across his moist forehead. "It can't be so. Why, the very thought of it— — —"

"I suppose I shall have to apologise to Lydia," said she calmly. "Your father will exact it of me, and I shall obey. How does it sound, coming from me? 'I am sorry, Lydia.' Do I say it prettily?"

"I don't understand you at all, Yvonne. I adore you, and yet, by Heaven, I—I actually believe I hated you just now. Listen to me. I've been treating Lydia vilely for a long, long time, but—she's the finest, best, dearest girl in the world. You—even you, Yvonne—shall not utter a word against— — —"

"*Aïe!* What heroics!" she cried ironically. "You are splendid when you are angry, my son. Yes, you are almost as splendid as your father. He, too, has been angry with me. He, too, has made me shudder. But he, too, has forgiven me, as you shall this instant. Say it, Freddy. You do forgive me? I was mean, nasty, ugly, vile—oh, everything that's horrid. I take it all back. Now be nice to me!"

She laid her hand on his arm, an appealing little caress that conquered him in a flash. He clasped her fingers fiercely in his and mumbled incoherently as he leaned forward, drawn resistlessly nearer by the strange magic that was hers.

"You—you are wonderful," he murmured. "I knew you'd regret what you said. You couldn't have meant it."

She smiled, patted his hand gently, and allowed her swimming eyes to rest on his for an instant to complete the conquest. Then she motioned him away. Brood's voice was heard in the doorway. She had, however, planted an insidious thing in Frederic's mind, and it would grow.

Her husband re-entered the room, his arm linked in Lydia's. Frederic was at the table lighting a cigarette.

"You did not mean all that you said a moment ago, Yvonne," said Brood levelly. "Lydia misinterpreted your jest. You meant nothing unkind, I am sure."

He was looking straight into her rebellious eyes. The last gleam of defiance died out of them as he spoke.

"I am sorry, Lydia darling," she said, and reached out her hand to the girl who approached reluctantly, uncertainly. "I confess that I was jealous. Why shouldn't I be jealous? You are so beautiful, so splendid." She drew the girl down beside her. "Forgive me, dear."

Lydia, whose honest heart had been so full of resentment the moment before, could not withstand the humble appeal in the voice of the penitent.

She smiled, first at Yvonne, then at Brood, and never quite understood the impulse that ordered her to kiss the warm, red lips that so recently had offended.

"James dear," fell softly, alluringly, from Yvonne's now tremulous lips. He sprang to her side. She kissed him passionately. "Now we are all ourselves once more," she gasped a moment later, her eyes still fixed inquiringly on those of the man beside her. "Let us be gay! Let us forget! Come, Frederic! Sit here at my feet. Lydia is not going home yet. Ranjab, the cigarettes!"

Frederic, white-faced and scowling, remained at the window, glaring out into the rain-swept night. A steady sheet of raindrops thrashed against the window-panes.

"Hear the wind!" cried Yvonne, after a single sharp glance at his tall, motionless figure. "One can almost imagine that ghosts from every graveyard in the world are whistling past our windows. Should we not rejoice? We have them safely locked outside. There are no ghosts in here to make us shiver—and—shake."

The sentence that began so glibly trailed off in a slow crescendo, ending abruptly. Ranjab was holding the lighted taper for her cigarette. As she spoke her eyes were lifted to his dark, saturnine face. She was saying there were no ghosts when his eyes suddenly fastened on hers. In spite of herself her voice rose in response to the curious dread that chilled her heart as she looked into the shining mirrors above her. She shivered as if in the presence of death! For an incalculably brief period their gaze remained fixed and steady, each reading a mystery. Then the Hindu lowered his heavy lashes and moved away. The little by-scene did not go unnoticed by the others, although its meaning was lost.

"There's nothing to be afraid of, Yvonne," said Brood, pressing the hand which trembled in his. "Your imagination carries you a long way. Are you really afraid of ghosts?"

She answered in a deep, solemn voice that carried conviction.

"I believe in ghosts. I believe the dead come back to us, not to flit about as we are told by superstition, but to lodge—actually to dwell—inside these warm, living bodies of ours. They come and go at will. Sometimes we feel that they are there, but—oh, who knows? Their souls may conquer ours and go on inhabiting———"

"Nonsense!" cried her husband. "Once dead, always dead, my dear."

"Do you really believe that, James?" she demanded seriously. "Have you never felt that something that was not you was living, breathing, speaking in this earthly shell of yours? Something that was not you, I say. Something that— — —"

"Never!" he exclaimed quickly, but his eyes were full of the wonder that he felt.

"Frederic," she called imperatively, "come away from that window!"

The young man joined the group. The sullen look in his face had given way to one of acute inquiry. The new note in her voice produced a strange effect upon him. It seemed like a call for help, a cry out of the darkness.

"It is raining pitchforks," he said, as if to explain his failure to respond at the first call.

"Oh, dear," sighed Lydia uncomfortably.

"You can't go out in the storm, my dear," cried Yvonne, tightening her grip on the girl's arm. "Draw up a chair, Freddy. Let's be cosy."

"Really, Mrs Brood, I should go at once. Mother— — —"

"Your mother is in bed and asleep," protested Yvonne.

"We should all be in bed," said Frederic.

"A bed is a sepulchre. We bury half our lives in it, Frederic. We spend too much time in bed. Why live in our dreams when we should be enjoying to-day and not our yesterdays? Do you want to hear about the concert, James? It was wonderful. The— — —"

"If it was so wonderful, why did you leave before it was over?" demanded her husband, his lips straightening.

She looked at him curiously.

"How do you know that we left before it was over?"

"You have been at home since ten."

They were all playing for time. They all realised that something sinister was attending their little conclave, unseen but vital. Each one knew that united they were safe, each against the other! Lydia was afraid because of Brood's revelations. Yvonne had sensed peril with the message delivered by Ranjab to Frederic. Frederic had come upstairs prepared for rebellion against the caustic remarks that were almost certain to come from his father. Brood was afraid of—himself! He was holding himself in check with the greatest difficulty. He knew that the smallest spark would create the explosion he dreaded and yet courted. Restraint lay heavily, yet shiftingly, upon all of them.

"Oh," said Yvonne easily, "there were still two numbers to be played, and I loathe both of them. Frederic was ready to come away, too."

"And Dr Hodder? Did he come away with you?" inquired Brood.

"No. He insisted on staying to the bitter end. We left him there."

Brood laughed shortly. "I see."

"He said he would come down with the Gunnings," explained Yvonne, her eyes flickering. "Besides, I always feel as though I were riding in an ambulance when he is in the car. He dissected every bit of music they played to-night. Now, James dear, you know he is quite dreadful." She said it pleadingly, poutingly.

"I offered to send the car back for him," said Frederic, speaking for the first time.

Brood drew a long breath. His glance met Lydia's and recognised the mute appeal that lay in her eyes. He smiled faintly, and hope rose in her troubled breast.

"The Gunnings were there," put in Yvonne, puffing more rapidly than usual at her cigarette. "They came to the box with Mr and Mrs Harbison during the intermission."

"What spiteful things did Mrs Harbison say about me?" demanded Brood, affecting a certain lightness of manner. "A cigarette, Ranjab. She despises me, I'm sure. Didn't she ask why I was not there to look after my beautiful and much-coveted wife?"

"She said that you interested her more than any man she knew, and, of course, I considered that particularly spiteful. Her husband declared he would rather shoot with you than with any man in the world. He's very tiresome."

"We've hunted a good bit together," said Brood.

"Harbison says you are the most deadly shot he's ever seen," said Frederic, relaxing slightly.

"What was it he said about your wonderful accuracy with a revolver? What was it, Frederic? Hitting a shilling at some dreadful distance—thirty yards, eh?"

"Thirty paces," said Frederic.

"My father often spoke of your shooting with a revolver, Mr Brood," said Lydia. "He said it was really marvellous."

Yvonne laughed. "How interesting to have a husband who can even see as far as thirty paces. But revolver shooting is a doubtful accomplishment in these days of peace, isn't it? What is there to shoot at?"

"Mad dogs and — men," said Brood. Lydia's look required an answer. "No, I've never shot a mad dog, Lydia."

"Who was the young woman with the lisp, Freddy?" asked Yvonne abruptly.

"Miss Dangerfield. Isn't she amusing? I love that soft Virginia drawl of hers. She's pretty, too. Old Hodder was quite taken with her."

A long, reverberating roll of thunder, ending in an ear-splitting crash that seemed no farther away than the window casement behind them, brought sharp exclamations of terror from the lips of the two women. The men, appalled, started to their feet.

"Good Lord, that *was* close!" cried Frederic. "There was no sign of a storm when we came in — just a steady, gentle spring rain."

"I am frightened," shuddered Yvonne, wide-eyed with fear. "Do you think — — —"

"It struck near by, that's all," said Brood. "Lightning bolts are deceptive. One may think they strike at one's very elbow, and yet the spot is really miles away. I hope your mother is not distressed, my dear," turning to Lydia. "She is afraid of the lightning, I know."

Lydia sprang to her feet. "I must go home at once, Mr Brood. She will be dreadfully frightened. I — —"

There came another deafening crash. The glare filled the room with a brilliant, greenish hue. Ranjab was standing at the window, holding the curtains apart while he peered upward across the space that separated them from the apartment building beyond the court.

"Take me home, Frederic!" cried Lydia frantically. She ran toward the door.

"Let me telephone to your mother, Lyddy," he cried, hurrying after her into the hall.

"No! no! no!" she gasped as she ran. "Don't come with me if you — —"

"I will come!" he exclaimed, as they raced down the stairs. "Don't be frightened, darling. It's all right. Listen to me! Mrs Desmond is as safe as — — —"

"Oh, Freddy, Freddy!" she wailed, breaking under a strain that he was not by way of comprehending. "Oh, Freddy dear!" Her nerves gave way. She was sobbing convulsively when they came to the lower hall.

In great distress he clasped her in his arms, mumbling incoherent words of love, encouragement — even ridicule for the fear she betrayed. Far from his mind was the real cause of her unhappy plight.

He held her close to his breast, and there she sobbed and trembled as with a mighty, racking chill. Her fingers clutched his arm with the grip of one who clings to the edge of a precipice with death below. Her face was buried against his shoulder.

"There! There!" he murmured, appalled by this wild display of fear. "Don't worry, darling. Everything is all right. Oh, you dear, dear girlie! Please, please! My little Lyddy!"

"Take me home, Freddy—take me home," she whispered brokenly. "I cannot stay here another second. Come, dearest—come home with me."

Still they stood there in the dark hall, clasped in each other's arms—stood there for many minutes without realising the lapse of time, thinking not of Mrs Desmond nor the storm that raged outside, but of the storm they were weathering together with the lightning racing through their veins, thunder in their heart-beats.

A footstep in the hall. Frederic looked up, dazed, bewildered. Jones, the butler, was retreating through a door near by, having come upon them unexpectedly.

"I—I beg pardon, sir. I———"

"Oh, Jones! Listen! My raincoat—and father's, quick. And Miss Lydia's things. Yes, yes, it's all right, Jones. It's quite all right." Frederic was calling out the sentences jerkily.

"Quite all right," repeated Jones, his throat swelling, his eyes suddenly dim. "Quite, sir. Yes, yes!" He rushed into the closet at the end of the hall, more grievously upset than he ever had been in all his life before.

"You will come with me, Freddy?" she was whispering, clinging to him as one in panic.

"Yes, yes. Don't be frightened, Lyddy. I—I know everything is all right now. I'm sure of it."

"Oh, I am sure, too, dear. I have always been sure," she cried, and he understood, as she had understood.

Despite the protests of Jones they dashed out into the blighting thunderstorm. The rain beat down in torrents, the din was infernal. As the door closed behind them Lydia, in the ecstasy of freedom from restraint bitterly imposed, gave vent to a shrill cry of relief. Words, the meaning of which he could not grasp, babbled from her lips as they descended the steps. One sentence fell vaguely clear from the others, and it puzzled him. He was sure that she said:

"Oh, I am so glad, so happy we are out of that house—you and I together."

Close together, holding tightly to each other, they breasted the swirling sheets of rain. The big umbrella was of little protection to them, although held manfully to break the force of the cold flood of waters. They bent their strong young bodies against the wind, and a sort of wild, impish hilarity took possession of them. It was freedom, after all! They were fighting a force in nature that they understood, and the sharp, staccato cries that came from their lips were born of an exultant glee which neither of them could have suppressed or controlled. Their hearts were as wild as the tempest about them.

They turned the corner and were flanked by the wind and rain. The long raincoats flattened their sleek, dripping folds tightly against their bodies. It was almost impossible to push forward into this mad deluge. The umbrella, caught by a gust, was turned inside out, and the full force of the storm struck upon their faces, almost taking the breath away. And they laughed as their arms tightened about each other. As one person they breasted the gale.

They were fairly blown through the doors of the apartment-house. Mrs Desmond threw open the door as their wet, soggy feet came sloshing down the hall. Frederic's arm was about Lydia as they approached, and both of their drenched faces were wreathed in smiles—gay, exalted smiles. The mother, white-faced and fearful, stared for a second at the amazing pair, and then held out her arms to them.

She was drenched in their embrace, but no one thought of the havoc that was being created in that swift, impulsive contact.

"It's a fine mess we've made of your rug, Mrs Desmond," said Frederic ruefully a few minutes later.

"Goodness!" cried Lydia, aghast. Then they all realised.

"Take those horrid things off at once, both of you," commanded Mrs Desmond. Her voice trembled. "And your shoes—and stockings. Dear, dear!"

"I must run back home!" exclaimed Frederic.

Lydia placed herself between him and the door.

"No! I want you to stay!" she cried.

"Stay?"

"You shall not go out in that dreadful storm again. I will not let you go, Frederic. Stay—stay here with me."

He stared. "What a funny idea!"

"Wait until the rain is over," added Mrs Desmond.

"No, no!" cried Lydia. "I mean for him to stay here the rest of the night. We can put you up, Freddy. I—I don't want you to go back there until— until to-morrow."

A glad light broke in his face. "By Jove, I—do you know, I'd like to stay? I—I really would, Mrs Desmond. Can you find a place for me?" His voice was eager, his eyes sparkling.

"Yes," said the mother quietly, almost serenely. "You shall have Lydia's bed, Frederic. She can come in with me. Yes, you must stay. Are you not our Frederic?"

"Thank you," he stammered, and his eyes fell.

"I will telephone to Jones when the storm abates," said Mrs Desmond. "Now get out of those coats, and—oh, dear, how wet you are! A hot drink for both."

"Would you mind asking Jones to send over something for me to wear in the morning?" said Frederic, grinning as he stood forth in his evening clothes.

Ten minutes later, in a dressing-gown and bare feet, he sat with them before an open fire and sipped the toddy she had brewed.

"I say, this is great!"

Lydia was suddenly shy and embarrassed.

"Good night," she whispered. Her fingers brushed his cheek lightly.

He drew her down to him and kissed her passionately.

"Good night, my Lyddy!" he said softly, his cheek flushing.

She went quickly from the room.

Later he stood in her sweet, dainty little bedroom and looked about him with a feeling of mingled awe and wonder. All of her intimate, exquisite belongings, the sanctified treasures of her most secret domain, were all about him.

He fingered the articles on her dressing-table; smelled of the perfume bottles and smiled as he recognised the sweet odours as being a part of her, and not a thing unto themselves; grinned delightedly at his own photograph in its silver frame that stood where she could see it the last thing at night and the first in the morning; caressed—aye, caressed—the little hand-mirror that had reflected her gay or troubled face so many times since the dear Christmas Day when he had given it to her with his love.

He stood beside her bed where she had stood, and the soft rug seemed to respond to the delightful tingling that ran through his bare feet. Her room! Her bed! Her domain!

Suddenly he dropped to his knees and buried his hot face in the cool white sheets and kissed them over and over again. Here was sanctuary! His eyes were wet with tears when he arose to his feet, and his arms went out to the closed door.

"My Lyddy!" he whispered chokingly.

Back there in the rose-hued light of James Brood's study Yvonne cringed and shook in the strong arms of her husband all through that savage storm. She was no longer the defiant, self-possessed creature he had come to know so well, but a shrinking, trembling child, stripped of all her bravado, all her arrogance, all her seeming guile. A pathetic whimper crooned from her lips in response to his gentle words of reassurance. She was afraid—desperately afraid—and she crept close to him in her fear.

And he? He was looking backward to another who had nestled close to him and whimpered as she was doing now—another who lived in terror when it stormed.

CHAPTER XIII

Frederic opened his eyes at the sound of a gentle, persistent tapping on the bedroom door. Resting on his elbow, he looked blankly, wonderingly, about the room, and—remembered. The sun streamed into the chamber, filling it with a radiance that almost dazzled him. He rubbed his eyes, and again, as in the night just gone, his thought absorbed the contents of the room.

He had not dreamed it, after all. He was there in Lydia's bed, attended by all the mute, inanimate sentinels that stood guard over her while she slept. The knocking continued. He dreamed on, his blinking eyes still seeking out the dainty, Lydia-like treasures in the enchanted room.

"Frederic!" called a voice outside the door.

He started guiltily.

"All right," was his cheery response.

"Get up! It's nine o'clock. Or will you have your breakfast in bed, sir?" It was Lydia who spoke, assuming a fine Irish brogue in imitation of their little maid of all work.

"I'll have to, unless my clothes have come over!"

"They are here. Now do hurry."

He sprang out of bed and bounded across the room. She passed the garments through the partly opened door.

"Morning!" he greeted, sticking his tousled head around the edge.

"Morning!" she responded as briefly.

"Don't wait breakfast for me. I'll skip over home———"

"It will be ready in fifteen minutes," she said arbitrarily. "Don't dawdle."

"How pretty, how sweet you are this morning," he cried, his dark eyes dancing.

"Silly!" she scoffed, but with a radiant smile. Then, with a perfectly childish giggle, she slammed the door and scurried away as if in fear of pursuit.

He was artistic, temperamental. Such as he have not the capacity for haste when there is the slightest opportunity to dream and dawdle. He was a full quarter of an hour taking his tub, and another was consumed in getting into his clothes. At home he was always much longer than this, for he was delayed by the additional task of selecting shirts, ties, socks, and scarf-pins, and changing his mind and all of them three or four times before being satisfied with the effect. He sallied forth in great haste at nine thirty-five, and was extremely proud of himself, although unshaved.

His first act, after warmly greeting Mrs Desmond, was to sit down at the piano. Hurriedly he played a few jerky, broken snatches of the haunting air he had heard the night before.

"I've been wondering if I could remember it," he apologised, as he followed them into the dining-room. "What's the matter, Lyddy? Didn't you sleep well? Poor old girl, I was a beast to deprive you of your bed."

"I have a mean headache, that's all," said the girl quickly. He noticed the dark circles under her eyes and the queer expression, as of trouble, in their depths. "It will go as soon as I've had my coffee."

Night, with its wonderful sensations, was behind them. Day revealed the shadow that had fallen. They unconsciously shrank from it and drew back into the shelter of their own misgivings. The joyous abandon of the night before was dead. Over its grave stood the leering spectre of unrest.

When he took her in his arms later on, and kissed her, there was not the shadow of a doubt in the mind of either that the restraining influence of a condition over which they had no control was there to mock their endeavour to be natural. They were not to be deceived by the apparent earnestness of the embrace. Each knew that the other was asking a question, even as their lips met and clung in the rather pathetic attempt to confirm the fond dream of the night before. They kissed as through a veil. They were awake once more, and they were wary, unconvinced. The answer to their questions came in the kiss itself, and constraint fell upon them.

Drawn by an impulse that had been struggling within him, Frederic found himself standing at the sitting-room window. It was a sly, covert, though intensely eager look that he directed at another window far below. If he hoped for some sign of life in his father's study he was to be disappointed. The curtains hung straight and motionless. He would have denied the charge that he longed to see Yvonne sitting in the casement, waiting to waft a sign of greeting up to him; he would have denied that the thought was in his mind when he went to the window; and yet he was conscious of a feeling of disappointment, even annoyance.

With considerable adroitness Lydia engaged his attention at the piano. Keyed up as she was, his every emotion was plain to her perceptions. She had anticipated the motive that led him to the window. She knew that it would assert itself in spite of all that he could do to prevent. She waited humbly for the thing to happen, pain in her heart, and when her reading proved true she was prepared to combat its effect. Music was her only ally.

"How does it go, Freddy—the thing you were playing before breakfast?" She was trying to pick up the elusive air. "It is such a fascinating, adorable thing. Is this right?"

He looked at his watch. The few bars she had mastered in her eagerness fell upon inattentive ears at first. But she persisted. He came over and stood beside her. His long, slim fingers joined hers on the keyboard, and the sensuous strains of the waltz responded to his touch. He smiled patiently as she struggled to repeat what he had played. The fever of the thing took hold of him at last, as she had known it would. Leaning over her shoulder, his cheek quite close to hers, he played. Her hands dropped into her lap.

She retained her seat on the bench. Her cunning brain told her that it would be a mistake to relinquish her place at the keyboard. He would play it through a time or two, mechanically perhaps, and then his interest would be gone. He would have gratified her simple request, and that would have been the end. She led him on by interrupting time and again in her eagerness to grasp the lesson he was giving. Finally she moved over on the bench, and he sat down beside her. He was absorbed in the undertaking. His brow cleared. His smile was a happy, eager one.

"It's a tricky thing, Lyddy," he said enthusiastically, "but you'll get it. Now listen."

For an hour they sat there, master and pupil, sweetheart and lover. The fear was less in the heart of one when, tiring at last, the other contentedly abandoned the rôle of taskmaster and threw himself upon the couch, remarking, as he stretched himself in luxurious ease:

"I like this, Lyddy. I wish you didn't have to go over there and dig away at that confounded journal. I like this so well that, 'pon my soul, I'd enjoy loafing here with you the whole day long."

Her heart leaped. "You shall have your wish, Freddy," she said, barely able to conceal the note of eagerness in her voice. "I am not going to work to-day. I—my head, you know. Mother telephoned to Mr Brood this morning before you were up."

"You're going to loaf?" he cried gladly. "Bully! And I may stay? But, gee, I forgot your headache. It will— — —" He was staring up from the couch when she hastily broke in, shaking her head vigorously.

"Lie still. My head is much better. I want you to stay, dear. I—I want to have you all to myself again. Oh, it will be so good—so good to while away an idle day with you!"

She was standing beside the couch. He reached forth and took her hand in his, laying it against his lips.

"It won't be an idle day," said he seriously. "We shall be very busy."

"Busy?" she inquired apprehensively.

"Talking things over," he said briefly. "Of course, I ought to go home and face the music."

"What do you mean?"

"It's something I can't talk about, Lyddy. Let's forget our troubles for to-day."

"Better still, let us share them. Stay here with me. Don't go home to-day, Freddy. I— — —"

"Oh, I've got to have it out with father some time," he said bitterly. "It may as well be now as later on. We've got to come to an understanding."

Her heart was cold. She was afraid of what would come out of that "understanding." All night long she had lain with wide-staring eyes, thinking of the horrid thing James Brood had said to her. Far in the night she aroused her mother from a sound sleep to put the question that had been torturing her for hours. Mrs Desmond confessed that her husband had told her that Brood had never considered Frederic to be his son, and then the two lay side by side for the remainder of the night without uttering a word, and yet keenly awake. They were thinking of the hour when Brood would serve notice on the intruder.

Lydia now realised that the hour was near. Frederic himself would challenge the wrath of all these bitter years, and it would fall upon his unsuspecting head with cruel, obliterating force.

The girl shivered as with a racking chill. "Have it out with father," he had said in his ignorance. He was preparing to rush headlong to his doom. To prevent that catastrophe was the single, all-absorbing thought in Lydia's mind. Her only hope lay in keeping the men apart until she could extract from Brood a promise to be merciful, and this she intended to accomplish if she had to go down on her knees and grovel before the man.

"Oh, Freddy," she cried earnestly, "why take the chance of making a bad matter worse?" Even as she uttered the words she realised how stupid, how ineffectual they were.

"It can't be much worse," he said gloomily. "I am inclined to think he'd relish a straight-out, fair, and square talk, anyhow. Moreover, I mean to take Yvonne to task for the thing she said—or implied last night. About you, I mean. She— — —"

"Oh, I beg of you, don't!"

"It was—unspeakable. I don't see what could have come over her."

"She was jealous. She admitted it, dear. If I don't mind, why should you incur— — —"

"Do you really believe she—she loves the governor enough to be as jealous as all that?" he exclaimed, a curious gleam in his eyes—an expression she did not like.

"Of course I think so!" she cried emphatically. "What a question! Have you any reason to suspect that she does not love your father?"

"No—certainly not," he said in some confusion. Then, after a moment: "Are you quite sure this headache of yours is real, Lyddy?"

"What do you mean?"

"Isn't it an excuse to stay away from—from Yvonne, after what happened last night? Be honest, dear."

She was silent for a long time, weighing her answer. Was it best to be honest with him?

"I confess that it has something to do with it," she admitted. Lydia could not be anything but truthful.

"I thought so. It's—it's a rotten shame, Lyddy. That's why I want to talk to her. I want to reason with her. It's all so perfectly silly, this misunderstanding. You've just got to go on as you were before, Lyddy—just as if it hadn't happened. It— — —"

"I shall complete the work for your father, Freddy," she said quietly. "Two or three days more will see the end. After that neither my services nor my presence will be required over there."

"You don't mean to say— —" he began, unbelievingly.

"It isn't likely I'd go there for pleasure, is it?" she interrupted dryly.

"But think of the old times, the— — —"

"I can think of them just as well here as anywhere else. No; I shan't annoy Mrs Brood, Freddy." It was on the tip of her tongue to say more, but she thought better of it.

"They're going abroad soon," he ventured. "At least, that's father's plan. Yvonne isn't so keen about it. She calls this being abroad, you know. Besides," he hurried on in his eagerness to excuse Yvonne, "she's tremendously fond of you."

Lydia was wise. "I would give a great deal to be able to really believe so, Freddy. I—I could be very fond of her."

He warmed to the cause.

"No end of times she's said you were the finest— — —" Her smile—an odd one, such as he had never seen on her lips before—checked his eager speech. He bridled. "Of course, if you don't choose to believe me, there's nothing more to be said. She meant it, however."

"I am sure she said it, Freddy," she hastened to declare. "Will she be pleased with our—our marriage?"

It required a great deal of courage on her part to utter these words, but she was determined to bring the true situation home to him.

He did not even hesitate, and there was conviction in his voice as he replied:

"It doesn't matter whether she's pleased or displeased. We're pleasing ourselves, are we not? There's no one else to consider, dear."

Her eyes were full upon his, and there was wonder in them.

"Thank you—thank you, Freddy," she cried. "I—I knew you'd— — —" The sentence remained unfinished.

"Has there ever been a doubt in your mind?" he asked uneasily, after a moment. He knew there had been misgivings, and he was ready, in his self-abasement, to resent them if given the slightest opening. Guilt made him arrogant.

"No," she answered simply.

The answer was not what he expected. He flushed painfully.

"I—I thought perhaps you'd—you'd get a notion in your head that— — —" He, too, stopped for want of the right words to express himself without committing the egregious error of letting her see that it had been in his thoughts to accuse her of jealousy.

She waited for a moment. "That I might have got the notion in my head you did not love me any longer? Is that what you started to say?"

"Yes," he confessed, averting his eyes.

"I've been unhappy at times, Freddy, but that is all," she said steadily. "You see, I know how honest you really are. I know it far better than you know it yourself."

"I wonder just how honest I am," he muttered. "I wonder what would happen if——— But nothing can happen. Nothing ever will happen. Thank you, old girl, for saying what you said just now. It's—it's bully of you."

He got up and began pacing the floor. She leaned back in her chair, deliberately giving him time to straighten out his thoughts for himself. Wiser than she knew herself to be, she held back the warm, loving words of encouragement, of gratitude, of belief.

But she was not prepared for the impetuous appeal that followed. He threw himself down beside her and grasped her hands in his. His face seemed suddenly old and haggard, his eyes burned like coals of fire. Then, for the first time, she had an inkling of the great struggle that had been going on inside of him for weeks and weeks.

"Listen, Lyddy," he began nervously; "will you marry me to-morrow? Are you willing to take the chance that I'll be able to support you, to earn enough———"

"Why, Freddy!" she cried, half starting up from the couch. She was dumbfounded.

"Will you? Will you? I mean it," he went on, almost argumentatively.

He was very much in earnest, but alas! the fire, the passion of the importunate lover was missing. She shrank back into the corner of the couch, staring at him with puzzled eyes. Comprehension was slow in arriving. As he hurried on with his plea she began to see clearly, her sound brain grasped the significance of this sudden decision on his part.

"There's no use waiting, dear. I'll never be more capable of earning a living than I am right now. I can go into the office with Brooks any day, and I—I think I can make good. God knows, I can try hard enough. Brooks says he's got a place there for me in the bond department. It won't be much at first, but I can work into a pretty good—what's the matter? Don't you think I can do it? Have you no faith in me? Are you afraid to take a chance?"

She had smiled sadly—it seemed to him reprovingly. His cheek flushed.

"What has put all this into your head, Freddy dear?" she asked shrewdly.

"Why, good Lord, haven't we had this very thing in mind for years?" he cried. "Haven't we talked about my———"

"What put it into your head—just now?" she insisted.

"I don't know what you're driving at," he floundered.

"Don't you think it would be safer—I mean wiser if you were to wait until you are quite certain of yourself, Freddy?"

"I am certain of myself," he exploded. "What do you mean? What sort of talk is this you are———"

"Hush! Don't be angry, dear. Be honest now Don't you understand just what I mean?" They looked squarely into each other's eyes.

"I want you to marry me at once," said he doggedly. "You know I love you, Lyddy. Is there anything more to say than that?"

"Don't you want to tell me, Freddy?"

His eyes wavered. "I can't go on living as I have been for the past few months. I've just got to end it, Lyddy. You don't understand—you can't, and there isn't any use in trying to explain the——"

"I think I do understand, dear," she said quietly, laying her hand on his. "I understand so completely that there isn't any use in your trying to explain. But don't you think you are a bit cowardly?"

"Cowardly?" he gasped, and then the blood rushed to his face.

"Is it quite fair to me—or to yourself?" He was silent. She waited for a moment and then went on resolutely. "I know just what it is that you are afraid of, Freddy. I shall marry you, of course. I love you more than anything else in all the world. But are you quite fair in asking me to marry you while you are still afraid, dear?"

"Before God, Lyddy, I love no one else but you!" he cried earnestly. "I know what it is you are thinking, and I—I don't blame you. But I want you *now*—you don't know how much I need you now! I want to begin a new life with you. I want to feel that you are with me—just you—strong and brave and enduring. I am adrift. I need you."

"I know you love me, Frederic. I am absolutely certain of it," she said slowly, weighing her words carefully. "But I cannot marry you to-morrow—nor for a long time after to-morrow. In a year—yes. But not now, dear; not just now. You—you understand, don't you? Say that you understand."

His chin sank upon his breast. "Of course I understand," he said in a very low voice.

"I shall never love you any more than I love you now, Freddy—never so much, perhaps, as at this moment."

"I know, Lyddy; I know," he said dully.

"If you insist, I will marry you to-morrow; but you cannot—you will not ask it of me, will you?"

"But you know I do love you," he cried. "There isn't any doubt in your mind, Lyddy. There is no one else I tell you."

"I think I am just beginning to understand men," she remarked enigmatically.

"And to wonder why they call women the weaker sex, eh?"

"Yes," she said, so seriously that the wry smile died on his lips. "I don't believe there are many women who would ask a man to be sorry for them. That's really what all this amounts to, isn't it, Freddy?"

"By Jove!" he exclaimed wonderingly.

"You are a strong, self-willed, chivalrous man, and yet you think nothing of asking a woman to protect you against yourself; You are afraid to stand alone. Wait! You need me because you are a strong man and are afraid that your very strength will lead you into ignoble warfare. You are afraid of your strength, not of your weakness. So you ask me to help you. Without thinking, you ask me to marry you to-morrow. The idea came to you like a flash of light in the darkness. Five minutes—yes, one minute before you asked it of me, Freddy dear, you were floundering in the darkness, uncertain which way to turn. You were afraid of the things you could not see. You looked for some place in which to hide. The flash of light revealed a haven of refuge. So you asked me to to marry you to-morrow."

All through this indictment she had held his hand clasped tightly in both of hers. He was looking at her with a frank acknowledgment growing in his eyes.

"Are you ashamed of me, Lyddy?" he asked.

"No," she said, meeting his gaze steadily. "I am a little disappointed, that's all. It is you who are ashamed."

"I am," said he simply. "It wasn't fair."

"Love will endure. I am content to wait," she said with a wistful smile.

"You will be my wife, no matter what happens? You won't let this make any difference?"

"You are not angry with me?"

"Angry? Why should I be angry with you, Lyddy? For shaking some sense into me? For seeing through me with that wonderful, far-sighted brain of yours? Why, I could go down on my knees to you. I could———"

"Let me think, Freddy," she cried, suddenly confronted by her own declaration of the night before. She had told James Brood that she would marry this discredited son of his the instant he was ready to take her unto himself. She had flung that in the older man's face, and she had meant every word of it.

"I—I take back what I said, dear. I will marry you to-morrow." She spoke rapidly, jerkily; her eyes were very dark and luminous.

"What has come over you?" He stared at her in astonishment. "What—oh, I see! You are not sure of me. You — — —"

"Yes, yes, I am! It isn't that. I did not know what I was saying when I refused to — — —"

"Oh, there you go, just like a woman!" he cried triumphantly. "Spoiling everything! You dear, lovable, inconsequent, regular girl! Hurray! Now we're back where we began, and I'm holding the whip. You bring me to my senses and then promptly lose your own." He clasped her in his arms and held her close. "You dear, dear Lyddy!"

"I mean it, dear heart." The whisper smothered in his embrace. "To-morrow—to-day, if you will. We will go away. We will — — —"

"No," he said, quite resolutely; "you have shown me the way. I've just got to make good in your estimation before I can hold you to your promise. You're splendid, Lyddy; you're wonderful, but—well, I was unfair a while ago. I mean to be fair now. We'll wait. It's better so. I will come again and ask you, but it won't be as it was just now. It would not be right for me to take you at your word. We'll wait."

Neither spoke for many minutes. It was she who broke the silence.

"You must promise one thing, Frederic. For my sake, avoid a quarrel with your father. I could not bear that. You will promise, dear? You must."

"I don't intend to quarrel with him; but if I am to remain in his house there has got to be — — —" He paused, his jaw set stubbornly.

"Promise me you will wait. He is going away in two weeks. When he returns—later on—next fall — — —"

"Oh, if it really distresses you, Lyddy, I'll — — —"

"It does distress me. I want your promise."

"I'll do my part," he said resignedly, "and next fall will see us married, so — — —"

The telephone-bell in the hall was ringing. Frederic released Lydia's hand and sat up rather stiffly, as one who suddenly suspects that he is being spied upon. The significance of the movement did not escape Lydia. She laughed mirthlessly.

"I will see who it is," she said, and arose. Two red spots appeared in his cheeks. Then it was that she realised he had been waiting all along for the bell to ring; he had been expecting a summons.

"If it's for me, please say—er—say I'll———" he began, somewhat disjointedly, but she interrupted him.

"Will you stay here for luncheon, Frederic? And this afternoon we will go to—oh, is there a concert or a recital———"

"Yes, I'll stay if you'll let me," he said wistfully. "We'll find something to do."

She went to the telephone. He heard the polite greetings, the polite assurances that she had not taken cold, two or three laughing rejoinders to what must have been amusing comments on the storm and its effect on timid creatures, and then:

"Yes, Mrs Brood, I will call him to the phone."

CHAPTER XIV

Frederic had the feeling that he slunk to the telephone. The girl handed the receiver to him and he met her confident, untroubled gaze for a second. Instead of returning to the sitting-room where she could have heard everything that he said, she went into her own room down the hall and closed the door. He was not conscious of any intention to temporise, but it was significant that he did not speak until the door closed behind her. Afterward he realised and was ashamed.

Almost the first words that Yvonne uttered were of a nature to puzzle and irritate him, although they bore directly upon his own previously formed resolution. Her voice, husky and low, seemed strangely plaintive and lifeless to him.

"Have you and Lydia made any plans for the afternoon?" she inquired. He made haste to declare their intention to attend a concert. "I am glad you are going to do that," she went on.

"Are you ill, Yvonne?" he queried suddenly. "I? Oh, no. I think I never felt better in my life than I do at this moment. The storm must have blown the cobwebs out of my brain. I believe I'm quite happy to-day, Frederic."

"Aren't you always happy?" he cried chidingly. "What an odd thing to say."

She did not respond to this.

"You will stay for luncheon with Lydia?"

"Yes. She's trying to pick up that thing of Feverelli's—the one we heard last night." There was silence at the other end of the wire, "Are you there?"

"Yes."

"I'm teaching it to her."

"I see."

"I will be home for dinner, of course. You—you don't need me for anything, do you?"

"No," she said. Then, with a low laugh: "You may be excused for the day, my son."

"What's wrong?" he demanded, lowering his voice.

"Wrong? Nothing is wrong. Everything seems right to me. Your father and I have been discussing the trip abroad."

"Is—is it settled?"

"Yes. We are to sail on the twenty-fifth—in ten days."

"Settled, eh?"

"Yes."

"I thought you—you were opposed to going."

"I've changed my mind. As a matter of fact, I've changed my heart."

"You speak in riddles."

"Your father has gone out to arrange for passage on the *Olympic*. He is lunching at the Lawyers' Club."

"You will lunch alone, then?"

"Naturally."

He suppressed an impulse.

"I'm sorry, Yvonne."

She was silent for a long time.

"Frederic, I want you to do something for me."

"I—I've promised Lydia to stay here———"

"Oh, it isn't that. Will you try to convince Lydia that I meant no offence last night when I———"

"She understands all that perfectly, Yvonne."

"No, she doesn't. A woman *wouldn't* understand."

"I will square everything," he said.

"It means a great deal to me,"

"In what way?"

There was a pause.

"No woman likes to be regarded as a fool," she said at last, apparently after careful reflection. "Oh, yes; there is something else. We are dining out this evening."

"You and I?" he asked, after a moment.

"Certainly not. Your father and I. I was about to suggest that you dine with Lydia—or, better still, ask her over here to share your dinner with you."

He was scowling.

"Where are you going?"

"Going? Oh, dining. I see. Well," slowly, deliberately, "we thought it would be great fun to dine alone at Delmonico's and see a play afterward."

"Just—you and father?"

"We two—no more."

"How cunning," he sneered.

"Will you ask Lydia to dine with you?"

"No."

"Perhaps you will go out somewhere?"

"I'll have dinner with Mr Dawes and — — —"

"That would be jolly. They will be pleased. A sort of—what do you call it—a sort of reunion, eh?"

"Are you making sport of me?" he demanded angrily.

"But no! It will be making sport for the old gentleman, though, aïe? And now au revoir! You will surely convince Lydia that I love her? I am troubled. You will — — —"

"What play are you going to see?" he cut in. She mentioned a Belasco production. "Well, I hope you enjoy it, Yvonne. By the way, how is the governor to-day? In a good humour?"

There was no response. He waited for a moment and then called out: "Are you there?".

"Good-bye," came back over the wire.

He started, as if she had given him a slap in the face. Her voice was cold and forbidding.

When Lydia rejoined him in the sitting-room he was standing at the window, staring across the courtyard far below.

"Are you going?" she asked steadily.

He turned toward her, conscious of the tell-tale scowl that was passing from his brow. It did not occur to him to resent her abrupt, uncompromising question. As a matter of fact, it seemed quite natural that she should put the question in just that way, flatly, incisively. He considered himself, in a way, to be on trial.

"No, I'm not," he replied. "You did not expect me to forget, did you?"

He was uncomfortable under her honest, inquiring gaze. A sullen anger against himself took possession of him. He despised himself for the feeling of loneliness and homesickness that suddenly came over him.

"I thought— — —" she began, and then her brow cleared. "I have been looking up the recitals in the morning paper. The same orchestra you heard last night is to appear again to-day at— — —"

"We will go there, Lydia," he interrupted, and at once began to hum the gay little air that had so completely charmed him. "Try it again, Lyddy. You'll get it in no time."

After luncheon, like two happy children they rushed off to the concert, and it was not until they were on their way home at five o'clock that his enthusiasm began to wane. She was quick to detect the change. He became moody, preoccupied; his part of the conversation was kept up with an effort that lacked all of the spontaneity of his earlier and more engaging flights.

They rode down town on the top of a Fifth Avenue stage, having it all to themselves. She found herself speculating on the change that had come over him, and soon lapsed into a reserve quite as pronounced as his own. By the time they were ready to get down at the corner above Brood's house there was no longer any pretence at conversation between them. The day's fire had burned out. Its glow had given way to the bleak, gray tone of dead coals.

Lydia went far back in her calculations and attributed his mood to the promise she had exacted in regard to his attitude toward his father. It occurred to her that he was smarting under the restraint that promise involved. She realised now, more than ever before, that there could be no delay, no faltering on her part. She would have to see James Brood at once; go down on her knees to him.

"I feel rather guilty, Freddy," she said as they approached the house. "Mr Brood will think it strange that I should plead a headache and yet run off to a concert and enjoy myself when he is so eager to finish the journal— especially as he is to sail so soon. I ought to see him; don't you think so? Perhaps there is something I can do to-night that will make up for the lost time." She was plainly nervous.

"He'd work you to death if he thought it would serve his purpose," said Frederic gloomily. And back of that sentence lay the thought that made it absolutely imperative for her to act without delay.

"I will go in for a few minutes," she said, at the foot of the steps. "Are you not coming, too?"

He had stopped. "Not just now, Lyddy. I think I'll run up to Tom's flat and smoke a pipe with him. Thanks, old girl, for the happy day we've had. You don't mind if I leave you here?"

Her heart gave a great throb of relief. It was best to have him out of the way for the time being.

"No, indeed," she said. "Do go and see Tom. I shan't be here long. We have had a glorious day, haven't we?" There was something wistful in her smile as she held out her hand to him.

He searched her face with tired, yearning eyes.

"We have thousands of them ahead of us, Lyddy—days that will be all our own, with nothing else in them but ourselves. I—I wish we could begin them to-morrow, after all."

A flush mounted to her cheek.

"Good-bye, Freddy."

He seemed reluctant to release her hand; her hand was cold, but her eyes were shining with a glorious warmth.

"I—I may run in to see you this evening," he said. "You won't mind?"

"Come, by all means."

"Well—so-long," he said diffidently. "So-long, Lyddy."

"So-long," she repeated, dropping into his manner of speech without thinking. There was a smothering sensation in her breast.

He looked back as he strode off in the direction from which they had come. She was at the top of the steps, her finger on the electric button. He wondered why her face was so white. He had always thought of it as being full of colour, rich, soft, and warm.

Inside the door Lydia experienced a strange sinking of the heart. Her limbs seemed curiously weak, and she was conscious of a feeling of utter loneliness, such as she had never known before. She looked about her in wonder, as if seeking an explanation for the extraordinary but fleeting impression that she was in a strange house. Never was she to find an interpretation of the queer fantasy that came and went almost in the span of a single breath.

"Is Mr Brood at———" she began nervously.

A voice at the top of the stairway interrupted the question she was putting to the footman.

"Is it you, Lydia? Come up to my room."

The girl looked up and saw Mrs Brood leaning over the banister-rail. She was holding her pink dressing-gown closely about her throat, as if it had been hastily thrown about her shoulders. One bare arm was visible— completely so.

"I came to see Mr Brood. Is he———"

"He is busy. Come up to my room," repeated Yvonne, somewhat imperiously.

As Lydia mounted the stairs she had a fair glimpse of the other's face. Always pallid—but of a healthy pallor—it was now almost ghastly. Perhaps it was the light from the window that caused it; Lydia was not sure, but a queer greenish hue overspread the lovely, smiling face. The lips were red, very red—redder than she had ever seen them. The girl suddenly recalled the face she had once seen of a woman who was addicted to the drug habit.

Mrs Brood met her at the top of the stairs. She was but half dressed. Her lovely neck and shoulders were now almost bare. Her hands were extended toward the visitor; the filmy lace gown hung loose and disregarded about her slim figure.

"Come in, dear. Shall we have tea? I have been so lonely. One cannot read the books they print nowadays. Such stupid things, *aïe?*"

She threw an arm about the tall girl, and Lydia was surprised to find that it was warm and full of a gentle strength. She felt her flesh tingle with the thrill of contact. Yes, it must have been the light from the window, for Yvonne's face was now aglow with the peculiar iridescence that was so peculiarly her own.

A door closed softly on the floor above them. Mrs Brood glanced over her shoulder and upward. Her arm tightened perceptibly about Lydia's waist.

"It was Ranjab," said the girl, and instantly was filled with amazement. She had not seen the Hindu, had not even been thinking of him, and yet she was impelled by some mysterious intelligence to give utterance to a statement in which there was conviction, not conjecture.

"Did you see him?" asked the other, looking at her sharply.

"No," admitted Lydia, still amazed. "I don't know why I said that."

Mrs Brood closed her boudoir door behind them. For an instant she stood staring at the knob, as if expecting to see it turn.

"I know," she said, "I know why you said it. Because it *was* Ranjab." She shivered slightly. "I am afraid of that man, Lydia. He seems to be watching me all the time. Day and night his eyes seem to be upon me."

"Why, should he be watching you?" asked Lydia bluntly.

Yvonne did not notice the question.

"Even when I am asleep in my bed, in the dead hour of night, he is looking at me. I can feel it. Oh, it is not a dream, for my dreams are of something or someone else—never of him. And yet he is there, looking at me. It—it is uncanny."

"Imagination," remarked Lydia quietly. "He never struck me as especially omnipresent."

"Didn't you *feel* him a moment ago?" demanded Yvonne irritably.

The other hesitated, reflecting.

"I suppose it must have been something like that." They were still facing the door, standing close together. "Why do you feel that he is watching you?"

"I don't know. I just feel it, that's all. Day and night. He can read my thoughts, Lydia, as he would read a book. Isn't—isn't it disgusting?" Her laugh was spiritless, obviously artificial.

"I shouldn't object to his reading my thoughts," said Lydia.

"Ah, but you are Lydia. It's different. I have thoughts sometimes, my dear, that would not—but there! Let us speak of more agreeable things. Take off your coat—here, let me help you. What a lovely waist! You will pardon my costume, won't you, or rather the lack of one? I shan't dress until dinner-time. Sit down here beside me. No tea? A cigarette, then. No?"

"I never smoke, you remember," said the other. She was looking at Yvonne now with a curious, new-found interest in her serious eyes. "I came to explain to Mr Brood how it happens that———"

"Poof! Never explain, my dear, never explain anything to a man!" cried Yvonne, lighting a cigarette. The flare of the match in the partially darkened room lit up her face with merciless candour. Lydia was conscious once more of the unusual pallor and a certain haggardness about the dark eyes.

"But he is so eager to complete the———"

"Do you forgive me for what I said to you last night?" demanded Yvonne, sitting down beside the girl on the *chaise longue*. The interruption was rude, perhaps, but it was impossible to resent it, so appealing was the expression in the offender's eyes.

"It was so absurd, Mrs Brood, that I have scarcely given it a moment's thought. Of course, I was hurt at the time. It was so unjust to Mr Brood. It was———"

"It is like you to say that!" cried Yvonne. "You are splendid, Lydia. Will you believe me when I tell you that I love you—that I love you very dearly?"

Lydia looked at her in some doubt, and not without misgivings.

"I should like to believe it," she said noncommittally.

"Ah, but you doubt it. I see. Well, I do not blame you. I have given you much pain, much distress. When I am far away you will be glad—you will be happy. Is not that so?"

"But you are coming back," said Lydia with a frank smile, not meant to be unfriendly.

Yvonne's face clouded.

"Yes, I shall probably come back. Nothing is sure in this queer world of ours." She threw her cigarette away. "I don't like it to-day. Ugh! how it tastes in my mouth!" She drew closer to the girl's side. Lydia's nostrils filled with the strange, sweet perfume that she affected, so individually hers, so personally Yvonne. "Oh, yes; I shall come back. Why not? Is not this my home?"

"You may call it your home, Mrs Brood," said Lydia, "but are you quite sure your thoughts always abide here? I mean in the United States, of course."

Yvonne had looked up at her quickly.

"Oh, I see. No; I shall never be an American." Then she abruptly changed the subject. "You have had a nice day with Frederic? You have been happy, both of you?"

"Yes—very happy, Mrs Brood," said the girl simply.

"I am glad. You must always be happy, you two. It is my greatest wish."

Lydia hesitated for a moment.

"Frederic asked me to be his wife—to-morrow," she said, and her heart began to thump queerly. She felt that she was approaching a crisis of some sort.

"To-morrow?" fell from Yvonne's lips. The word was drawn out, as if in one long breath. Then, to Lydia's astonishment, an extraordinary change came over the speaker.

"Yes, yes; it should be—it must be to-morrow. Poor boy—poor, poor boy! You will marry, yes, and go way at once, aïe?" Her voice was almost shrill in its intensity, her eyes were wide and eager and—anxious.

"I— — — Oh, Mrs Brood, is it for the best?" cried Lydia. "Is it the best thing for Frederic to do? I—I feared you might object. I am sure his father will refuse permission— — —"

"But you love each other—that is enough. Why ask the consent of anyone? Yes, yes, it is for the best. I know—oh, you cannot realise how well I know. You must not hesitate." The woman was trembling in her eagerness. Lydia's astonishment gave way to perplexity.

"What do you mean? Why are you so serious—so intent on this— — —"

"Frederic has no money," pursued Yvonne, as if she had not heard Lydia's words. "But that must not deter you—it must not stand in the way. I shall find a way; yes, I shall find a way. I— — —"

"Do you mean that you would provide for him for us?" exclaimed Lydia.

"There is a way, there is a way," said the other, fixing her eyes appealingly on the girl's face, to which the flush of anger was slowly mounting.

"His father will not help him—if, that is what you are counting upon, Mrs Brood," said the girl coldly.

"I know. He will not help him; no."

Lydia started.

"What do you know about—what has Mr Brood said to you?" Her heart was cold with apprehension. "Why are you going away next week? What has happened?"

Brood's wife was regarding her with narrowing eyes.

"Are you attributing my motives to something that my husband has said to me? Am I expected to say that he has—what you call it—that he has put his foot down?"

"I am sorry you misunderstood my— — —"

"Oh, I see now. You think my husband suspects that Frederic is too deeply interested in his beautiful stepmother; is not that so? Poof! It has nothing to do with it." Her eyes were sullen, full of resentment now. She was collecting herself.

The girl's eyes expressed the disdain that suddenly took the place of apprehension in her thoughts. A sharp retort leaped to her lips, but she suppressed it.

"Mr Brood does not like Frederic," she said instead, and could have cut out her tongue the instant the words were uttered. Yvonne's eyes were glittering with a light that she had never seen in them before. Afterward she described it to herself as baleful.

"So! He has spoken ill—evil—of his son to you?" she said, almost in a monotone, "He has hated him for years—is not that so? I am not the original cause, *aïe?* It began long ago—long, long ago?"

"Oh, I beg of you, Mrs Brood———" began Lydia, shrinking back in dismay.

"You are free to speak your thoughts to me. I shall not be offended. What has he said to you about Frederic—and me?"

"Nothing, I swear to you; nothing!" cried the girl.

"But you have the power of observation. You do not have to be told in so many words. You have been with him a great deal, alone. His manner tells you what his lips hold back. Tell me." Lydia resolved to take the plunge. Now was the time to speak plainly to this woman of the thing that was hurting her almost beyond the limits of endurance. Her voice was rather high-pitched. She had the fear that she would not be able to control it.

"I should be blind not to have observed the cruel position in which you are placing Frederic. Is it surprising that your husband has eyes as well as I? What must be his thoughts, Mrs Brood?"

She expected an outburst, a torrent of indignation, an angry storm of words, and was therefore unprepared for the piteous, hunted expression that came swiftly into the lovely eyes, bent so appealing upon her own, which were cold and accusing. Here was a new phase to this extraordinary creature's character. She was a coward, after all, and Lydia despised a coward. The look of scorn deepened in her eyes, and out from her heart rushed all that was soft and tender in her nature, leaving it barren of all compassion.

"I do not want to hurt Frederic," murmured Yvonne. "I—I am sorry if———"

"You are hurting him dreadfully," said Lydia, suddenly choking up with emotion.

"He is not—not in love with me," declared Yvonne,

"No," said the girl, regaining control of herself, "he is not in love with you. That is the whole trouble. He is in love with me. But—but can't you see?"

"You are a wise young woman to know men so well," said the other enigmatically. "I have never believed in St Anthony."

"Nor I," said Lydia, and was surprised at herself.

"I prefer to put my faith in the women who tempted him," said Yvonne, drawing a little closer to the girl.

"Perhaps you are right. They at least were not pretending."

"I am not so sure of that. At any rate, they succeeded in making a saint of him eventually."

"I suppose you are undertaking a similar office in—in Frederic's behalf," said Lydia with fine irony.

"Do you consider me to be a bad woman, Lydia?" Her lips trembled. There was a suspicious quiver to her chin.

"No; I do not," pronounced the girl flatly. "If I could only think that of you it would explain everything, and I should know just how to treat you. But I do not think it of you."

With a long, deep sigh Yvonne crept closer and laid her head against Lydia's shoulder. The girl's body stiffened, her brow grew dark with annoyance.

"I am afraid you do not understand, Mrs Brood. The fact still remains that you have not considered Frederic's peace of mind."

"Nor yours," murmured the other.

"Nor mine," confessed Lydia, after a moment.

"I did not know that you and Frederic were in love with each other until I had been here for some time," Mrs Brood explained, suddenly fretful.

Lydia stared hard at the soft white cheek that lay exposed below the black crown of hair.

"What had that to do with it?"

"A great deal more than you can imagine," said the other, looking up into Lydia's face with a curious gleam in her eyes.

"You admit, then, that you deliberately———"

"I admit nothing, except that I am sorry to have made you unhappy."

"What kind of a woman are you?" burst out Lydia's indignant soul. "Have you no conception of the finer, nobler———"

Yvonne deliberately put her hand over the girl's lips, checking the fierce outburst. She smiled rather plaintively as Lydia tried to jerk her head to one side in order to continue her reckless indictment.

"You shall not say it, Lydia. I am not all that you think I am. No, no; a thousand times no. God pity me, I am more accursed than you may think with the finer and nobler instincts. If it were not so, do you think I should be where I am now—cringing here like a beaten child? No, you cannot understand—you never will understand. I shall say no more. It is ended. I swear on my soul that I did not know you were Frederic's sweetheart. I did not know———"

"But you knew almost immediately after you came here!" exclaimed Lydia harshly. "It is not myself I am thinking of, Mrs Brood, but of Frederic. Why have you done this abominable thing to him? Why?"

"I—I did not realise what it would mean to him," said the other desperately. "I—I did not count all the cost. But, dearest Lydia, it will come out all right. Everything shall be made right again, I promise you. I have made a horrible, horrible mistake. I can say no more. Now let me lie here with my head upon your breast. I want to feel the beating of your pure, honest heart—the heart I have hurt. I can tell by its throbs whether it will ever soften toward me. Do not say anything now—let us be still."

It would be difficult to describe the feelings of Lydia Desmond as she sat there with the despised, though to be adored, head pillowed upon her breast, where it now rested in a sort of confident repose, as if there was safety in the very strength of the young girl's disapproval. Yvonne had twisted her lithe body on the *chaise longue* so that she half faced Lydia. Her free arm, from which the loose sleeve had fallen, leaving it bare to the shoulder, was about the girl's neck.

For a long time Lydia stared straight before her, seeing nothing, positively dumb with wonder, and acknowledging a sense of dismay over her own disposition to submit to this extraordinary situation. She was asking herself why she did not cast the woman away, why she lacked the power to resent by deed as well as by thought.

At last she lowered her eyes, conquered by an impulse she had resisted for many minutes. Her now perplexed gaze rested upon the gleaming white arm, and then moved wonderingly to the smooth cheek and throat. She saw the pulse beating in that slender neck. Fascinated, she watched it for a long, long time.

Suddenly there ran through her heart a strange wave of tenderness. That faint, delicate throb in the throat of this woman represented the rush of life's blood—the warm, sweet flood of a lovely living thing. Yvonne's eyes were closed. The long, dark lashes lay feathery above the alabaster cheek; there were delicate blue lines in the lids. A faint, almost imperceptible depression as of pain appeared between the eyebrows. The black, glossy hair filled Lydia's nostrils with its living perfume.

Life—marvellous, adorable life rested there on her breast. This woman had hurt her—had hurt her wantonly—and yet there came stealing over her, subtly, the conviction that she could never hurt her in return. She could never bring herself to the point of hurting this wondrous living, breathing, throbbing creature who pleaded, not only with her lips and eyes, but with the gentle heart-beats that rose and fell in her throat.

Like velvet was the smooth, glossy skin of her arm and breast. Never had Lydia dreamed that flesh could be so soft and white and so aglow with vitality. There was a sheen to it, a soft sheen that seemed fairly to radiate light itself.

Still in a maze of wonder and something bordering on sheer delight, she fell to studying the perfections that the cheek and lips revealed.

Scarlet, pensively drooping were the lips, and almost opalescent the clear-cut cheek and chin. The delicate nostrils vibrated with the quickened breath that stirred the firm, full breast which rose and fell softly, gently; there were firm, hitherto invisible blue lines in the gleaming skin. Slowly, resistlessly Lydia's arm tightened about the slender, seductive body.

After a long time, in which there was conflict, she suddenly pressed her warm lips to Yvonne's in a kiss that thrilled through every nerve in her body—a kiss that lingered because it was returned with equal fervour and abandon. They were clasped tightly in each other's arms and their eyes were closed as with pain.

Then, in an abrupt revulsion of feeling, in a desperate awakening, Lydia relaxed. Her arms fell away from the warm, sweet body and her eyes widened with something that passed for confusion, but which was in reality shame. Almost roughly she pushed Yvonne away from her.

"I—I didn't mean to do that!" she gasped.

The other withdrew her arm and straightened up slowly, all the time regarding the girl with a strange, wondering look in her eyes—a look that quickly resolved itself into sadness so poignant that the girl, even in her confused state of mind, recognised it as such and was abashed.

"I knew that you would," said Yvonne in a very low voice, and shook her head drearily.

"I am sorry," murmured Lydia in great distress.

The other smiled, but it was a sad, plaintive effort on her part.

"I knew that you would," she repeated.

Lydia sprang to her feet, her face suddenly flaming with embarrassment. She felt unaccountably guilty of—she knew not what.

"I must see Mr Brood. I stepped in to tell him that———" she began, trying to cover her confusion, but Yvonne interrupted.

"I know that you could not help it, my dear," she said. Then, after a pause: "You will let me know what my husband has to say about it?"

"To—to say about it?"

"About your decision to marry Frederic in spite of his objections."

Lydia felt a little shiver race over her as she looked toward the door.

"You will help us?" she said tremulously, turning to Yvonne. Again she saw the drawn, pained look about the dark eyes and was startled.

"You can do more with him than I," was the response.

CHAPTER XV

Lydia stopped for a moment in the hall, after closing the door behind her, to pull herself together for the ordeal that was still to come. She was trembling; a weakness had assailed her. She had left Yvonne's presence in a dazed, unsettled condition of mind.

There was a lapse of some kind that she could neither account for nor describe even to herself. She tried to put it into seconds and minutes, and then realised that it was not a matter to be reckoned as time. Yet there had been a distinct, unmistakable gap in her existence. Something had stopped— she knew not for how long—and then she had found herself breathing, thinking once more. In spite of the conviction that she had passed through a period of utter oblivion, she could account for every second of time with an absolute clearness of memory.

There was not an instant, nor a sensation, nor an impulse that was not fully recorded in her alert brain. She remembered everything; she could have described every emotion; and yet she felt that there had been a period of complete absence, as real as it was improbable.

She felt now as she always felt after sipping champagne—in a warm glow of intoxication. She was drunk with the scent that filled her nostrils, the scent that lay on her lips, that lived and breathed with her. Her heart was throbbing rapidly, as if earnestly seeking to regain the beats that it had lost.

Suddenly there came to her an impulse to go back and lay bare before Yvonne all of the wretched story that had fallen from the lips of James Brood the night before. She conceived the strange notion that Yvonne alone could avert the disaster, that she could be depended upon to save Frederic from the blow that seemed so sure to fall. She even went so far as to turn toward the door and to take a step in its direction.

Then came the revolt against the impulse. Was it fair to Frederic? Had she the right to reveal this ugly thing to one whose sympathies might, after all, be opposed to the wife who had preceded her in James Brood's affections—the wife who had been first in his heart, and whose memory, for all she knew, might still be a worthy adversary even in this day of apparent supremacy?

What right had she to conclude that this woman would take up the cause of Frederic's mother and jeopardise her own position by seeking to put her husband in the wrong in that unhappy affair of long ago? Would Yvonne do this for Frederic? Would she do all this for Frederic's mother?

Lydia turned away and went slowly toward the stairs, despising herself for the thought. The black velvet coat that formed a part of her trig suit hung limply in her hand, dragging along the floor as she moved with hesitating steps in the direction of James Brood's study. A sickening estimate of her own strength of purpose confronted her. She was suddenly afraid of the man who had always been her friend. Somehow she felt that he would turn upon and rend her, this man who had always been gentle and considerate—and who had killed things!

She found herself at last standing stock-still at the bottom of the steps, looking upward, trying to concentrate all of her determination on what now appeared to her to be an undertaking of the utmost daring, as one who risks everything in an encounter in the dark.

Ranjab appeared at the head of the stairs. She waited for his signal to ascend, somehow feeling that Brood had sent him forth to summon her. Her hand sought the stair-rail and gripped it tightly. Her lips parted in a stiff smile. Now she knew that she was turning coward, that she longed to put off the meeting until to-morrow—*to-morrow!*

The Hindu came down the stairs, quickly, noiselessly.

"The master say to come to-morrow, to-morrow as usual," he said, as he paused above her on the steps.

"It—it must be to-day," she said doggedly, even as the chill of relief shot through her.

"To-morrow," said the man. His eyes were kindly inquiring. "*Sahib* say you are to rest." There was a pause. "To-morrow will not be too late."

She started. Had he read the thought that was in her mind?

"Thank you, Ranjab," she said, after a moment of indecision. "I will come to-morrow."

Then she slunk downstairs and out of the house, convinced that she had failed Frederic in his hour of greatest need, that to-morrow would be too late.

Frederic did not come in for dinner until after his father and Yvonne had gone from the house. He did not inquire for them, but instructed Jones to say to the old gentlemen that he would be pleased to dine with them if they could allow him the time to "change." He also told Jones to open a single bottle of champagne and to place three glasses.

"If you please, sir, Mrs Brood has given strict orders— —"

"That's all right, Jones. She won't mind for to-night. We expect to drink the health of the bride, Jones."

"Yes, sir."

"That is to say, *my* bride."

"Your bride, Mr Frederic?"

"I'm going to be married."

"Bless my soul, sir!"

"You seem surprised."

"Ahem! I should 'ave said, 'God be praised,' sir."

"Now that I think of it, don't mention it to Mr Dawes and Mr Riggs. Let me make the announcement, Jones."

"Certainly, sir. It is most confidential, of course. Bless my—I mean to say, Golden Seal, sir?"

"Any old thing, Jones."

"May I offer my congratulations, Mr Frederic? Thank you, sir. Ahem! Aw—ahem! Anyways soon, sir?"

"Very soon, Jones."

"Bless—very good, sir. Of course, if I may be so bold as to inquire, sir, it's—it's—ahem?"

"Certainly, Jones. Who else could it be?"

"To be sure, sir, it *couldn't* be anyone else. Thank you, sir. Yes, sir. She is the finest young lady in this 'ere world, Mr Frederic. You did say Golden Seal, Cliquot, ninety-eight, sir? It's the best in the 'ouse, sir, quite the best at present."

Later on Frederic made his announcement to the old men. In the fever of an excitement that caused him to forget that Lydia might be entitled to some voice in the matter, he deliberately committed her to the project that had become a fixed thing in his mind the instant he set foot in the house and found it empty—oh, so empty!

Jones's practised hand shook slightly as he poured the wine. The old men drank rather noisily. They, too, were excited. Mr Riggs smacked his lips and squinted at the chandelier, as if trying to decide upon the vintage, but in reality doing his best to keep from coughing up the wine that had gone the wrong way in a moment of profound paralysis.

"The best news I've heard since Judas died," said Mr Dawes manfully. "Fill 'em up again, Jones. I want to propose the health of Mrs Brood."

"The future Mrs Brood," hissed Mr Riggs wheezily, glaring at his comrade. "Ass!"

"I'm not married yet, Mr Dawes," explained Frederic, grinning.

"Makes no difference," said Mr Dawes stoutly. "Far as I'm concerned, you are. We'll be the first to drink to Lydia Brood! The first to call her by that name, gentlemen. God bless her!"

"God bless her!" shouted Mr Riggs.

"God bless her!" echoed Frederic, and they drained their glasses to Lydia Brood.

"Jones, open another bottle," commanded Mr Dawes loftily.

Frederic shook his head, and two faces fell. Right bravely, however, the old men maintained a joyous interest in the occasion. They expounded loudly upon the virtues and graces of John Desmond's daughter; they plied the young man with questions and harangued him with advice; they threatened him with hell-fire if he ever gave the girl a minute of unhappiness; they were very firm in their contention that he "oughtn't to let the grass grow under his feet," not for an instant! In the end they waxed tearful. It was quite too much joy to be borne with equanimity.

The young man turned moody, thoughtful; the unwonted exhilaration died as suddenly as it had come into existence. A shadow crossed his vision and he followed it with his thoughts. The gabbling of the old men irritated him as the makeshift feast of celebration grew old, and he made no pretence of keeping up his end of the conversation.

The gloomy, uneasy look deepened in his face. It was a farce, after all, this attempt to glorify an impulse conceived in desperation. A sense of utter loneliness came over him with a swiftness that sickened, nauseated him. The food was flat to his taste; he could not eat. Self-commiseration stifled him. He suddenly realised that he had never been so lonely, so unhappy, in all his life as he was at this moment.

His thoughts were of his father. A vast, inexplicable longing possessed his soul—a longing for the affection of this man who was never tender, who stood afar off and was lonely, too. He could not understand this astounding change of feeling. He had never felt just this way before. There had been times—and many—when his heart was sore with longing, but they were of other days, childhood days. To-night he could not crush out the thought of how ineffably happy, how peaceful life would be if his father were to lay his hands upon his shoulders and say: "My son, I love you—I love you dearly." There would be no more lonely days; all that was bitter in his life would be swept away in the twinkling of an eye; the world would be full of joy for him and for Lydia.

If anyone had told him an hour earlier that he would have been possessed of such emotions as these he could have sneered in the face of him. When he entered the house that evening he was full of resentment toward his father and sullen with the remains of an ugly rage. And now to be actually craving the affection of the man who humbled him, even in the presence of servants. It was unbelievable. He could not understand himself. A wonderful, compelling tenderness filled his heart. He longed to throw himself at his father's feet and crave his pardon for the harsh, vengeful thoughts he had spent upon him in those black hours. He hungered for a word of kindness or of understanding on which he could feed his starving soul. He wanted his father's love. He wanted, more than anything else in the world, to love his father.

Lydia slipped out of his mind, Yvonne was set aside in that immortal moment. He had not thought of them except in their relation to a completed state of happiness for his father. Indistinctly he recognised them as essentials.

In the library, later on, he smoked with the old men, moodily staring up through the blue clouds into a space that seemed limitless. The expression of pain, and the self-pity that attended it, increased in his eyes. The old men rambled on, but he scarcely heard them. They wrangled, and he was not impatient with them. He was lonely. He felt deserted, forsaken. The sweet companionship of the day just closing stood for naught in this hour of a deeper longing. He wanted to hear his father say, from his heart: "Frederic, my son, here is my hand. It is no longer against you."

Aye, he was lonely. The house was as bleak as the steppes of Siberia. He longed for companionship, friendship, kindness, and suddenly in the midst of it all he leaped to his feet.

"I'm going out, gentlemen," he exclaimed, breaking in upon an unappreciated tale that Mr Riggs was relating at some length and with considerable fierceness in view of the fact that Mr Dawes had pulled him up rather sharply once or twice in a matter of inaccuracies. "Excuse me, please."

He left them gaping with astonishment and dashed out into the hall for his coat and hat. Even then he had no definite notion as to what his next move would be, save that he was going out—somewhere, anywhere; he did not care. All the time he was employed in getting into his light overcoat his eyes were fixed on the front door, and in his heart was the strange, indescribable hope that it would open to admit his father, who, thinking of him in his loneliness and moved by a suddenly aroused feeling of love, had abandoned an evening of selfish pleasure in order to spend it with him.

And if his father should walk in, with eagerness in his long unfriendly eyes, what joy it would be for him to rush up to him and cry out: "Father, let's be happy! Let's make each other happy!"

Somehow, as he rushed down the front steps with the cool night air blowing in his face, there surged up within him a strong, overpowering sense of filial duty. It was his duty to make the first advances. It was for him to pave the way to peace and happiness. Something vague but disturbing tormented him with the fear that his father faced a great peril and that his own place was beside him and not against him, as he had been for all these illy directed years. He could not put it away from him, this thought that his father was in danger—in danger of something that was not physical, something from which, with all his valour, he had no adequate form of defence.

At the corner he paused, checked by an irresistible impulse to look backward at the house he had just left. To his surprise there was a light in the drawing-room windows facing the street. The shade in one of them had been thrown wide open and a stream of light flared out across the sidewalk.

Standing in this stream of light was the figure of a man. Slowly, as if drawn by a force he could not resist, the young man retraced his steps until he stood directly in front of the window. A questioning smile was on his lips. He was looking up into Ranjab's shadowy, unsmiling face, dimly visible in the glow from the distant street-lamp. For a long time they stared at each other, no sign of recognition passing between them. The Hindu's face was as rigid, as emotionless as if carved out of stone; his eyes were unwavering. Frederic could see them, even in the shadows. He had the queer feeling that, though the man gave no sign, he had something he wanted to say to him, that he was actually calling to him to come back into the house.

Undecided, the man outside took several halting steps toward the doorway, his gaze still fixed on the face in the window. Then he broke the spell. It was a notion on his part, he argued, If he had been wanted, his father's servant would have beckoned to him. He would not have stood there like a graven image, staring out into the night.

Having convinced himself of this, Frederic wheeled and swung off up the street once more, walking rapidly, as one who is pursued. Turning, he waved his hand at the man in the window. He received no response. Farther off, he looked back once more. The Hindu still was there. Long after he was out of sight of the house he cast frequent glances over his shoulder, as if still expecting to see the lighted window and its occupant.

Blocks away, in his hurried, aimless flight, he slackened his pace and began to wonder whither he was going. He had no objective point in mind. He was drifting. His footsteps lagged and he looked about him for marks of locality. Union Square lay behind him, and beyond, across Eighteenth Street, was the Third Avenue Elevated. He had not meant to come in this direction. It was not his mind alone that wandered.

As he made his way back to Broadway, somewhat hazily bent on following that thoroughfare up to the district where the night glittered and the stars were shamed, he began turning over in his mind a queer notion that had just suggested itself to him, filtering through the maze of uncertainty in which he had been floundering. It occurred to him that he had been mawkishly sentimental in respect to his father. He was seriously impressed by the feelings that had mastered him, but he found himself ridiculing the idea that his father stood in peril of any description. And suddenly, out of no particular trend of thought, groped the sly, persistent suspicion that he had not been altogether responsible for the sensations of an hour ago. Some outside influence had moulded his emotions, some cunning brain had been doing his thinking for him!

Then came the sharp recollection of that motionless, commanding figure in the lighted window, and his own puzzling behaviour on the side-walk outside. He recalled his impression that someone has called out to him just before he turned to look up at the window. It was all quite preposterous, he kept on saying over and over again to himself, and yet he could not shake off the uncanny feeling.

Like a shot there flashed into his brain the startling question: was Ranjab the solution? Was it Ranjab's mind and not his own that had moved him to such tender resolves? Could such a condition be possible? Was there such a thing as mind control?

He laughed aloud, and was startled by the sound of his own voice. The idea was preposterous. Such a thing could not have been possible. They were his own thoughts, his own emotions, coming from his own brain, his own heart.

An hour later Frederic approached the box-office of the theatre mentioned by Yvonne over the telephone that morning. The play was half over and the house was sold out. He bought a ticket of admission, however, and lined up with others who were content to stand at the back to witness the play.

He had walked past the theatre three or four times before finally making up his mind to enter, and even then his intentions were not quite clear. He only knew that he was consciously committing an act that he was ashamed of, an act so inexcusable that his face burned as he thought of the struggle he had had with himself up to the moment he stood at the box-office window.

Inside the theatre he leaned weakly against the railing at the back of the auditorium and wiped his brow. What was it that had dragged him there against his will, in direct opposition to his dogged determination to shun the place? The curtain was up, the house was still, save for the occasional coughing of those who succumb to a habit that can neither be helped nor explained.

There were people moving on the stage, but Frederic had no eyes for them. He was seeking in the darkness for the two figures that he knew were somewhere in the big, tense throng.

Hundreds of backs confronted him, no faces. A sensation not far removed from stealth took possession of him. His searching eyes were furtive in their quest. If he had been lonely before, he was doubly so now. The very presence of the multitude filled him with a sickening sense of emptiness. He was friendless there, with all those contented backs for company. Not one among them all had a thought for him, not one turned so much as an inch from the engrossing scene that held them in its grip. Straight, immovable, unresponsive backs—nothing but backs!

Again he asked of himself, why was he there? And he pitied himself so vastly that his throat contracted as with pain. His soul sickened. The truth was being revealed to him as he stood there and with aching eyes searched throughout the serried rows of backs. It came home to him all of a sudden that his quest was a gleaming white back and a small, exquisitely poised head crowned with black.

With a sharp execration, a word of disgust for himself, he tore himself away from the railing and rushed toward the doors. At the same instant a tremendous burst of applause filled the house and he whirled just in time to see the curtain descending. Curiously interested, he paused near the door, his gaze fixed on the great velvet wall that rose and fell at least a half-dozen times in response to the clamour of the delighted crowd.

The backs all at once seemed to become animated and friendly. He drew near the last row of seats again and stared at the actor and the actress who came out to take the "curtain-call"—stared as if at something he had never seen before.

And they had been up there all the time, developing the splendid climax that had drawn people out of their seats, that had put life into all those insufferable backs.

The lights went up and the house was bright. Men began scurrying up the aisles. Here and there broad, black backs rose up in the centre of sections and moved tortuously toward the aisles. Pretty soon, when the theatre was dark again and the curtain up, they would return, politely hiss something about being sorry or "Don't get up, please," and even more tortuously move into their places, completing once more the sullen, arrogant row of backs.

Frederic experienced a sudden shock of dismay. It was not at all unlikely that his father would be among those heading for the lobby, although the chance was remote. His father was the peculiar type of gentleman, now almost extinct, that subsists without fresh air quite as long as the lady who sits in the seat beside him. He was a bit old-fashioned for a New Yorker, no doubt, but he was rather distinguished for his good manners. In fact, he was almost unique. He would not leave Yvonne between the acts, Frederic was quite sure. In spite of this, the young man discreetly hid himself behind two stalwart figures and watched the aisles with alert, shifty eyes.

Presently the exodus was over and the danger past. He moved up to the railing again and resumed his eager scrutiny of the throng. He could not find them. At first he was conscious of disappointment, then he gave way to an absurd rage. Yvonne had misled him, she had deceived him— aye, she had *lied* to him. They were not in the audience, they had not even contemplated coming to this theatre. He had been tricked, deliberately tricked.

No doubt they were seated in some other place of amusement, serenely enjoying themselves.

The thought of it maddened him. And then, just as he was on the point of tearing out of the house, he saw them, and the blood rushed to his head so violently that he was almost blinded.

He caught sight of his father far down in front, and then the dark, half-obscured head of Yvonne. He could not see their faces, but there was no mistaking them for anyone else. He only marvelled that he had not seen them before, even in the semi-darkness. They now appeared to be the only people in the theatre; he could see no one else.

James Brood's fine, aristocratic head was turned slightly toward his wife, who, as Frederic observed after charging his position to one of better advantage, apparently was relating something amusing to him. They undoubtedly were enjoying themselves. Once more the great, almost suffocating wave of tenderness for his father swept over him, mysteriously as before and as convincing. He experienced a sudden, inexplicable feeling of pity for the strong, virile man who had never revealed the slightest symptoms of pity for him. The same curious desire to put his hands on his father's shoulders and tell him that all was well with them came over him again.

Involuntarily he glanced over his shoulder, and the fear was in his heart that somewhere in the shifting throng his gaze would light upon the face of Ranjab.

Long and intently his searching gaze went through the crowd, seeking the remote corners and shadows of the foyer, and a deep breath of relief escaped him when it became evident that the Hindu was not there. He had, in a measure, proved his own cause; his emotions were genuinely his own and not the outgrowth of an influence for good exercised over him by the Brahmin.

He began what he was pleased to term a systematic analysis of his emotions covering the entire evening, all the while regarding the couple in the orchestra chairs with a gaze unswerving in its fidelity to the sensation that now controlled him—a sensation of impending peril.

All at once he slunk farther back into the shadow, a guilty flush mounting to his cheek. Yvonne had turned and was staring rather fixedly in his direction. Despite the knowledge that he was quite completely concealed by the intervening group of loungers, he sustained a distinct shock. He had the uncanny feeling that she was looking directly into his eyes. She had turned abruptly, as if someone had called out to attract her attention and she had obeyed the sudden impulse. A moment later her calmly impersonal gaze swept on, taking the sections to her right and the balcony, and then went back to her husband's face.

Frederic was many minutes in recovering from the effects of the queer shock he had received. He could not get it out of his head that she knew he was there, that she actually turned in answer to the call of his mind. She had not searched for him; on the contrary, she directed her gaze instantly to the spot where he stood concealed.

Actuated by a certain sense of guilt, he decided to leave the theatre as soon as the curtain went up on the next act, which was to be the last. Instead of doing so, however, he lingered to the end of the play, secure in his conscienceless espionage. It had come to him that if he met them in front of the theatre as they came out he could invite them to join him at supper in one of the near-by restaurants. The idea pleased him. He coddled it until it became a sensation.

When James Brood and his wife reached the side-walk they found him there, directly in their path as they wedged their way to the curb to await the automobile. He was smiling frankly, wistfully. There was an honest gladness in his fine, boyish face and an eager light in his eyes. He no longer had the sense of guilt in his soul. It had been a passing qualm, and he felt regenerated for having experienced it, even so briefly. Somehow it had purged his soul of the one longing doubt as to the sincerity of his impulses.

"Hello!" he said, planting himself squarely in front of them.

There was a momentary tableau. He was vividly aware of the fact that Yvonne had shrunk back in alarm and that a swift look of fear leaped into her surprised eyes. She drew closer to Brood's side—or was it the jostling of the crowd that made it seem to be so? He realised then that she had not seen him in the theatre. Her surprise was genuine. It was not much short of consternation, a fact that he realised with a sudden sinking of the heart.

Then his eyes went quickly to his father's face. James Brood was regarding him with a cold, significant smile, as one who understands and despises.

"They told me you were here," faltered Frederic, the words rushing hurriedly through his lips, "and I thought we might run in somewhere and have a bite to eat. I—I want to tell you about Lydia and myself and what——"

The carriage-man bawled a number in his ear and jerked open the door of a limousine that had pulled up to the curb.

Without a word James Brood handed his wife into the car and then turned to the chauffeur.

"Home," he said, and, without so much as a glance at Frederic, stepped inside. The door was slammed and the car slid out into the maelstrom.

Yvonne had sunk back into a corner, huddled down as if suddenly deprived of all her strength. Frederic saw her face as the car moved away. She was staring at him with wide-open, reproachful eyes, as if to say: "Oh, what have you done? What a fool you are!"

For a second or two he stood as if petrified, then everything turned red before him, a wicked red that blinded him. He staggered, as if from a blow in the face.

"My God!" slipped from his stiff lips, and tears leaped to his eyes— tears of supreme mortification. Like a beaten dog he slunk away, feeling himself pierced by the pitying gaze of every mortal in the street.

CHAPTER XVI

Long past midnight the telephone in the Desmond apartment rang sharply, insistently. Lydia, who had just fallen asleep, awoke with a start and sat bolt upright in her bed. A clammy perspiration broke out all over her body. There in the darkness she shivered with a dread so desolating that every vestige of strength forsook her and she could only stare helplessly into the black pall that surrounded her.

Never before in all her life had she been aroused from sleep by the jangling of a telephone-bell. The sound struck terror to her heart. She knew that something terrible had happened. She knew there had been a catastrophe.

She sat there chattering until she heard her mother's door open and then the click of the receiver as it was lifted from the hook. Then she put her fingers to her ears and closed her eyes. The very worst had happened; she was sure of it. The blow had fallen. The one thought that seared her brain was that she had failed him, failed him miserably in the crisis. Oh, if she could only reclaim that lost hour of indecision and cowardice!

The light in the hallway suddenly smote her in the face, and she realised for the first time that her eyes were tightly closed, as if to shut out some abhorrent sight.

"Lydia!" Her mother was standing in the open door. "Oh, you are awake?" Mrs Desmond stared in amazement at the girl's figure.

"What is it, mother? Tell me what has happened? Is he————"

"He wants to speak to you. He is on the wire. His voice sounds queer——"

The girl sprang out of bed and hurried to the telephone.

"Don't go away, mother—stay here," she cried as she sped past the white-clad figure in the doorway. Mrs Desmond flattened herself against the wall and remained there as motionless as a statue, her sombre gaze fixed on her daughter's face.

"Yes, Frederic, it is I, Lydia. What is it, dear?" Her voice was high and thin.

His words came jerking over the wire, sharp and querulous. She closed her eyes in anticipation of the blow, her body rigid.

"I'm sorry to disturb you," he was saying, "but I just had to call you up." The words were disjointed, as if he forced them from his lips in a supreme effort at coherency.

"Yes, yes—it's all right. I don't mind. You did right. What is it?"

"I want you to release me from my promise."

"Release you? Oh, Freddy!" It was a wail that issued from her lips. Her body sagged limply, she steadied herself by leaning against the wall for support.

"You've got to, Lydia. There's no other way. Something has happened to-night, dear. You've got to———"

"Has he—has he———" Her throat closed up as if gripped by a strong hand.

"I'm sorry to drag you out of bed to tell you———"

"Freddy, Freddy!"

"To tell you that I must withdraw my promise, even if you refuse to release me. Oh, I'm not excited, I'm not crazy, I'm not drunk! I never was so steady in my life. To-night has made a man of me. I know just where I stand at last. Now go back to bed, dearest, and don't worry about anything. I couldn't go ahead until I'd asked you to release me from the promise I made."

"You mean—the promise—but, Freddy, I can't release you. I love you. I *will* be your wife, no matter what has happened, no matter———"

"Oh, Lord, Lyddy—it isn't that! It's the other—the promise to say nothing to my father———"

"Oh!" she sighed weakly, a vast wave of relief almost suffocating her.

"He has made it impossible for me to go on without———"

"Where are you, Frederic?" she cried in sudden alarm.

"Oh, I'm all right. I shan't go home, you may be sure of that. To-morrow will be time enough."

"Where are you? I must know. How can I reach you by telephone—"

"Don't be frightened, dear. It's got to be, that's all. It might as well be ended now as later on. The last straw was laid on to-night. Now don't ask questions. I'll see you in the morning. Good night, sweetheart. I've—I've told you that I can't stick to my promise. You'll understand. I couldn't rest until I'd told you and heard your dear voice. Forgive me for calling you up. Tell your mother I'm sorry. Good night!"

"Freddy, listen to me! You must wait until I— — — Oh!" He had hung up the receiver. She heard the whir of the open wire.

There was little comfort for her in the hope held out by her mother as they sat far into the night and discussed the possibilities of the day so near at hand. She could see nothing but disaster, and she could think of nothing but her own lamentable weakness in shrinking from the encounter that might have made the present situation impossible. Between them mother and daughter constructed at random a dozen theories as to the nature of the fresh complication that had entered into the already serious situation, and always it was Lydia who advanced the most sickening of conjectures.

Nor was it an easy matter for Mrs Desmond to combat these fears. In her heart she felt that an irreparable break had occurred and that the final clash was imminent. She tried to make light of the situation, however, prophesying a calmer attitude for Frederic after he had slept over his grievance, which, after all, she argued was doubtless exaggerated.

She promised to go with Lydia to see James Brood in the morning, and to plead with him to be merciful to the boy she was to marry, no matter what transpired. The girl at first insisted on going over to see him that night, notwithstanding the hour, and was dissuaded only after the most earnest opposition.

It was four o'clock before they went back to bed, and long after five before either closed her eyes.

Mrs Desmond, utterly exhausted, was the first to awake. She glanced at the little clock on her dressing-table and gave a great start of consternation. It was long past nine o'clock. She arose at once and hurried to her daughter's door, half expecting to find the room empty and the girl missing from the apartment.

But Lydia was lying there sound asleep. Mrs Desmond's lips parted to give voice to a gentle call, but it was never uttered. A feeling of infinite pity for the tired, harassed girl came over her. For a long time she stood there watching the gentle rise and fall of the sleeper's breast. Then she closed the door softly and stole back to her own room, inspired by a sudden resolve.

While she was dressing the little maid-servant brought in her coffee and toast and received instructions not to awaken Miss Lydia but to let her have her sleep out. A few minutes later she left the apartment and walked briskly around the corner to Brood's home.

She had resolved to take the matter out of her daughter's hands. As she stood at the bedroom door watching Lydia's sweet, troubled face, there arose within her the mother instinct to fight for her young. It was not unlikely that James Brood could be moved by Lydia's pleading, in spite of his declaration that Frederic should never marry her, but the mother recognised the falseness of a position gained by such means.

Over Lydia's head would hang the perpetual reminder that he had submitted out of consideration for her, and not through fairness or justice to Frederic; all the rest of her life she would be made to feel that he tolerated Frederic for her sake. The girl would never know a moment in which she could be free from that ugly sense of obligation. God willing, Frederic would be her daughter's husband. Lydia might spare him the blow that James Brood could deal, but all of her life would be spent in contemplation of that one bitter hour in which she went on her knees to beg for mercy.

The mother saw all this with a foresightedness that stripped the situation of every vestige of romance. Lydia might rejoice at the outset, but there would surely come a time of heartache for her. It would come with the full realisation that James Brood's pity was hard to bear.

Fearing that she might be too late, she walked so rapidly that she was quite out of breath when she entered the house. Mr Riggs and Mr Dawes were putting on their coats in the hall preparatory to their short morning constitutional. They greeted her profusely, and with one accord proceeded to divest themselves of the coats, announcing in one voice their intention to remain for a good, old-fashioned chat.

"It's dear of you," she said hurriedly, "but I must see Mr Brood at once. Why not come over to my apartment this afternoon for a cup of tea and——"

Mrs Brood's voice interrupted her.

"What do you want, Mrs Desmond?" came from the landing above.

The visitor looked up with a start, not so much of surprise as uneasiness. There was something sharp, unfriendly, in the low, level tones.

Yvonne, fully dressed—a most unusual circumstance at that hour of the day—was leaning over the banister-rail.

"I came to see Mr Brood on a very important—"

"He is occupied. Won't I do as well?"

"It is really quite serious, Mrs Brood. I am afraid it would be of no avail to—to take it up with you."

"Have you been sent here by someone else?" demanded Mrs Brood.

"I have not seen Frederic," fell from the other's lips before she thought.

"I dare say you haven't," said the other with ominous clearness. "He has been here since seven this morning, waiting for a chance to speak to his father in private."

"Heaven help me! I—I am too— — —"

"Unless he spent the night in your apartment, I fancy you haven't seen him," went on Yvonne languidly.

She was descending the stairs slowly, almost lazily as she uttered the remark.

"They are together now?" gasped Mrs Desmond.

"Will you come into the library? Good morning, gentlemen. I trust you may enjoy your long walk."

Mrs Desmond followed her into the library. Yvonne closed the door almost in the face of Mr Riggs, who had opened his mouth to accept the invitation to tea, but who said he'd "be blasted" instead, so narrow was his escape from having his nose banged. He emphasised the declaration by shaking his fist at the door.

The two women faced each other. For the first time since she had known Yvonne Brood, Mrs Desmond observed a high touch of colour in her cheeks. Her beautiful eyes were alive with an excitement she could not conceal. Neither spoke for a moment.

"You are accountable for this, Mrs Brood," said Lydia Desmond's mother sternly, accusingly. She expected a storm of indignant protest. Instead, Yvonne smiled slightly.

"It will not hurt my husband to discover that Frederic is a man and not a milksop," she said, but despite her coolness there was a perceptible note of anxiety in her voice.

"You know, then, that they are—that they will quarrel?"

"I fancy it was in Frederic's mind to do so when he came here this morning. He was still in his evening clothes, Mrs Desmond."

"Where are they now?"

"I think he has them on," said Yvonne lightly.

Mrs Desmond regarded her for a moment in perplexity. Then her eyes flashed dangerously.

"I do not think you misunderstood me, Mrs Brood. Where are Frederic and his father?"

"I am not accustomed to that tone of voice, Mrs Desmond."

"I am no longer your housekeeper," said the other succinctly. "You do not realise what this quarrel may mean. I insist on going up to them before it has gone too far."

"My husband can take care of himself, thank you."

"I am not thinking of your husband, but of that poor boy who is———"

"And if I am to judge by Frederic's manner this morning, he is also able to take care of himself," said Yvonne coolly. Her voice shook a little.

Mrs Desmond shot a quick glance of comprehension at the speaker.

"You are worried, Mrs Brood. Your manner betrays you. I command you to tell me how long they have been upstairs together. How long———"

"Will you be so good, Mrs Desmond, as to leave this house instantly?" cried Yvonne angrily.

"No," said the other quietly. "I suppose I am too late to prevent trouble between those two men, but I shall at least remain here to assure Frederic of my sympathy, to help him if I can, to offer him the shelter of my home."

A spasm of alarm crossed Yvonne's face.

"Do you really believe it will come to that?" she demanded nervously.

"If what I fear should come to pass, he will not stay in this house another hour. He will go forth from it cursing James Brood with all the hatred that his soul can possess. And now, Mrs Brood, shall I tell you what I think of you?"

"No. It isn't at all necessary. Besides, I've changed my mind. I'd like you to remain. I do not want to mystify you any farther, Mrs Desmond, but I now confess to you that I am losing my courage. Don't ask me to tell you why, but———"

"I suppose it is the custom with those who play with fire. They shrink when it burns them."

Mrs Brood looked at her steadily. The rebellious, sullen expression died out of her eyes. She sighed deeply, almost despairingly.

"I am sorry you think ill of me, but yet I cannot blame you for considering me to be a—a——— I'll not say it. Mrs Desmond, I—I wish I had never come to this house."

"Permit me to echo your words."

"You will never be able to understand me. And, after all, why should I care? You are nothing to me. You are merely a good woman who has no real object in life. You———"

"No real object in life?"

"Precisely. Sit down. We will wait here together, if you please. I—I *am* worried. I think I rather like to feel that you are here with me. You see, the crisis has come."

"You know, of course, that he turned one wife out of this house, Mrs Brood," said Mrs Desmond deliberately.

Something like terror leaped into the other's eyes. The watcher experienced an incomprehensible feeling of pity for her—she who had been despising her so fiercely the instant before.

"He—he will not turn me out," murmured Yvonne, and suddenly began pacing the floor, her hands clenched. Stopping abruptly in front of the other woman, she exclaimed: "He made a great mistake in driving that other woman out. He is not likely to repeat it, Mrs Desmond."

"Yes—I think he *did* make a mistake," said Mrs Desmond calmly. "But he does not think so. He is a man of iron. He is unbending."

"He is a wonderful man—a great, splendid man," cried Yvonne fiercely. "It is I—Yvonne Lestrange—who proclaim it to the world. I cannot bear to see him suffer. I———"

"Then, why do you———"

"Ah, you would say it, eh? Well, there is no answer. Poof! Perhaps it will not be so bad as we think. Come! I am no longer uneasy. See! I am very calm. Am I not an example for you? Sit down. We will wait together."

They sat far apart, each filled with dark misgivings, though radically opposed in their manner of treating the situation. Mrs Desmond was cold with apprehension. She sat immovable, tense. Yvonne sank back easily in a deep, comfortable chair and coolly lighted a cigarette. It would have been remarked by a keen observer that her failure to offer one to her visitor was evidence of an unwonted abstraction. As a matter of fact, inwardly she was trembling like a leaf.

"I suppose there is nothing to do," said Mrs Desmond in despair, after a long silence. "Poor Lydia will never forgive herself."

Yvonne blew rings of smoke toward the ceiling.

"I dare say you think I am an evil person, Mrs Desmond."

"Curiously, Mrs Brood, I have never thought of you in that light. Your transgressions are the greater for that reason."

"Transgressions? An amiable word, believe me."

"I did not come here, however, to discuss your actions."

Yvonne leaned forward suddenly.

"You do not ask what transpired last night to bring about this crisis. Why do you hesitate?"

Mrs Desmond shook her head slowly. "I do not want to know."

"Well, it was not what you have been thinking it was," said Yvonne levelly.

"I am relieved to hear it," said the other rather grimly.

Mrs Brood flushed to the roots of her hair.

"I do not want to appear unfair to my husband, but I declare to you, Mrs Desmond, that Frederic is fully justified in the attitude he has taken this morning. His father humiliated him last night in a manner that made forbearance impossible. That much I must say for Frederic. And permit me to add, from my soul, that he is vastly more sinned against than sinning."

"I can readily believe that, Mrs Brood."

"This morning Frederic came into the breakfast-room while we were having our coffee. You look surprised. Yes, I was having breakfast with my husband. I knew that Frederic would come. That was my reason. When I heard him in the hall I sent the servants out of the dining-room. He had spent the night with a friend. His first words on entering the room were these—I shall never forget them: 'Last night I thought I loved you, father, but I have come home just to tell you that I hate you. I can't stay in this house another day. I'm going to get out. But I just wanted you to know that I thought I loved you last night, as a son should love his father. I just wanted you to know it.'

"He did not even look at me, Mrs Desmond. I don't believe he knew I was there. I shall never forget the look in James Brood's face. It was as if he saw a ghost or some horrible thing that fascinated him. He did not utter a word, but stared at Frederic in that terrible, awe-struck way.

"'I'm going to get out,' said Frederic, his voice rising. 'You've treated me like a dog all of my life, and I'm through. I shan't even say good-bye to you. You don't deserve any more consideration from me than I've received from you. I hope I'll never see you again. If I ever have a son I'll not treat him as you've treated your son. You don't deserve the honour of being called father; you don't deserve to have a son. I wish to God I had never been obliged to call you father! I don't know what you did to my mother, but if you treated her as— — —'

"Just then my husband found his voice. He sprang to his feet, and I've never seen such a look of rage. I thought he was going to strike Frederic, and

I think I screamed—just a little scream, of course. I was so terrified. But he only said—and it was horrible the way he said it—'You fool—you bastard!' And Frederic laughed in his face and cried out, unafraid: 'I'm glad you call me a bastard! I'd rather be one than be your son. It would at least give me something to be proud of—a real father!'"

"Good Heaven!" fell from Mrs Desmond's white lips.

Yvonne seemed to have paused to catch her breath. Her breast heaved convulsively, the grip of her hands tightened on the arms of the chair.

Suddenly she resumed her recital, but her voice was hoarse and tremulous.

"I was terribly frightened. I thought of calling out to Jones, but I—I had no voice! Ah, you have never seen two angry men waiting to spring at each other's throats, Mrs Desmond. My husband suddenly regained control of himself. He was very calm. 'Come with me,' he said to Frederic. 'This is not the place to wash our filthy family linen. You say you want something to be proud of. Well, you shall have your wish. Come to my study.' And they went away together, neither speaking a word to me—they did not even glance in my direction. They went up the stairs. I heard the door close behind them—away up there. That was half an hour ago. I have been waiting, too—waiting as you are waiting now—to comfort Frederic when he comes out of that room a wreck."

Mrs Desmond started up, an incredulous look in her eyes.

"You are taking his side? You are against your husband? Oh, now I know the kind of woman you are. I know— — —"

"Peace! You do not know the kind of woman I am. You will never know. Yes, I shall take sides with Frederic."

"You do not love your husband!"

A strange, unfathomable smile came into Yvonne's face and stayed there. Mrs Desmond experienced the same odd feeling she had had years ago on first seeing the Sphinx. She was suddenly confronted by an unsolvable mystery.

"He shall not drive me out of his house, Mrs Desmond," was her answer to the challenge.

A door slammed in the upper regions of the house. Both women started to their feet.

"It is over," breathed Yvonne with a tremulous sigh.

"We shall see how well they were able to take care of themselves, Mrs Brood," said Mrs Desmond in a low voice.

"We shall see—yes," said the other mechanically. Suddenly she turned on the tall, accusing figure beside her. "Go away! Go now! I command you to go. This is *our* affair, Mrs Desmond. You are not needed here. You were too late, as you say. I beg of you, go!" She strode swiftly toward the door. As she was about to place her hand on the knob it was opened from the other side, and Ranjab stood before them.

"*Sahib* begs to be excused, Mrs Desmond. He is just going out."

"Going out?" cried Yvonne, who had shrunk back into the room.

"Yes, *sahibah*. You will please excuse, Mrs Desmond. He regret very much."

Mrs Desmond passed slowly through the door, which he held open for her. As she passed by the Hindu she looked full into his dark, expressive eyes, and there was a question in hers. He did not speak, but she read the answer as if it were on a printed page. Her shoulders drooped.

She went back to Lydia.

CHAPTER XVII

When James Brood and Frederic left the dining-room, nearly an hour prior to the departure of Mrs Desmond, there was in the mind of each the resolution to make short work of the coming interview. Each knew that the time had arrived for the parting of the ways, and neither had the least desire to prolong the suspense.

Frederic, far from suspecting the ordeal in store for him, experienced a curious sense of exaltation as he followed the master of the house up the stairway. He was about to declare his freedom; the very thought of it thrilled him. He had at last found the courage to revolt, and there was cause for rejoicing in the prospect of a lively triumph over what he was pleased to call oppression.

He would not mince matters! Oh, no; he would come straight to the point. There wasn't any sense in temporising. There were years of pent-up grievances that he could fling at his father, but he would crystallise them into a few withering minutes and have done with the business. He knew he was as pale as a ghost and his legs were strangely weak, but he was not cognisant of the slightest sensation of fear, nor the least inclination to shrink from the consequences of that brief, original challenge.

The study door was closed. James Brood put his hand on the knob, but before turning it faced the young man with an odd mixture of anger and pity in his eyes.

"Perhaps it will be better if we had nothing more to say to each other," he said with an effort. "I have changed my mind. I cannot say the thing to you that I— —"

"Has it got anything to do with Yvonne and me?" demanded Frederic ruthlessly, jumping at conclusions in his new-found arrogance.

Brood threw open the door.

"Step inside," he said in a voice that should have warned the younger man, it was so prophetic of disaster. Frederic had touched the open sore with that unhappy question. Not until this instant had James Brood admitted to himself that there was a sore and that it had been festering all these weeks.

Now it was laid bare and it smarted with pain. Nothing could save Frederic after that reckless, deliberate thrust at the very core of the malignant growth that lay so near the surface.

It had been in James Brood's heart to spare the boy. An unaccountable wave of compassion had swept through him as he mounted the stairs, leading his victim to the sacrifice. He would have allowed him to go his way in ignorance of the evil truth; he would have spared the son of Matilde and been happier, far happier, he knew, for having done so. He would have let him fare forth, as he elected to go, rejoicing in his foolish independence, scorning to the end of his days, perhaps, the man who posed as father to him.

But Frederic had touched the hateful sore. His chance was gone.

Hot words were on Frederic's lips. Brood held up his hand, and there was in the gesture a command that silenced the young man. He was somewhat shocked to find that he still recognised the other's right to command. The older man went quickly to the door of the Hindu's closet. He rapped on the panel, and in an instant the door was opened. Ranjab stepped out and quickly closed the door behind him. A few words, spoken in lowered tones and in the language of the East, passed between master and man.

Frederic turned his back to them. Moved by a sudden impulse, he strode to the window and pulled the curtains apart. A swift glance upward showed him the drawn shades in Lydia's bedroom windows. Somehow he was glad that she was asleep. An impulse as strong as the other ordered him to shift his glance downward to the little balcony outside of Yvonne's windows. Then he heard the door close softly behind him and turned to face his father.

They were alone in the room. He squared his shoulders.

"I suppose you think I am in love with her," he said defiantly. He waited a moment for the response that did not come. Brood was regarding him with eyes from which every spark of compassion had disappeared. "Well, it may interest you to know that I intend to marry Lydia this very day."

Brood advanced a few steps toward him. In the subdued light of the room his features were not clearly distinguishable. His face was gray and shadowy; only the eyes were sharply defined. They glowed like points of light, unflickering.

"I shall be sorry for Lydia," he said levelly.

"You needn't be," said Frederic hotly. "She understands everything."

"You were born to be dishonest in love."

"What do you mean by that?"

"It is my purpose to tell you precisely what I mean. Lydia understands far more than you think. If she marries you it will be with her eyes open; she will have no one to blame but herself for the mistake."

"Oh, I haven't tried to deceive her as to my prospects. She knows how poor we will be at the———"

"Does she know that this love you profess for her is at the very outset disloyal?"

Frederic was silent for a moment. A twinge shot through his heart.

"She understands everything," he repeated stubbornly.

"Have you lied to her?"

"Lied? You'd better be careful how you———"

"Have you told her that you love her and no one else?"

"Certainly!"

"Then you *have* lied to her."

There was silence—tense silence.

"Do you expect me to strike you for that?" came at last from Frederic's lips, low and menacing.

"You have always considered yourself to be my son, haven't you?" pursued Brood deliberately. "Can you say to me that you have behaved of late as a son should———"

"Wait! We'll settle that point right now. I *did* lose my head. Head, I say, not heart. I shan't attempt to explain—I can't, for that matter. As for Yvonne—well, she's as good as gold. She understands me far better than I understand myself. She knows that even honest men lose their heads sometimes—and she knows the difference between love and—the other thing. I can say to you now that I would sooner have cut my own throat than do more than envy you the possession of someone you do not deserve. I *have* considered myself your son. I have no apology to make for my— we'll call it infatuation. I shall only admit that it has existed and that I have despaired. So God is my witness, I have never loved anyone but Lydia. I have given her pain, and the amazing part of it is that I can't help myself. Naturally, you can't understand what it all means. You are not a young man any longer. You cannot understand."

"Good God!" burst from Brood's lips. Then he laughed aloud— grotesquely.

"Yvonne is the most wonderful thing that has ever come into my life. She has shown me that life is beautiful and rich and full of warmth. I had always thought it ugly and cold. Something inside of me awoke the instant I looked into her eyes—something that had always been there, and yet undeveloped. She spoke to me with her eyes, if you can believe such a thing possible, and I understood. I adored her the instant I saw her. I have felt sometimes that I knew her a thousand years ago. I have felt that I loved her a thousand years ago." A calm seriousness now attended his speech, in direct contrast to the violent mood that had gone before. "I have thought of little else but her. I confess it to you. But through it all there has never been an instant in which I did not worship Lydia Desmond. I—I do not pretend to account for it. It is beyond me."

Brood waited patiently to the end.

"Your mother before you had a somewhat similar affliction," he said, still in the steady, repressed voice. "Perhaps it is a gift—a convenient gift—this ability to worship without effort."

"Better leave my mother out of it," said Frederic sarcastically. A look of wonder leaped to his eyes. "That's the first time you've condescended to acknowledge that I ever had a mother."

"I shall soon make you regret that you were ever so blessed as to have had one."

"You've always made it easy for me to regret that I ever had a father."

Brood's smile was deadly.

"If you have anything more to say to me, you had better get it over. Purge your soul of all the gall that embitters it. I grant you that privilege. Take your innings."

A spasm of pain crossed Frederic's face.

"Yes, I am entitled to my innings. I'll go back to what I said downstairs. I thought I loved and honoured you last night. I would have forgiven everything if you had granted me a friendly—friendly, that's all—just a friendly word. You denied———"

"I suppose you want me to believe that it was love for me that brought you slinking to the theatre," said the other ironically.

"I don't expect you to believe anything. I was lonely. I wanted to be with you and Yvonne. Curse you! Can't you understand how lonely I've been all my life? Can't you understand how hungry I am for the affection that every other boy I've known has had from his parents? I've never asked you about my mother. I used to wonder a good deal. Every other boy had a mother. I never had one. I couldn't understand it. And they all had fathers, but they were not like my father. Their fathers were kind and loving, they were interested in everything their sons did — good or bad. I used to love the fathers of all those other lucky boys at school. They came often — and so did the mothers. No one ever came to see me — no one!

"I used to wonder why you never told me of my own mother. Long ago I gave up wondering. Something warned me not to ask you about her. Something told me it was best to let sleeping dogs lie. I never inquired of anyone after I was old enough to think for myself. I was afraid to ask, so I waited, hoping all the time that you would some day tell me of her. But you've never breathed her name to me. I no longer wonder. I know now that she must have hated you with all the strength of her soul. God, how she must have hated to feel the touch of your hands upon her body! Something tells me she left you, and if she did, I hope she afterward found someone who — but no, I won't say it. Even now I haven't the heart to hurt you by saying that." He stopped, choking up with the rush of bitter words. "Well, why don't you say something?"

"I'm giving you your innings. Go on," said Brood softly.

"She must have loved you once — or she wouldn't have married you. She must have loved you or I wouldn't be here in this world. She — — —"

"Ha!" came sharply from Brood.

" — didn't find you out until it was too late. She was lovely, I know. She was sweet and gentle and she loved happiness. I can see that in her face, in her big, wistful eyes. You — — —"

"What's this?" demanded Brood, startled. "What are you saying?"

"Oh, I've got her portrait — an old photograph. For a month I've carried it here in this pocket-case over my heart. I wouldn't part with it for all the money in the world. When I look at the dear, sweet, girlish face and her eyes look back into mine, I know that *she* loved me."

"Her portrait?" said Brood, unbelieving.

"Yes — and I have only to look at it to know that she couldn't have hurt you — so it must have been the other way round. She's dead now, I know, but she didn't die for years after I was born. Why was it that I never saw her? Why was I kept up there in that damnable village — — —"

"Where did you get that photograph?" demanded Brood hoarsely. "Where, I say? What interfering fool — — —"

"I wouldn't be too nasty, if I were you," said Frederic, a note of triumph in his voice. "Yvonne gave it to me. I made her promise to say nothing to you about it. She— — —"

"Yvonne? Are you— — — Impossible! She could not have had— — —"

"It was lying under the marble top of that old bureau in her bedroom. She found it there when the men came to take it away to storage. It hadn't been moved in twenty years or more."

"In—her—bedroom?" murmured Brood, passing his hand over his eyes. "The old bureau—marble top—good Lord! It was our bedroom. Let me see it—give it to me this instant!"

"I can't do that. It's mine now. It's safe where it is."

"Yvonne found it? Yvonne? And gave it to you? What damnable trick of fate is this? But— — — Ah, it may not be a portrait of your—your mother. Some old photograph that got stuck under the— — —"

"No; it is my mother. Yvonne saw the resemblance at once and brought it to me. And it may interest you to know that she advised me to treasure it all my life, because it would always tell me how lovely and sweet my mother was—the mother I have never seen."

"I insist on seeing that picture," said Brood with deadly intensity.

"No," said Frederic, folding his arms tightly across his breast. "You didn't deserve her then and you— — —"

"You don't know what you are saying, boy!"

"Ah, don't I? Well, I've got just a little bit of my mother safe here over my heart—a little faded card, that's all—and you shall not rob me of that. I wish to God I had her here, just as she was when she had the picture taken. Don't glare at me like that. I don't intend to give it up. Last night I was sorry for you. I had the feeling that somehow you have always been unhappy over something that happened in the past, and that my mother was responsible. And yet when I took out this photograph, this tiny bit of old cardboard— see, it is so small that it can be carried in my waistcoat pocket—when I took it out and looked at the pure, lovely face, I—by Heaven, I knew she was not to blame!"

"Have you finished?" asked Brood, wiping his brow. It was dripping.

"Except to repeat that I am through with you for ever. I've had all that I can endure, and I'm through. My greatest regret is that I didn't get out long ago. But like a fool—a weak fool—I kept on hoping that you'd change and that there were better days ahead for me. I kept on hoping that you'd be a real father to me. Good Lord, what a libel on the name!" He laughed raucously. "I'm sick of calling you father. You did me the honour downstairs of calling me 'bastard.' You had no right to call me that; but, by Heaven, if it were not for this bit of cardboard here over my heart, I'd laugh in your face and be happy to shout from the housetops that I am no son of yours. But there's no such luck as that! I've only to look at my mother's innocent, soulful face to————"

"Stop!" shouted Brood in an awful voice. His clenched hands were raised above his head. "The time has come for me to tell you the truth about this innocent mother of yours. Luck is with you. I am not your father. You are————"

"Wait! If you are going to tell me that my mother was not a good woman, I want to go on record in advance of anything you may say, as being glad that I am her son no matter who my father was. I am glad that she loved me because I was her child, and if you are not my father, then I still have the joy of knowing that she loved some one man well enough to———" He broke off the bitter sentence and with nervous fingers drew a small leather case from his waistcoat pocket. "Before you go any farther, take one look at her face. It will make you ashamed of yourself. Can you stand there and lie about her after looking into————"

He was holding the window curtains apart, and a stream of light fell upon the lovely face, so small that Brood was obliged to come quite close to be able to see it. His eyes were distended.

"It is not Matilde—it is like her, but—yes, yes; it is Matilde! I must be losing my mind to have thought———" He wiped his brow. "But it was startling—positively uncanny." He spoke as to himself, apparently forgetting that he had a listener.

"Well, can you lie about her now?" demanded Frederic.

Brood was still staring, as if fascinated, at the tiny photograph.

"But I have never seen that picture before. She never had one so small as that. It————"

"It was made in Vienna," interrupted Frederic, not without a strange thrill of satisfaction in his soul, "and before you were married, I'd say. On the back of it is written 'To my own sweetheart,' in Hungarian, Yvonne says. There! Look at her. She was like that when you married her. How adorable she must have been. 'To my own sweetheart'! O—ho!"

A hoarse cry of rage and pain burst from Brood's lips. The world grew red before his eyes.

"'To my own sweetheart'!" he cried out. He sprang forward and struck the photograph from Frederic's hand. It fell to the floor at his feet. Before the young man could recover from his surprise, Brood's foot was upon the bit of cardboard. "Don't raise your hand to me! Don't you dare to strike me! Now I shall tell you who that sweetheart was!"

Half an hour later James Brood descended the stairs alone. He went straight to the library, where he knew that he could find Yvonne. Ranjab, standing in the hall, peered into his white, drawn face as he passed, and started forward as if to speak to him. But Brood did not see him. He did not lift his gaze from the floor. The Hindu went swiftly up the stairs, a deep dread in his soul.

The shades were down. Brood stopped inside the door and looked dully about the library. He was on the point of retiring when Yvonne spoke to him out of the shadowy corner beyond the fireplace.

"Close the door," she said huskily. Then she emerged slowly, almost like a spectre, from the dark background formed by the huge mahogany bookcases that lined the walls from floor to ceiling. "You were a long time up there," she went on.

"Why is it so dark in here, Yvonne?" he asked lifelessly.

"So that it would not be possible for me to see the shame in your eyes, James."

He leaned heavily against the long table. She came up and stood across the table from him, and he felt that her eyes were searching his very soul.

"I have hurt him beyond all chance of recovery," he said hoarsely.

She started violently.

"You—you struck him down? He—he is dying?" Her voice trailed off into a whisper.

"He will be a long time in dying. It will be slow. I struck him down, not with my hand, not with a weapon that he could parry, but with words— words! Do you hear? I have crushed his soul with words!"

"Oh, you coward!" she cried, leaning over the table, her eyes blazing. "I can understand it in you. You have no soul of your own. What have you done to your son, James Brood?"

He drew back as if from the impact of a blow. "Coward? If I have crushed his soul, it was done in time, Yvonne, to deprive you of the glory of doing it."

"What did he say to you about me?"

"You have had your fears for nothing. He did not put you in jeopardy," he said scornfully.

"I know. He is not a coward," she said calmly.

"In your heart you are reviling me. You judge me as one guilty soul judges another. Suppose that I were to confess to you that I left him up there with all the hope, all the life blasted out of his eyes—with a wound in his heart that will never stop bleeding—that I left him because I was sorry for what I had done and could not stand by and look upon the wreck I had created. Suppose———"

"I am still thinking of you as a coward. What is it to me that you are sorry now? What have you done to that wretched, unhappy boy?"

"He will tell you soon enough. Then you will despise me even more than I despise myself. He—he looked at me with his mother's eyes when I kept on striking blows at his very soul. Her eyes—eyes that were always pleading with me! But, curse them—always scoffing at me! For a moment I faltered. There was a wave of love—yes, love, not pity, for him—as I saw him go down before the words I hurled at him. It was as if I had hurt the only thing in all the world that I love. Then it passed. He was not meant for me to love. He was born for me to despise. He was born to torture me as I have tortured him."

"You poor fool!" she cried, her eyes glittering.

"Sometimes I have doubted my own reason," he went on, as if he had not heard her scathing remark. "Sometimes I have felt a queer gripping of the heart when I was harshest toward him. Sometimes, his eyes—*her eyes*— have melted the steel that was driven into my heart long ago, his voice and the touch of his hand have gently checked my bitterest thoughts. Are you listening?"

"Yes."

"You ask what I have done to him. It is nothing in comparison to what he would have done to me. It isn't necessary to explain. You know the thing he has had in his heart to do. I have known it from the beginning. It is the treacherous heart of his mother that propels that boy's blood along its craven way. She was an evil thing—as evil as God ever put life into."

"Go on."

"I loved her as no woman was ever loved before—or since. I thought she loved me; I believe she did. He—Frederic had her portrait up there to flash in my face. She was beautiful; she was as lovely as—but no more! I was not the man. She loved another. You may have guessed, as others have guessed, that she betrayed me. Her lover was that boy's father."

Dead silence reigned in the room, save for the heavy breathing of the man. Yvonne was as still as death itself. Her hands were clenched against her breast.

"That was years ago," resumed the man hoarsely.

"You—you told him this?" she cried, aghast.

"He stood before me up there and said that he hoped he might some day discover that he was not my son."

"You told him *then*?"

"He cursed me for having driven his mother out of my house."

"You told him?"

"He uttered the hope that she might come back from the grave to torture me for ever—to pay me back for what I had done to her."

"Then you told him!"

"He said she must have loathed me as no man was ever loathed before. Then I told him."

"You told him because you knew she did *not* loathe you!"

"Yvonne! You are laughing!"

"I laugh because after he had said all these bitter things to you, and you had paid him back by telling him that he was not your son, it was you—not he—who was sorry!"

"I did not expect sympathy from you, but—to have you laugh in my face! I———"

"Did you expect sympathy from him?" she cried.

"I told him in the end that as he was not my son he need feel no compunction in trying to steal my wife away from me. I———"

"And what did he say to that?" she broke in shrilly.

"Nothing! He did not speak to me after that. Not one word!"

"Nor should I speak to you again, James Brood!"

"Yvonne—I—I love you. I———"

"And you loved Matilde—God pity your poor soul! For no more than I have done, you drove her out of your house. You accuse me in your heart when you vent your rage on that poor boy. Oh, I know! You suspect *me!* And you suspected the other one. I swear to you that you have more cause to suspect me than Matilde. She was not untrue to you. She could not have loved anyone else but you. I know—I know! Don't come near me! Not now! I tell you that Frederic is your son. I tell you that Matilde loved no one but you. You drove her out. You drive Frederic out. *And you will drive me out!*"

She stood over him like an accusing angel, her arms extended. He shrank back, glaring.

"Why do you say these things to me? You cannot know—you have no right to say———"

"I *am* sorry for you, James Brood," she murmured, suddenly relaxing. Her body swayed against the table, and then she sank limply into the chair alongside.

"Yvonne!"

"You will never forget that you struck a man who was asleep, absolutely asleep, James Brood. That's why I am sorry for you."

"Asleep!" he murmured, putting his hand to his eyes. "Yes, yes—he was asleep! Yvonne, I—I have never been so near to loving him as I am now. I—I———"

"I am going up to him. Don't try to stop me. But first let me ask you a question. What did Frederic say when you told him his mother was was what you claim?"

Brood lowered his head.

"He said that I was a cowardly liar."

"And it was then that you began to feel that you loved him. Ah, I see what it is that you need, James. You are a great, strong man, a wonderful man in spite of all this. You have a heart—a heart that still needs breaking before you can ever hope to be happy."

"As if my heart hasn't already been broken," he groaned.

"Your head has been hurt, that's all. There is a vast difference. Are you going out?"

He looked at her in dull amazement. Slowly he began to pull himself together.

"Yes. I think you should go to him. I—I gave him an hour to—to———"

"To get out?"

"Yes. He must go, you see. See him, if you will. I shall not oppose you. Find out what he expects to do."

She passed swiftly by him as he started toward the door. In the hall, which was bright with the sunlight from the upper windows, she turned to face him. To his astonishment her cheeks were aglow and her eyes bright with eagerness. She seemed almost radiant.

"Yes; it needs breaking, James," she said, and went up the stairs, leaving him standing there dumbfounded. Near the top she began to hum a blithe tune. It came down to him distinctly—the weird little air that had haunted him for years—Feverelli's!

CHAPTER XVIII

To Brood's surprise she came half-way down the steps again, and, leaning over the railing, spoke to him with a voice full of irony.

"Will you be good enough to call off your spy, James?"

"What do you mean?" He had started to put on his light overcoat.

"I think you know," she said briefly.

"Do you consider me so mean, so infamous as———" he began hotly.

"Nevertheless, I feel happier when I know he is out of the house. Call off your dog, James."

He smothered an execration and then called out harshly to Jones:

"Ask Ranjab to attend me here, Jones. He is to go out with me," he said to the butler a moment later.

Yvonne was still leaning over the banister, a scornful smile on her lips.

"I shall wait until you are gone. I intend to see Frederic alone," she said, with marked emphasis on the final word.

"As you like," said he coldly.

She crossed the upper hall and disappeared from view down the corridor leading to her own room. Her lips were set with decision; a wild, reckless light filled her eyes, and the smile of scorn had given way to one of exaltation. Her breath came fast and tremulously through quivering nostrils as she closed her door and hurried across to the little vine-covered balcony.

"The time has come—the time has come, thank God!" she was saying to herself, over and over again. The French doors stuck. She was jerking angrily at them when her maid hurried in from the bedroom, attracted by the unusual commotion.

"*Que faites vous, madame?*" she cried anxiously.

Her mistress turned quickly.

"Listen! Go downstairs at once and tell them that I have dismissed you. At once, do you hear?"

"*Oui madame!*" cried Céleste, her eyes dancing with a sudden, incomprehensible delight.

"You are to leave the house immediately. I dismiss you. You have been stealing from me, do you understand?"

"*Oui, madame. Je comprendes parfaitement, madame!*" cried the maid, actually clapping her hands.

"You will pack two steamer-trunks and get them out of the house before five o'clock. You are going back to Paris. You are dismissed."

The little Frenchwoman beamed.

"*Certainement, madame! Par le premier bateau. Je comprend.*"

"The first boat for Havre—do you know the hour for sailing? Consult the morning paper, Céleste."

"*En bien, madame. La Provence. Il part demain. Je— — —*"

"Go at once!" cried the mistress, waving her hands excitedly.

"*Vous me renvoyez!*" And the little maid dashed out of the room.

As she descended the back stairs an amazing change came over her. Her sprightly face became black with sullen rage and her eyes snapped with fury. So violent was her manner when she accosted Jones in the servants' hall that he fell back in some alarm. She was not long in making him understand that she had been dismissed, however, and that she would surely poison the diabolical creature upstairs if she remained in the house another hour. Even the cook, who had a temper of her own, was appalled by the exhibition; other servants were struck dumb.

Jones, perspiring freely, said something about calling in an officer, and then Céleste began to weep bitterly. All she wanted was to get out of the house before she did something desperate to the cruel tyrant upstairs, and she'd be eternally grateful to Jones if he'd get her trunks out of the storeroom as soon as— — — But Jones was already on his way to give instructions to the furnace-man.

Céleste took the occasion to go into hysterics, and the entire servant body fell to work hissing "*Sh—h!*" in an agony of apprehension lest the turmoil should penetrate the walls and reach the ears of the "woman upstairs." They closed all of the doors and most of the windows, and the upstairs maid thought it would be a good idea to put a blanket over the girl's head.

Left alone, Yvonne turned her attention to the window across the court and two floors above her the heavily curtained window in Brood's "retreat."

There was no sign of life there, so she hurried to the front of the house to wait for the departure of James Brood and his man. The two were going down the front steps. At the bottom Brood spoke to Ranjab, and the latter, as imperturbable as a rock, bowed low and moved off in an opposite direction to that taken by his master. She watched until both were out of sight. Then she rapidly mounted the stairs to the top floor.

Frederic was lying on the couch near the jade room door. She was able to distinguish his long, dark figure after peering intently about the shadowy interior in what seemed at first to be a vain search for him. She shrank back, her eyes fixed in horror upon the prostrate shadow. Suddenly he stirred and then half raised himself on one elbow to stare at the figure in the doorway.

"Is it *you?*" he whispered hoarsely, and dropped back with a great sigh on his lips.

Her heart leaped. The blood rushed back to her face. Quickly closing the door, she advanced into the room, her tread as swift and as soft as a cat's.

"He has gone out. We are quite alone," she said, stopping to lean against the table, suddenly faint with excitement.

He laughed, a bitter, mirthless, snarling laugh.

"Get up, Frederic. Be a man! I know what has happened. Get up! I want to talk it over with you. We must plan. We must decide now at once—before he returns." The words broke from her lips with sharp, staccato-like emphasis.

He came to a sitting posture slowly, all the while staring at her with a dull wonder in his heavy eyes.

"Pull yourself together," she cried hurriedly. "We cannot talk here. I am afraid in this room. It has ears, I know. That awful Hindu is always here, even though he may seem to be elsewhere. We will go down to my boudoir."

He slowly shook his head and then allowed his chin to sink dejectedly into his hands. With his elbows resting on his knees, he watched her movements in a state of increasing interest and bewilderment. She turned abruptly to the Buddha, whose placid, smirking countenance seemed to be alive to the situation in all of its aspects. Standing close, her hands behind her back, her figure very erect and theatric, she proceeded to address the image in a voice full of mockery.

"Well, my chatterbox friend, I have pierced his armour, haven't I? He will creep up here and ask you, his wonderful god, to tell him what to do about it, *aïe?* His wits are tangled. He doubts his senses. And when he comes to you, my friend, and whines his secret doubts into your excellent and trustworthy ear, do me the kindness to keep the secret I shall now whisper to you, for I trust you, too, you amiable fraud."

Standing on tiptoe, she put her lips to the idol's ear and whispered. Frederic, across the room, roused from his lethargy by the strange words and still stranger action, rose to his feet and took several steps toward her.

"There! Now you know everything. You know more than James Brood knows, for you know what his charming wife is about to do next." She drew back and regarded the image through half-closed, smouldering eyes. "But he will know before long—before long."

"What are you doing, Yvonne?" demanded Frederic unsteadily.

She whirled about and came toward him, her hands still clasped behind her back.

"Come with me," she said, ignoring his question.

"He—he thinks I am in love with you," said he, shaking his head.

"And are you not in love with me?"

He was startled. "Good Lord, Yvonne!"

She came quite close to him. He could feel the warmth that travelled from her body across the short space that separated them. The intoxicating perfume filled his nostrils; he drew a deep breath, his eyes closing slowly as his senses prepared to succumb to the delicious spell that came over him. When he opened them an instant later she was still facing him, as straight and fearless as a soldier, and the light of victory was in her dark, compelling eyes.

"Well," she said deliberately, "I am ready to go away with you."

He fell back stunned beyond the power of speech. His brain was filled with a thousand clattering noises.

"He has turned you out," she went on rapidly. "He disowns you. Very well; the time has come for me to exact payment of him for that and for all that has gone before. I shall go away with you. I———"

"Impossible!" he cried, finding his tongue and drawing still farther away from her.

"Are you not in love with me?" she whispered softly.

He put his hands to his eyes to shut out the alluring vision.

"For God's sake, Yvonne—leave me. Let me go my way. Let me———"

"He cursed your mother! He curses you! He damns you—as he damned her. You can pay him up for everything. You owe nothing to him. He has killed every———"

Frederic straightened up suddenly and, with a loud cry of exultation, raised his clenched hands above his head.

"By Heaven, I will break him! I will make him pay! Do you know what he has done to me? Listen to this: he boasts of having reared me to manhood, as one might bring up a prize beast, that he might make me pay for the wrong that my poor mother did a quarter of a century ago. All these years he has had in mind this thing that he has done to-day. All my life has been spent in preparation for the sacrifice that came an hour ago. I have suffered all these years in ignorance of — — —"

"Not so loud!" she whispered, alarmed by the vehemence of his reawakened fury.

"Oh, I'm not afraid!" he cried savagely. "Can you imagine anything more diabolical than the scheme he has had in mind all these years? To pay back my mother—whom he loved and still loves—yes, by Heaven, he still loves her—he works to this beastly end! He made her suffer the agonies of the damned up to the day of her death by refusing her the right to have the child that he swears is no child of his. Oh, you don't know the story—you don't know the kind of man you have for a husband—you don't— — —"

"Yes, yes; I do know!" she cried violently, beating her breast with clenched hands. "I *do* know! I know that he still loves the poor girl who went out of this house with his curses ringing in her ears a score of years ago, and who died still hearing them. And I had almost come to the point of pitying him—I was failing—I was weakening. He is a wonderful man. I—I was losing myself. But that is all over. Three months ago I could have left him without a pang—yesterday I was afraid that it would never be possible. To-day he makes it easy for me. He has hurt you beyond all reason, not because he hates you, but because he loved your mother."

"But you do love him!" cried Frederic in stark wonder. "You don't care the snap of your fingers for me. What is all this you are saying, Yvonne? You must be mad. Think! Think what you are saying."

"I have thought—I am always thinking. I know my own mind well enough. It is settled: I am going away, and I am going with you."

"You can't be in earnest!"

"I am desperately in earnest. You owe nothing to him now. He says you are not his son. You owe nothing but hatred to him, and you should pay. You owe vengeance for your mother's sake—for the sake of her whose face you have come to love, who loved you to the day she died, I am sure. He will proclaim to the world that you are not his son, he will brand you with the mark of shame, he will drive you out of New York. You are the son of a music-master, he shouts from the housetops! Your mother was a vile woman, he shouts from the housetops You cannot remain here. You *must* go. You must take me with you. Ah, you are thinking of Lydia! Well, are you thinking of dragging her through the mire that he will create? Are you willing to give her the name he declares is not yours to give? Are you a craven, whipped coward who will not strike back when the chance is offered to give a blow that will———"

"I cannot listen to you, Yvonne!" cried Frederic, aghast. His heart was pounding so fiercely that the blood surged to his head in great waves, almost stunning him with its velocity.

"We go to-morrow!" she cried out in an ecstasy of triumph. She was convinced that he would go! "La Provence!"

"Good Heaven!" he gasped, dropping suddenly into a chair and burying his face in his shaking hands. "What will this mean to Lydia—what will she do—what will become of her?"

A quiver of pain crossed the woman's face, her eyelids fell as if to shut out something that shamed her in spite of all her vainglorious protestations. Then the spirit of exaltation resumed its sway. She lifted her eyes heavenward, and inaudible words trembled on her lips. A moment later she stood over him, her hands extended as if in blessing.

Had he looked up at that instant he would have witnessed a Yvonne he did not know. No longer was she the alluring, sensuous creature who had been in his thoughts for months, but a transfigured being whose soul looked out through gentle, pitying eyes, whose wiles no longer were employed in the devices of which she was past-mistress, whose real nature was revealed now for the first time since she entered the house of James Brood.

There was pain and suffering in the lovely eyes, and there was a strange atmosphere of sanctuary attending the very conquest she had made. But Frederic did not look up until all this had passed and the smile of triumph was on her lips again and the glint of determination in her eyes. He had missed the revelation that would have altered his estimate of her for the future.

"You cannot marry Lydia now," she said, affecting a sharpness of tone that caused him to shrink involuntarily. "It is your duty to write her a letter to-night, explaining all that has happened to-day. She would sacrifice herself for you to-day, but there is—to-morrow! A thousand to-morrows, Frederic. Don't forget them, my dear. They would be ugly, after all, and she is too good, too fine to be dragged into———"

"You are right!" he exclaimed, leaping to his feet. "It would be the vilest act that a man could perpetrate. Why—why, it would be proof of what he says of me—it would stamp me for ever the dastard he—no, no; I could never lift my head again if I were to do this utterly vile thing to Lydia. He said to me here—not an hour ago—that he expected me to go ahead and blight that loyal girl's life, that I would consider it a noble means of self-justification! What do you think of that? He——— But wait! What is this that we are proposing to do? Give me time to think! Why—why, I can't take you away from him, Yvonne! What am I thinking of? Have I no sense of honour? Am I———"

"You are not his son," she said significantly.

"But that is no reason why I should stoop to a foul trick like this. Do—do you know what you are suggesting?" He drew back from her with a look of disgust in his eyes. "No! I'm not that vile! I———"

"Frederic, you must let me———"

"I don't want to hear anything more, Yvonne. What manner of woman are you? He is your husband, he loves you, he trusts you; oh, yes, he does! And you would leave him like this? You would———"

"Hush! Not so loud!" she cried in great agitation.

"And let me tell you something more. Although I can never marry Lydia, by Heaven, I shall love her to the end of my life. I will not betray that love. To the end of time she shall know that my love for her is real and true and———"

"Frederic, you must listen to me," she cried, wringing her hands. "You must hear what I have to say to you. Wait! Do not leave me!"

"What is it, Yvonne—what is it?" he cried, pausing in utter amazement after taking a few steps toward the door.

"Where are you going?" she whispered, following him with dragging steps. "Not to *him?*"

"Certainly not! Do you think I would betray you to him?"

"Wait! Give me time to think," she pleaded. He shook his head resolutely. "Do not judge me too harshly. Hear what I have to say before you condemn me. I am not the vile creature you think, Frederic. Wait! Let me think!"

He stared at her for a moment in deep perplexity and then slowly drew near.

"Yvonne, I do not believe you mean to do wrong—I do not believe it of you. You have been carried away by some horrible———"

"Listen to me," she broke in fiercely. "I would have sacrificed you—aye, sacrificed you, poor boy—in order to strike James Brood the cruellest blow that man ever sustained. I would have destroyed you in destroying him—God forgive me! But you have shown me how terrible I am, how utterly terrible! Love you? No! No! Not in that way. I would have put a curse, an undeserved curse, upon your innocent head, and all for the joy it would give me to see James Brood grovel in misery for the rest of his life. Oh!"

She uttered a groan of despair and self-loathing so deep and full of pain that his heart was chilled.

"Yvonne!" he gasped, dumbfounded.

"Do not come near me!" she cried out, covering her face with her hands. For a full minute she stood before him, straight and rigid as a statue, a tragic figure he was never to forget. Suddenly she lowered her hands. To his surprise, a smile was on her lips.

"You would never have gone away with me. I know it now. All these months I have been counting on you for this very hour, this culminating hour—and now I realise how little hope I have really had, even from the beginning. You are honourable. There have been times when my influence over you was such that you resisted only because you were loyal to yourself—not to Lydia, not to my husband—but to yourself. I came to this house with but one purpose in mind. I came here to take you away from the man who has always stood as your father. I would not have become your mistress—pah! how loathsome it sounds!—but I would have enticed you away, believing myself to be justified. I would have struck James Brood that blow. He would have gone to his grave believing himself to have been paid in full by the son of the woman he had degraded, by the boy he had reared for the slaughter, by the blood———"

"In God's name, Yvonne, what is this you are saying? What have you against my—against him?"

"Wait! I shall come to that. I did not stop to consider all that I should have to overcome. First, there was your soul, your honour, your integrity to consider. I did not think of all those things. I did not stop to think of the damnable wrong I should be doing to you. I was blind to everything except my one great, long-enduring purpose. I could see nothing else but triumph over James Brood. To gain my end it was necessary that I should be his wife. I became his wife—I deliberately took that step in order to make complete my triumph over him. I became the wife of the man I had hated with all my soul, Frederic. So you can see how far I was willing to go to—ah, it was a hard thing to do! But I did not shrink. I went into it without faltering, without a single thought of the cost to myself. He was to pay for all that, too, in the end. Look into my eyes, Frederic. I want to ask you a question. Will you go away with me? Will you take me?"

He returned her look steadily.

"No!"

"That is all I want to hear you say. It means the end. I have done all that could be done, and I have failed. Thank God, I have failed!" She came swiftly to him and, before he was aware of her intention, clutched his hand and pressed it to her lips. He was shocked to find that a sudden gush of tears was wetting his hand.

"Oh, Yvonne!" he cried miserably.

She was sobbing convulsively. He looked down upon her dark, bowed head and again felt the mastering desire to crush her slender, beautiful body in his arms. The spell of her was upon him again, but now he realised that the appeal was to his spirit and not to his flesh—as it had been all along, he was beginning to suspect.

"Don't pity me," she choked out. "This will pass, as everything else has passed. I am proud of you now, Frederic. You are splendid. Not many men could have resisted in this hour of despair. You have been cast off, despised, degraded, humiliated. You were offered the means to retaliate. You———"

"And I was tempted!" he cried bitterly. "For the moment I was———"

"And now what is to become of *me?*" she wailed.

His heart grew cold.

"You—you will leave him? You will go back to Paris? Yvonne, it will be a blow to him. He has had one fearful slash in the back. This will break him."

"At least, I may have that consolation," she cried, straightening up in an effort to revive her waning purpose. "Yes, I shall go. I cannot stay here now. I—" She paused and shuddered.

"What, in Heaven's name, have you against my—against him? What does it all mean? How you must have hated him to———"

"Hated him? Oh, how feeble the word is! Hate! There should be a word that strikes more terror to the soul than that one. But wait! You shall know everything. You shall have the story from the beginning. There is much to tell, and there will be consolation—aye, triumph for you in the story I shall tell. First, let me say this to you: when I came here I did not know that there was a Lydia Desmond. I would have hurt that poor girl; but it would not have been a lasting pain. In my plans, after I came to know her, there grew a beautiful alternative through which she should know great happiness. Oh, I have planned well and carefully, but I was ruthless. I would have crushed her with him rather than to have failed. But it is all a dream that has passed, and I am awake.

"It was the most cruel, but the most magnificent dream—ah, but I dare not think of it. As I stand here before you now. Frederic, I am shorn of all my power. I could not strike him as I might have done a month ago. Even as I was cursing him but a moment ago I realised that I could not have gone on with the game. Even as I begged you to take your revenge, I knew that it was not myself who urged, but the thing that was having its death-struggle within me."

"Go on. Tell me. Why do you stop?"

She was glancing fearfully toward the Hindu's door. "There is one man in this house who knows. He reads my every thought. He does not know all, but he knows *me*. He has known from the beginning that I was not to be trusted. That man is never out of my thoughts. I fear him, Frederic—I fear him as I fear death. If he had not been here I—I believe I should have dared anything. I *could* have taken you away with me months ago. But he worked his spell and I was afraid. I faltered. He knew that I was afraid, for he spoke to me one day of the beautiful serpents in his land that were cowards in spite of the death they could deal with one flash of their fangs. You were intoxicated. I *am* a thing of beauty. I can charm as the———"

"God knows that is true," he said hoarsely.

"But enough of that! I am stricken with my own poison. Go to the door! See if he is there. I fear———"

"No one is near," said he, after striding swiftly to both doors, listening at one and peering out through the other.

"You will have to go away, Frederic. I shall have to go. But we shall not go together. In my room I have kept hidden the sum of ten thousand dollars, waiting for the day to come when I should use it to complete the game I have played. I knew that you would have no money of your own. I was prepared even for that. Look again! See if anyone is there? I feel—I feel that someone is near us. Look, I say!"

He obeyed.

"See! There is no one near." He held open the door to the hall. "You must speak quickly. I am to leave this house in an hour. I was given the hour."

"Ah, I can see by your face that you hate him! It is well. That is something. It is but little, I know, after all I have wished for—but it is something for me to treasure—something for me to take back with me to the one sacred little spot in this beastly world of men and women."

"Yvonne, you are the most incomprehensible———"

"Am I not beautiful, Frederic? Tell me!" She came quite close to him.

"You are the most beautiful woman in all the world," he said abjectly.

"And I have wasted all my beauty—I have lent it to unloveliness, and it has not been destroyed! It is still with me, is it not? I have not lost it in———"

"You are beautiful beyond words—beyond anything I have ever imagined," said he, suddenly passing his hand over his brow.

"You would have loved me if it had not been for Lydia?"

"I couldn't have helped myself. I—I fear I—faltered in my—are you still trying to tempt me? Are you still asking me to go away with you?"

A hoarse cry came from the doorway behind them—a cry of pain and anger that struck terror to their souls.

CHAPTER XIX

Transfixed, they watched James Brood take two or three steps into the room. At his back was the swarthy Hindu, his eyes gleaming like coals of fire in the shadowy light.

"James!" fell tremulously from the lips of Yvonne. She swayed toward him as Ranjab grasped his arm from behind.

Frederic saw the flash of something bright as it passed from the brown hand to the white one. He did not at once comprehend.

"It happened once." came hoarsely from the throat of James Brood. "It shall not happen again. Thank you, Ranjab."

Then Frederic knew. The Hindu had slipped a revolver into his master's hand!

"It gives me great pleasure, Yvonne, to relieve you of that worthless thing you call your life."

As he raised his arm Frederic sprang forward with a shout of horror. Scarcely realising what he did, he hurled Yvonne violently to one side.

It was all over in the twinkling of an eye. There was a flash, the crash of an explosion, a puff of smoke, and the smell of burned powder.

Frederic stood perfectly still for an instant, facing the soft cloud that rose from the pistol-barrel, an expression of vague amazement in his face. Then his hand went uncertainly to his breast.

Already James Brood had seen the red blotch that spread with incredible swiftness—blood-red against the snowy white of the broad shirt bosom. Glaring with wide-open eyes at the horrid spot, he stood there with the pistol still levelled.

"Good God, father, you've—why, you've———" struggled from Frederic's writhing lips, and then his knees sagged; an instant later they gave way with a rush and he dropped heavily to the floor.

There was not a sound in the room. Suddenly Brood made a movement, quick and spasmodic. At the same instant Ranjab flung himself forward and grasped his master's arm. He had turned the revolver upon himself!

The muzzle was almost at his temple when the Hindu seized his hand in a grip of iron.

"*Sahib! Sahib!*" he hissed. "What would you do?" Wrenching the weapon from the stiff, unresisting fingers, he hurled it across the room.

Brood groaned. His tall body swerved forward, but his legs refused to carry him. The Hindu caught him as he was sinking limply to his knees. With a tremendous effort of the will, Brood succeeded in conquering the black unconsciousness that was assailing him. He straightened up to his full height and with trembling fingers pointed to the prostrate figure on the floor.

"The pistol, Ranjab! Where is it? Give it to me! Man, can I live after *that*? I have killed my son—my own son! Quick, man!"

"*Sahib!*" cried the Hindu, wringing his hands. "I cannot! I cannot!"

"I command you! The pistol!"

Without a word the Hindu, fatalist, slave, pagan that he was, turned to do his master's bidding. It was not for him to say nay, it was not for him to oppose the will of the master, but to obey.

All this time Yvonne was crouching against the table, her horrified gaze upon the great red blotch that grew to terrible proportions as she watched. She had not moved, she had not breathed, she had not taken her hands from her ears where she had placed them at the sound of the explosion.

"Blood! It is blood!" she moaned, and for the first time since the shot was fired her husband glanced at the one for whom the bullet had originally been intended.

An expression of incredulity leaped into his face, as if he could not believe his senses. She was alive and unhurt! His bullet had not touched her. His brain fumbled for the explanation of this miracle. He had not aimed at Frederic, he had not fired at him, and yet he lay stretched out there before him, bleeding, while the one he had meant to destroy was living— incomprehensively living! How had it happened? What agency had swept his deadly bullet out of its path to find lodgment in the wrong heart? There was no blood gushing from her breast; he could not understand it.

She did not take her eyes from the great red blot; she was fascinated by the horror that spread farther and farther across the gleaming white. She was alone, utterly alone with the most dreadful thing she had ever known; alone with that appalling thing called death. A life was leaving its warm, beautiful home as she watched, leaving in a path of red, creeping away across a stretch of white!

"Blood!" she wailed again, a long, shuddering word that came not from her lips but from the very depths of her terror-stricken soul.

Slowly Brood's mind worked out of the maze. His shot had gone straight, but Frederic himself had leaped into its path to save this miserable creature who would have damned his soul if life had been spared to him.

Ranjab crawled to his side, his eyes covered with one arm, the other extended. Blindly the master felt for the pistol, not once removing his eyes from the pallid figure against the table. His fingers closed upon the weapon. Then the Hindu looked up, warned by the strange voice that spoke to him from the mind of his master. He saw the arm slowly extend itself with a sinister hand directed straight at the figure of the woman. This time Brood was making sure of his aim, so sure that the lithe Hindu had time to spring to his feet weapon.

"Master! Master!" he cried out.

Brood turned to look at his man in sheer bewilderment. What could all this mean? What was the matter with the fellow?

"Down, Ranjab!" he commanded in a low, cautious tone, as he would have used in speaking to a dog when the game was run to earth.

"There is but one bullet left, *sahib!*" cried the man.

"Only one is required," said the master hazily.

"You have killed your son. This bullet is for yourself."

"Yes! But—but see! She lives! She— — —"

The Hindu struck his own breast significantly.

"Thy faithful servant remains, *sahib*. Die, if thou wilt, but leave her to Ranjab. There is but one bullet left. It is for you. You must not be here to witness the death Ranjab, thy servant, shall inflict upon her. Shoot thyself now, if so be it, but spare thyself the sight of— — —"

He did not finish the sentence, but his strong, bony fingers went through the motion that told a more horrible story than words could have expressed. There was no mistaking his meaning. He had elected himself her executioner.

A ghastly look of comprehension flitted across Brood's face. For a second his mind slipped from one dread to another more appalling. He knew this man of his. He remembered the story of another killing in the hills of India. His gaze went from the brown fanatic's face to the white, tender, lovely throat of the woman, and a hoarse gasp broke from his lips.

"No! No! Not that!" he cried, and as the words rang out Yvonne removed her horrified gaze from the blot of red and fixed it upon the face of her husband. She straightened up slowly and her arms fell limply to her sides.

"It was meant for me. Shoot, James!" she said, almost in a whisper.

The Hindu's grasp tightened at the convulsive movement of his master's hand. His fingers were like steel bands.

"Shoot!" she repeated, raising her voice. "Save yourself, for if he is dead I shall kill you with my own hands! This is your chance—shoot!"

Brood's fingers relaxed their grip on the revolver. A fierce, wild hope took all the strength out of his body; he grew faint with it.

"He—he can't be dead! I have not killed him. He shall not die, he shall not!"

Flinging the Hindu aside, he threw himself down beside the body on the floor. The revolver, as it dropped, was caught in the nimble hand of the Hindu, who took two long, swift strides toward the woman who now faced him instead of her husband. There was a great light in his eyes as he stood over her, and she saw death staring upon her.

But she did not quail. She was past all that. She looked straight into his eyes for an instant and then, as if putting him out of her thoughts entirely, turned slowly toward the two men on the floor. The man half-raised the pistol, but something stayed his hand, something stronger than any mere physical opposition could have done.

He glared at the half-averted face, confounded by the most extraordinary impression that ever had entered his incomprehensible brain. Something strange and wonderful was transpiring before his very eyes, something so marvellous that even he, mysterious seer of the Ganges, was stunned into complete amazement and unbelief.

That strange, uncanny intelligence of his, born of a thousand mysteries, was being tried beyond all previous exactions. It was as if he now saw this woman for the first time, as if he had never looked upon her face before. A mist appeared to envelop her, and through this veil he saw a face that was new to him, the face of Yvonne, and yet *not* hers at all. Absolute wonder crept into his eyes.

As if impelled by the power of his gaze, she faced him once more. For what seemed hours to him, but in reality only seconds, his searching eyes looked deep into hers. He saw at last the soul of this woman, and it was not the soul he had known as hers up to that tremendous moment. And he came to know that she was no longer afraid of him or his powers. His hand was lowered, his eyes fell, and his lips moved; but there were no words, for he addressed a spirit. All the venom, all the hatred fled from his soul. His knee bent in sudden submission, and his eyes were raised to hers once more, but now in their sombre depths was the fidelity of the dog.

"Go at once," she said, and her voice was as clear as a bell.

He shot a swift glance at the prostrate Frederic and straightened his tall figure, as would a soldier under orders. His understanding gaze sought hers again. There was another command in her eyes. He placed the weapon on the table. It had been a distinct command to him.

"One of us will use it," she said monotonously. "Go!"

With incredible swiftness he was gone. The curtains barely moved as he passed between them, and the heavy door made no sound in opening and closing. There was no one in the hall. The sound of the shot had not gone beyond the thick walls of that proscribed room on the top floor. Somewhere at the rear of the house an indistinct voice was uttering a jumbled stream of French.

Many minutes passed. There was not a sound, not a movement in the room. Brood, kneeling beside the outstretched figure of his unintended victim, was staring at the graying face with wide, unblinking eyes. He looked at last upon features that he had searched for in vain through all the sullen years. There was blood on his hands and on his cheek, for he had listened at first for the beat of the heart. Afterward his agonised gaze had gone to the bloodless face. There it was arrested.

A dumb wonder possessed his soul. He knelt there petrified by the shock of discovery. In the dim light he no longer saw the features of Matilde, but his own, and his heart was still. In that revealing moment he realised that he had never seen anything in Frederic's countenance save the dark, never-to-be-forgotten eyes, and they were his Matilde's. Now those eyes were closed. He could not see them, and the blindness was struck from his own.

He had always looked into the boy's eyes, he had never been able to seek farther than those haunting, inquiring eyes, but now he saw the lean, strong jaw and the firm chin, the straight nose and the broad forehead, and none of these was Matilde's. These were the features of a man, and of but one man. He was seeing himself as he was when he looked into his mirror at twenty-one.

All these years he had been blind; all these years he had gone on cursing his own image. In that overpowering thought came the realisation that it was too late for him to atone. His mind slowly struggled out of the stupefied bondage of years. He was looking at his own face. Dead, he would look like that! Matilde was gone for ever, the eyes were closed, but he was there; James Brood was still there, turning grayer and grayer of face all the time.

All the pent-up rage of years rushed suddenly to his lips and an awful curse issued, but it was delivered against himself. He started to rise to his feet, his mind bent on the one way to end the anguish that was too great to bear. The revolver!

It had been cruel, it should be kind. His heart leaped. He had a few seconds to live, not longer than it would take to find the weapon and place it against his breast—just so long and no longer would he be compelled to live.

He had forgotten the woman. She was standing just beyond the body that stretched itself between them. Her hands were clasped against her breast and her eyes were lifted heavenward. She had not moved throughout that age of oblivion.

He saw her and suddenly became rigid. Slowly he sank back, his eyes distended, his jaw dropping. He put out a hand and saved himself from falling, but his eyes did not leave the face of the woman who prayed, whose whole being was the material representation of prayer. But it was not Yvonne, his wife, that he saw standing there. It was another Matilde!

A hoarse, inarticulate sound came from his gaping mouth, and then issued the words that his mind had created unknown to him while he knelt, but now were uttered in a purely physical release from the throat that had held them back through a period of utter unconsciousness. He never knew that he spoke them; they were not the words that his conscious mind was now framing for deliverance. He said what he had already started to say when his soul was full of hatred for Yvonne.

"You foul, cringing— — —" and then came the new cry—"Matilde, Matilde! Forgive! Forgive!"

Slowly her eyes were lowered until they fell full upon his stricken face.

"Am I going mad?" he whispered hoarsely. As he stared the delicate, wan face of Matilde began to fade and he again saw the brilliant, undimmed features of Yvonne. "But it *was* Matilde! What trick of— — —"

He sprang to his feet and advanced upon her, stepping across the body of his son in his reckless haste. For many seconds they stood with their faces close together, he staring wildly, she with a dull look of agony in her eyes, but unflinching. What he saw caused an icy chill to sweep through his tense body and a sickness to enter his soul. He shrank back.

"Who—who are you?" he cried out in sudden terror. He felt the presence of Matilde. He could have stretched out his hand and touched her, so real, so vivid was the belief that she was actually there before him. "Matilde was here—I saw her, I saw her. And—and now it is you! She is still here. I can feel her hand touching mine—I can feel—no, no! It is gone—it—has passed. She has left me again. I—I————"

The cold, lifeless voice of Yvonne was speaking to him, huskier than ever before.

"Matilde *has* been here. She has always been with her son. She is always near you, James Brood."

"What—are—you—saying?" he gasped.

She turned wearily away and pointed to the weapon on the table.

"Who is to use it—you or I?"

He opened his mouth, but uttered no sound. His power of speech was gone.

She went on in a deadly monotone.

"You intended the bullet for me. It is not too late. Kill me, if you will. I give you the first chance—take it, for if you do not I shall take mine."

"I—I cannot kill you, I cannot kill the woman who stood where you are standing a moment ago. Matilde was there! She was alive; do you hear me? Alive and—ah!"

The exclamation fell from his lips as she suddenly leaned forward, her intense gaze fixed on Frederic's face.

"See! Ah, see! I prayed, and I have been answered. See!"

He turned. Frederic's eyes were open. He was looking up at them with a piteous appeal, an appeal for help, for life, for consciousness.

"He is not dead! Frederic, Frederic, my son——" Brood dropped to his knees and frantically clutched at the hand that lay stretched beside the limp figure. The pain-stricken eyes closed slowly.

Yvonne knelt beside Brood. He saw a slim, white hand go out and touch the pallid brow.

"I shall save your soul, James Brood," a voice was saying, but it seemed far away. "He shall not die. Your poor, wretched soul may rest secure. I shall keep death away from him. You shall not have to pay for this; no, not for this. The bullet was meant for me. I owe my life to him, you shall owe his to me. But you have yet to pay a greater debt than this can ever become.

He is your son. You owe another for his life, and you will never be out of her debt, not even in hell, James Brood!"

Slowly Frederic's eyes opened again. They wavered from one face to the other and there was in them the unsolvable mystery of divination. As the lids drooped once more, Brood's manner underwent a tremendous change. The stupefaction of horror and doubt fell away in a flash and he was again the clear-headed, indomitable man of action. The blood rushed back into his veins, his eyes flashed with the returning fire of hope, his voice was steady, sharp, commanding.

"The doctor!" he cried in Yvonne's ear, as his strong fingers went out to tear open the shirt-bosom. "Be quick! Send for Hodder; we must save him." She did not move. He whirled upon her fiercely. "Do as I tell you! Are you so——"

"Dr Hodder is on the way now," she said dully.

His hands ceased their operations as if checked by a sudden paralysis.

"On the way here?" he cried incredulously. "Why———"

"He is coming," she said fiercely. "I sent for him. Don't stop now, be quick! You know what to do. Stanch the flow of blood. Do something, man! You have seen men with mortal wounds, and this man *must* be saved!"

He worked swiftly, deftly, for he did know what to do. He had worked over men before with wounds in their breasts, and he had seen them through the shadow of death. But he could not help thinking, as he now worked, that he was never known to miss a shilling at thirty paces.

She was speaking. Her voice was low, with a persistent note of accusation in it.

"It was an accident, do you understand? You did not shoot to kill him. The world shall never know the truth, unless he dies, and that is not to happen. You are safe. The law cannot touch you, for I shall never speak. This is between you and me. Do you understand?"

He glanced at her set, rigid face.

"Yes. It was an accident. And this is between you and me. We shall settle it later on. Now I see you as you are—as Yvonne. I—wonder———" His hand shook with a sudden spasm of indecision. He had again caught that baffling look in her dark eyes.

"Attend!" she cried, and he bent to the task again. "He is not going to die. It would be too cruel if he were to die now and miss all the joy of victory over you, his lifelong foe. He———"

The door opened behind them and they looked up to see the breathless Hindu. He came straight to the woman.

"He comes. Ranjab has obey. I have told him that the revolver was discharge accidentally, by myself, by the unhappy son of a dog, I. It is well. Ranjab is but a dog. He shall die to-day and his lips be sealed for ever. Have no fear. The dead shall be silent." His voice trailed off into a whisper, for his eyes were looking into hers. "No," he whispered, after a moment, "no; the dead are not silent. One who is dead has spoken to Ranjab."

"Hush!" said the woman. Brood's hands were shaking again, shaking and uncertain. "The doctor? He comes?"

"Even now," said the Hindu, turning toward the door.

Dr Hodder came blinking into the room. A gaping assistant from his office across the street followed close behind, carrying a box of instruments.

"Turn up the lights," said the surgeon crisply. It seemed hours before the soft glow was at its full and the room bathed in its mellow light. All this time not a word was uttered. "Ah!" exclaimed Dr Hodder at last. "Now we'll see."

He was kneeling beside Frederic an instant later.

"Bad!" he said after a single glance. "Wiley, get busy now. Clear that table, Ranjab. Water, quick, Wiley. Lively, Ranjab. Shove 'em off, don't waste time like that. Ah, now lend a hand, both of you. Easy! So!" Three strong, nerveless pairs of hands raised the inert figure.

"Hello! What's this?" The incomprehensible Hindu in his ruthless clearing of the table had left the revolver lying where Yvonne had placed it. "Good Lord, take it away! It's done enough damage already." It was Wiley, the assistant, who picked it up gingerly and laid it on a chair near by. "Now, where's the butler? Send for an ambulance, and—you, Wiley, call up the hospital and say———"

"No!" came in Yvonne's husky, imperative voice. "No, not the hospital. He is not to be taken away."

"But, madam, you———"

"I insist! It is not to be thought of, Dr Hodder. He must remain in this house. I will get his room ready for him. He is—to—stay—here!"

"Well, we'll see," said the surprised surgeon, and forthwith put her out of his mind.

James Brood was standing stock-still and rigid in the centre of the room. He had not moved an inch from the position he had taken when the doctor pushed him aside in order to clear the way to the table. Yvonne came straight to him. The matter of half a yard separated them as she stopped and spoke to him, her voice so low that the bustling doctor could not have distinguished a word.

"You owe it to Frederic to allow Ranjab's story to stand. There is no one to dispute it. I command you to protect the good name of your son. That weapon was accidentally discharged by your servant, and you will have to swear to it, James Brood, if called upon to do so, for I shall swear to it, and Ranjab, too."

"I shall conceal nothing," he groaned. "Do you think I am a craven coward as well as a — — —"

"Nevertheless, you will do as I command. He is going to live. That is why I demand it of you. If he were to die — well, even then you would not be permitted to speak. I shall stand here beside you, James Brood, and if you utter one word to contradict Ranjab's story I shall shoot you down. Can you not see how desperately in earnest I am?" She reached over and caught up the revolver from the chair as she was speaking.

For a full minute they looked into each other's eyes, and he — the strong, invulnerable Brood — was the first to give way. The steely glitter faded before the swift rush of a new feeling that swept over him — an extraordinary feeling of tenderness toward this woman who fought him with something more than her own cause at stake.

"I understand. You are right. If he gets well, this beastly thing must never be known. We will leave it to him. If he chooses to tell the truth, then — — —"

"I have your promise — *now?*" she demanded intensely.

"Yes. Now go!" Involuntarily he straightened his tall figure and pointed toward the door.

"He is not to be removed from this house," she insisted.

"Ten minutes ago you were suggesting a different — — —" he began sneeringly.

"The whole world has changed since then, James Brood," she said, and her shoulders drooped. Almost instantly she recovered her poise. "I have a great deal to say to you later on."

"Not a great deal," he said meaningly.

He saw her flinch and was conscious of a curious pang, a poignant yet indefinable pang of remorse.

She went swiftly from the room. He looked for the revolver. It was gone. Somehow he found himself wondering if she had taken it away with her in the fear that he would turn it against himself in case——

"No powder stains," he heard Hodder saying to his assistant. "Not a sign of 'em."

"That's right," said the assistant, shaking his head.

"Couldn't have been—no, of course not," went on the first speaker in a matter-of-fact tone.

"Doesn't look that way," agreed the assistant.

"Fired from some little distance, I'd say."

"Fifteen or twenty feet, perhaps."

It suddenly dawned upon Brood that they were talking of suicide.

"Good Heaven, Hodder, it—it wasn't *that!*" he cried hoarsely. "What right have you to doubt my word? I tell you I———"

"Your word, Jim? This is the first word you've spoken since I came into the room."

"Is—is it a mortal wound?" broke from the other's lips.

"Can't tell. First aid now, that's the point. We'll get him downstairs in a few minutes. More light. I can't see a thing in this—hello! What's this? A photograph? Fell out of his pocket when I—oh, I see! Your wife. Sorry I got blood on it." He laid the small bit of pasteboard on the table. "Wiley! See if you can get a mattress. We'll move him at once. Lively, my lad. He's alive, all right, Jim. Do our best. Looks bad. Poor kid. He's not had a very happy life of it, I'm afraid—I beg pardon!"

In considerable embarrassment he brought his comments to an end and bent lower to examine the small black hole in the left breast of his patient.

Frederic's lips moved. The doctor's ear caught the strangled whisper that issued.

"Curious," he remarked, turning to Brood with something like awe in his eyes. "I'm sure he said 'Mother.' But he never knew his mother, did he?"

CHAPTER XX

Hours afterward Brood sat alone in the room where the tragedy occurred. Much had transpired in the interim to make those hours seem like separate and distinct years to him, each hour an epoch in which a vital and memorable incident had been added to his already overfull measure of experience.

He had refused to see the newspaper men who came. Dr Hodder wisely had protested against secrecy.

"Murder will out," he had said fretfully, little realising how closely the trite old saying applied to the situation. He had accepted the statements of Yvonne and Ranjab as to the accidental discharge of the weapon, but for some reason had refrained from asking Brood a single question, although he knew him to be a witness to the shooting.

Yvonne saw the reporters and, later on, an inspector of police. Ranjab told his unhappy story. He had taken the weapon from a hook on the wall for the purpose of cleaning it. It had been hanging there for years, and all the time there had been a single cartridge left in the cylinder unknown to anyone. He had started to remove the cylinder as he left the room.

All these years the hammer had been raised; death had been hanging over them all the time that the pistol occupied its insecure position on the wall. Somehow, he could not tell how, the hammer fell as he tugged at the cylinder. No one could have known that the revolver was loaded. That was all that he could say, except to declare that if his master's son died he would end his own miserable, valueless life.

His story was supported by the declarations of Mrs Brood, who, while completely exonerating her husband's servant, had but little to say in explanation of the affair. She kept her wits about her. Most people would have made the mistake of saying too much. She professed to know nothing except that they were discussing young Mr Brood's contemplated trip abroad and that her husband had given orders to his servants to pack a revolver in his son's travelling-bag.

She had paid but little attention to the Hindu's movements. All she could say was that it was an accident—a horrible, blighting accident. For the present it would not be possible for anyone to see the heart-broken father. Doubtless later on he would be in the mood to discuss the dreadful catastrophe, but not now. He was crushed with the horror of the thing that had happened. And so she explained.

The house was in a state of subdued excitement. Servants spoke in whispers and tiptoed through the halls. Nurses and other doctors came. Two old men, shaking as with palsy, roamed about the place, intent only on worming their way into the presence of their friend and supporter to offer consolation and encouragement to him in his hour of tribulation. They shuddered as they looked into each other's faces, and they shook their heads without speaking, for their minds were filled with doubt. They did not question the truth of the story as told, but they had their own opinions.

In support of the theory that they did not believe there was anything accidental in the shooting of Frederic it is only necessary to speak of their extraordinary attitude toward Ranjab. They shook hands with him and told him that Allah would reward him. Later on, after they had had time to think it all out for themselves, being somewhat slow of comprehension, they sought out James Brood and offered to accept all the blame for having loaded the revolver without consulting him, their object having been to destroy a cat that infested the alley hard by. They felt that it was absolutely necessary to account for the presence of the unexploded cartridge.

"As a matter of fact, Jim, old man," insisted Mr Riggs, "I am entirely to blame for the whole business. I ought to have had more sense than to leave a shell in———"

"You had nothing to do with it," said Mr Dawes fiercely. "It was I who loaded the devilish thing, and I'm going to confess to the police. To be perfectly honest about it, I sort of recollect cocking it before I hung it up on the nail. I sort of recollect it, I say, and that's more than you can do. No, sir, Jim; I'm the one to blame. I ought to be shot for my carelessness. It was———"

"There's no sense in your lying at a time like this," said Mr Riggs caustically, glaring at his lifelong friend. "I suppose it's because he can't help it, Jim. Lying has got to be such a habit with him that———"

"Well," interrupted Mr Dawes vigorously, "to show you that I am not lying, I intend to give myself up to the police and take the full penalty for criminal and contributory negligence. I suppose you'll still say I'm lying after they've sent me to jail for a couple of years for———"

"Yes, sir; I will," said Mr Riggs with conviction. "And I shall have you arrested for perjury if you try any of your tricks on me. I loaded it, I cocked sir; I will," said Mr Riggs with conviction.

"And I suppose you fired it off!" exclaimed Mr Dawes savagely.

Mr Riggs took a long breath. "Yes, sir, you scoundrel, I am ready to swear that I *did* fire it off!" They glared at each other with such ferocity that Brood, coming between them, laid his hands on their shoulders, shaking his head as he spoke to them gently.

"Thank you, old pals. I understand what it is you are trying to do. It's no use. I fired the shot. It isn't necessary to say anything more to you, I'm sure, except that, as God is my witness, I did not intend the bullet for Frederic. It was an accident in that respect. Thank you for what you would do. It isn't necessary, old pals. The story that Ranjab tells must stand for the time being. Later on—well, I may *write* my own story and give it to the world."

"Write it?" said Mr Dawes, and Brood nodded his head slowly, significantly.

"Oh, Jim, you—you mustn't do that!" groaned Mr Dawes, appalled. "You ain't such a coward as to do that!"

"There is one bullet left in that revolver. Ranjab advised me to save it—for myself. He's a thoughtful fellow," said Brood.

"Jim," said Mr Riggs, squaring himself, "it's too bad that you didn't hit what you shot at."

Mr Dawes turned on him in a flash. "None o' that, Joe," he said, and this time he was very much in earnest. "She's all right. You'll all find out she's all right. I tell you a woman can't nurse a feller back from the edge of the grave, yes, from the very bottom of it almost, and not betray her true nature to that same feller in more———"

"Jim," interrupted Mr Riggs, ignoring his comrade's defence, "I see she's going to nurse Freddy. Well, sir, if I was you, I'd———"

Brood stopped him with an impatient gesture.

"I must ask you not to discuss Mrs Brood."

"I was just going to say, Jim, that if I was you I'd thank the Lord that she's going to do it," substituted Mr Riggs somewhat hastily. "She's a wonderful nurse. She told me a bit ago that she was going to save his life in spite of the doctor."

"What does Dr Hodder say?" demanded Brood, pausing in his restless pacing of the floor.

"He says the poor boy is as good as dead," said Mr Riggs,

"Ain't got a chance in a million," said Mr Dawes.

They were surprised to see Brood wince. He hadn't been so thin-skinned in the olden days. His nerve was going back on him, that's what it was; poor Jim! Twenty years ago he would have stiffened his back and taken it like a man. It did not occur to them that they might have broken the news to him with tact and consideration.

"But you can depend on us, Jim, to pull him through," said Mr Riggs quickly. "Remember how we saved you back there in Calcutta when all the fool doctors said you hadn't a chance? Well, sir, we're still— — —"

"If any feller can get well with a bullet through his— —" began Mr Dawes encouragingly, but stopped abruptly when he saw Brood put his hands over his eyes and sink dejectedly into a chair, a deep groan on his lips.

"I guess we'd better go," whispered Mr Riggs, after a moment of indecision, and then, inspired by a certain fear for his friend, struck the gong resoundingly. Silently they made their way out of the room, encountering Ranjab just outside the door.

"You must stick to it, Ranjab," said Mr Riggs sternly.

"With your dying breath," added Mr Dawes, and the Hindu, understanding, gravely nodded his head.

"Well?" said Brood, long afterward, raising his haggard face to meet the gaze of the motionless brown man who had been standing in his presence for many minutes.

"She ask permission of *sahib* to be near him until the end," said the Hindu. "She will not go away. I have heard the words she say to the *sahibah*, and the *sahibah* is silent as the tomb. She say no word for herself, just sit and look at the floor and never move. Then she accuse the *sahibah* of being the cause of the young master's death, and the *sahibah* only nod her head to that and go out of the room and up to the place where the young master is, and they cannot keep her from going in. She just look at the woman in the white cap and the woman step aside. The *sahibah* is now with the young master and the doctors. She is not of this world, *sahib*, but of another."

"And Miss Desmond? Where is she?"

"She wait in the hall outside his door. Ranjab have speech with her. She does not believe Ranjab. She look into his eye and his eye is not honest; she see it all. She say the young master shoot himself and— — —"

"I shall tell her the truth, Ranjab," said Brood stolidly. "She must know, she and her mother. To-night I shall see them, but not now. Suicide! Poor, poor Lydia!"

"Miss Lydia say she blame herself for everything. She is a coward, she say, and Ranjab he understand. She came yesterday and went away. Ranjab tell her the *sahib* no can see her."

"Yesterday? I know. She came to plead with me. I know," groaned Brood bitterly.

"She will not speak her thoughts to the world, *sahib*," asserted Ranjab. "Thy servant have spoken his words and she will not deny him. It is for the young master's sake. But she say she *know* he shoot himself because he no can bear the disgrace———"

"Enough, Ranjab," interrupted the master. "To-night I shall tell her everything. Go now and fetch me the latest word."

The Hindu remained motionless just inside the door. His eyes were closed.

"Ranjab talk to the winds, *sahib*. The winds speak to him. The young master is alive. The great doctor he search for the bullet. It is bad. But the *sahibah* stand between him and death. She hold back death. She laugh at death. She say it no can be. Ranjab know her now. Here in this room he see the two woman in her, and he no more will be blind. She stand there before Ranjab, who would kill, and out of the air came a new spirit to shield her. Her eyes are the eyes of another who does not live in the flesh, and Ranjab bends the knee. He see the inside. It is not black. It is full of light, a great big light, *sahib*. Thy servant would kill his master's wife, but, Allah defend! He cannot kill the wife who is already dead. His master's wives stand before him—two, not one—and his hand is stop."

Brood was regarding him through wide—open, incredulous eyes. "You—you saw it, too?" he gasped.

"The serpent is deadly. Many time Ranjab have take the poison from its fangs and it becomes his slave. He would have take the poison from the serpent in his master's house, but the serpent change before his eye and he become the slave. She speak to him on the voice of the wind and he obey. It is the law. Kismet! His master have of wives two. Two, *sahib*, the living and the dead. They speak with Ranjab to-day and he obey."

There was dead silence in the room for many minutes after the remarkable utterances of the mystic. Master and man looked into each other's eyes and spoke no more, yet something passed between them.

"The *sahibah* has sent Roberts for a priest," said the Hindu at last.

"A priest? But I am not a Catholic—nor Frederic."

"Madam is. The servants are saying that the priest will be here too late. They are wondering why you have not already killed me, *sahib*."

"Kill you, *too?*"

"They are now saying that the last stroke of the gong, *sahib*, was the death-sentence for Ranjab. It called me here to be slain by you. I have told them all that I fired the — — —"

"Go down at once, my friend," said Brood, laying his hand on the man's shoulder. "Let them see that I do not blame you, even though we permit them to believe this lie of ours. Go, my friend!"

The man bent his head and turned away. Near the door he stopped stock-still and listened intently.

"The *sahibah* comes."

"Aye, she said she would come to me here," said Brood, and his jaw hardened. "Hodder—sent for me, Ranjab, an hour ago, but—but he was conscious then. His eyes were open. I—I could not look into them. There would have been hatred in them—hatred for me, and I—I could not go. I was a coward. Yes, a coward, after all. She would have been there to watch me as I cringed. I was afraid of what I might do to her then."

"He is not conscious now, *sahib*" said the Hindu slowly.

"Still," said the other, compressing his lips, "I am afraid—I am afraid. Ranjab, you do not know what it means to be a coward! You— — —"

"And yet, *sahib*, you are brave enough to stand on the spot where he fell, where his blood flowed, and that is not what a coward would do."

The door opened and closed swiftly and he was gone. Brood allowed his dull, wondering gaze to sink to his feet. He was standing on the spot where Frederic had fallen. There was no blood there now. The rug had been removed, and before his own eyes the swift-moving Hindu had washed the floor and table and put the room in order. All this seemed ages ago. Since that time he had bared his soul to the smirking Buddha, and receiving no consolation from the smug image, had violently cursed the thing.

Since then he had waited—he had waited for many things to happen. He knew all that took place below stairs. He knew when Lydia came and he denied himself to her. The coming of the police, the nurses and the anæsthetician, and later on Mrs John Desmond and the reporters. All this he had known, for he had listened at a crack in the open door. And he had heard his wife's calm, authoritative voice in the hall below, giving directions. Now for the first time he looked about him and felt himself attended by ghosts. In that instant he came to hate this once-loved room, this cherished retreat, and all that it contained. He would never set his foot inside of its four walls again. It was filled with ghosts!

On the corner of the table lay a great heap of manuscript, the story of his life up to the escape from Thassa. The sheets of paper had been scattered over the floor by the surgeon, but now they were back in perfect order, replaced by another hand. He thought of the final chapter that would have to be written if he went on with the journal. It would have to be written, for it was the true story of his life. He strode swiftly to the table. In another instant the work of many months would have been torn to bits of waste paper. But his hand was stayed. Someone had stopped outside his door. He could not hear a sound, and yet he knew that a hand was on the heavy latch. He suddenly recalled his remark to the old men. He would have to *write* the final chapter, after all.

He waited. He knew that she was out there, collecting all of her strength for the coming interview. She was fortifying herself against the crisis that was so near at hand. To his own surprise and distress of mind he found himself trembling and suddenly deprived of the fierce energy that he had stored up for the encounter. He wondered whether he would command the situation, after all, notwithstanding his righteous charge against her.

She had wantonly sought to entice Frederic, she had planned to dishonour her husband, she had proved herself unwholesome and false, and her heart was evil. And yet he wondered whether he would be able to stand his ground against her.

So far she had ruled. At the outset he had attempted to assert his authority as the master of the house in this trying, heart-breaking hour, and she had calmly waved him aside. His first thought had been to take his proper place at the bedside of his victim and there to remain until the end, but she had said: "You are not to go in. You have done enough for one day. If he must die, let it be in peace and not in fear. You are not to go in," and he had crept away to hide!

He remembered her words later on when Hodder sent for him to come down. "Not in fear," she had said.

On the edge of the table, where it had reposed since Dr Hodder dropped it there, was the small photograph of Matilde. He had not touched it, but he had bent over it for many minutes at a time, studying the sweet, never-to-be-forgotten, and yet curiously unfamiliar features of that long-ago loved one. He looked at it now as he waited for the door to open, and his thoughts leaped back to the last glimpse he had ever had of that adorable face. Then it was white with despair and misery; here it looked up at him with smiling eyes and the languor of unbroken tranquillity.

Suddenly he realised that the room was quite dark. He dashed to the window and threw aside the broad, thick curtains. A stream of afternoon sunshine rushed into the place. He would have light this time; he would not be deceived by the darkness, as he had been once before. This time he would see her face plainly. There should be no sickening illusion. He straightened his tall figure and waited for the door to open.

The window at his back was open. He heard a penetrating but hushed voice speaking from one of the windows across the court, from his wife's window, he knew without a glance of inquiry.

Céleste, her maid, was giving orders in great agitation to the furnace-man in the yard below.

"No, no, you big fool! I am not dismiss. I am not going away—no. Tak' *zem* back. *Madame* has change her mind. I am not fire non, *non!* Tak' zem back, *vitement!* I go some other day!"

The door was opened suddenly and Yvonne came into the room.

CHAPTER XXI

If she had hesitated outside the room to summon the courage to face the man who would demand so much of her, there was nothing in her manner when she entered to indicate that such had been the case. She approached him without a symptom of nervousness or irresolution. Her dark eyes met his without wavering, and there was purpose in them.

She devoted a single glance of surprise to the uncurtained window on entering the door, and an instant later scrutinised the floor with unmistakable interest, as if expecting to find something there to account for his motive in admitting the glare of light, something to confound and accuse her. But there was no fear in the look.

She had put on a rather plain white blouse, open at the neck. The cuffs were rolled up nearly to the elbows, evidence that she had been using her hands in some active employment and had either forgotten or neglected to restore the sleeves to their proper position. A chic black walking-skirt lent to her trim, erect figure a suggestion of girlishness.

Her arms hung straight down at her sides, limply it would have seemed at first glance, but in reality they were rigid.

"I have come, as I said I would," she said, after a long, tense silence. Her voice was low, huskier than ever, but without a tremor of excitement. "You did not say you would wait for me here, but I knew you would do so. The hour of reckoning has come. We must pay, both of us. I am not frightened by your silence, James, nor am I afraid of what you may say or do. First of all, it is expected that Frederic will die. Dr Hodder has proclaimed it. He is a great surgeon. He ought to know. But he doesn't know—do you hear? He does not know. I shall not let him die."

"One moment, if you please," said her husband coldly. "You may spare me the theatrics. Moreover, we will not discuss Frederic. What we have to say to each other has little to do with that poor boy downstairs. This is *your* hour of reckoning, not his. Bear that———"

"You are very much mistaken," she interrupted, her gaze growing more fixed than before. "He is a part of our reckoning. He is the one great character in this miserable, unlooked-for tragedy. Will you be so kind as to draw those curtains? And do me the honour to allow me to sit in your presence."

There was infinite scorn in her voice. "I am very tired. I have not been idle. Every minute of my waking hours belongs to your son, James Brood, but I owe this half-hour to you. You shall know the truth about me, as I know it about you. I did not count on this hour ever being a part of my life, but it has to be, and I shall face it without weeping over what might have been. Will you draw the curtains?"

He hesitated a moment and then jerked the curtains together, shutting out the pitiless glare.

"Will you be seated there?" he said quietly, pointing to a chair at the end of the table.

She switched on the light in the big lamp, but instead of taking the chair indicated, sank into one on the opposite side of the table, with the mellow light full upon her lovely, serious face.

"Sit there," she said, signifying the chair he had requested her to take. "Please sit down," she went on impatiently, as he continued to regard her forbiddingly from his position near the window.

"I shall be better able to say what I have to say standing," he said significantly.

"Do you expect me to plead with you for forgiveness?" she inquired, with an unmistakable look of surprise.

"You may save yourself the humiliation of such— —"

"But you are gravely mistaken," she interrupted. "I shall ask nothing of you."

"Then we need not prolong the— — —"

"I have come to explain, not to plead," she went on resolutely. "I want to tell you why I married you. You will not find it a pleasant story, nor will you be proud of your conquest. It will not be necessary for you to turn me out of your house. I entered it with the determination to leave it in my own good time. I think you had better sit down."

He looked at her fixedly for a moment, as if striving to materialise a thought that lay somewhere in the back of his mind. He was vaguely conscious of an impression that he could unfathom all this seeming mystery without a suggestion from her if given the time to concentrate his mind on the vague, hazy suggestion that tormented his memory.

He sat down opposite her and rested his arms on the table. The lines about his mouth were rigid, uncompromising, but there was a look of wonder in his eyes.

She leaned forward in her chair, the better to watch the changing expression in his eyes as she progressed with her story. Her hands were clenched tightly under the table's edge.

"You are looking into my eyes, as you have looked a hundred times," she said after a moment. "There is something in them that has puzzled you since the night when you looked into them across that great ballroom in London. You have always felt that they were not new to you, that you have had them constantly in front of you for ages. Do you remember when you first saw me, James Brood?"

He stared, and his eyes widened.

"I never saw you in my life until that night in London, I———"

"Look closely. Isn't there something more than doubt in your mind as you look into them now?"

"I confess that I have always been puzzled by by something I cannot understand in—but all this leads to nothing," he broke off harshly. "We are not here to mystify each other, but to———"

"To explain mysteries, that's it, of course. You are looking. What do you see? Are you not sure that you looked into my eyes long, long ago? Are there not moments when my voice is familiar to you, when it speaks to you out of———"

He sat up, rigid as a block of stone.

"Yes, by Heaven, I have felt it all along! To-day I was convinced that the unbelievable had happened. I saw something that———" He stopped short, his lips parted.

She waved her hand in the direction of the Buddha.

"Have you never petitioned your too-stolid friend over there to unravel the mystery for you? In the quiet of certain lonely, speculative hours have you not wondered where you had seen me before, long, long before the night in London? In all the years that you have been trying to convince yourself that Frederic is not your son has there not been the vision of———"

"What are you saying to me? Are you trying to tell me that you are Matilde?"

"If not Matilde, then who am I, pray?" she demanded.

He sank back frowning.

"It cannot be possible. I would know her a thousand years from now. You cannot trick me into believing—but, who are you?" He leaned forward again, clutching the edge of the table. "I sometimes think you are a ghost come to haunt me, to torture me. What trick, what magic is behind all this? Has her soul, her spirit, her actual being found a lodging-place in you, and have you been sent to curse me for———"

She rose half-way out of her chair, leaning farther across the table.

"Yes, James Brood. I represent the spirit of Matilde Valeska, if you will have it so. Not sent to curse you, but to love you. That's the pity of it all. I swear to you that it is the spirit of Matilde that urges me to love you and to spare you now. It is the spirit of Matilde that stands between her son and death. But it is not Matilde who confronts you here and now, you may be sure of that. Matilde loved you. She loves you now, even in her grave. You will never be able to escape from that wonderful love of hers. If there have been times—and God help me, there were many, I know—when I appeared to love you for myself, I swear to you that I was moved by the spirit of Matilde. I—I am as much mystified, as greatly puzzled as yourself. I came here to hate you, and I have loved you; yes, there were moments when I actually loved you."

Her voice died away into a whisper. For many seconds they sat looking into each other's eyes, neither possessing the power to break the strange spell of silence that had fallen upon them.

"No, it is not Matilde who confronts you now, but one who would not spare you as she did up to the hour of her death. You are quite safe from ghosts from this hour on, my friend. You will never see Matilde again, though you look into my eyes till the end of time. Frederic may see, may feel the spirit of his mother, but you—ah, no! You have seen the last of her. Her blood is in my veins, her wrongs are in my heart. It was she with whom you fell in love, and it was she you married six months ago, but now the curtain is lifted. Don't you know me now, James? Can your memory carry you back twenty-three years and deliver you from doubt and perplexity? Look closely, I say. I was six years old then, and———"

Brood was glaring at her as one stupefied. Suddenly he cried out in a loud voice. "You are you are the little sister? The little Thérèse?"

She was standing now, leaning far over the table, for he had shrunk down into his chair.

"The little Thérèse, yes! Now do you begin to see? Now do you begin to realise what I came here to do? Now do you know why I married you? Isn't it clear to you? Well, I have tried to do all these things so that I might break your heart as you broke hers. I came to make you pay!"

She was speaking rapidly, excitedly now. Her voice was high-pitched and unnatural. Her eyes seemed to be driving him deeper and deeper into the chair, forcing him down as though with a giant's hand.

"The little, timid, heart-broken Thérèse who would not speak to you, nor kiss you, nor say goodbye to you when you took her darling sister away from the Bristol in the *Kartnerring* more than twenty years ago. Ah, how I loved her, how I loved her! And how I hated you for taking her away from me. Shall I ever forget that wedding night? Shall I ever forget the grief, the loneliness, the hatred that dwelt in my poor little heart that night? Everyone was happy, the whole world was happy; but was I? I was crushed with grief. You were taking her away across the awful sea, and you were to make her happy, so they said, *aïe*, so said my beloved, joyous sister.

"You stood before the altar in St Stephens's with her and promised, promised, promised everything. I heard you. I sat with my mother and turned to ice, but I heard you. All Vienna, all Budapest said that you promised naught but happiness to each other. She was twenty-one. She was lovely; ah, far lovelier than that wretched photograph lying there in front of you. It was made when she was eighteen. She did not write those words on the back of the card. I wrote them, not more than a month ago, before I gave it to Frederic. To this house she came twenty-three years ago. You brought her here the happiest girl in all the world. How did you send her away? How?"

He stirred in the chair. A spasm of pain crossed his face.

"And I was the happiest man in all the world," he said hoarsely. "You are forgetting one thing, Thérèse." He fell into the way of calling her Thérèse as if he had known her by no other name. "Your sister was not content to preserve the happiness that———"

"Stop!" she commanded. "You are not to speak evil of her now. You will never think evil of her after what I am about to tell you. You will curse yourself. Somehow I am glad that my plans have gone awry. It gives me the opportunity to see you curse yourself."

"Her sister!" muttered the man unbelievingly. "I have married the child Thérèse. I have held her sister in my arms all these months and never knew. It is a dream. I———"

"Ah, but you have *felt*, even though———"

He struck the table violently with his fist. His eyes were blazing.

"What manner of woman are you? What were you planning to do to that unhappy boy—her son? Are you a fiend to———"

"In good time, James, you will know what manner of woman I am," she interrupted quietly. Sinking back in the chair, she resumed the broken strain, all the time watching him through half—closed eyes. "She died ten years ago. Her boy was twelve years old. She never saw him after the night you turned her away from this house. On her death-bed, as she was releasing her pure, undefiled soul to God's keeping, she repeated to the priest who went through the unnecessary form of absolving her, she repeated her solemn declaration that she had never wronged you by thought or deed. I had always believed her, the holy priest believed her, God believed her. You would have believed her, too, James Brood. She was a good woman. Do you hear? And you put a curse upon her and drove her out into the night. That was not all. You persecuted her to the end of her unhappy life. You did that to my sister!"

"And yet you married me," he muttered thickly.

"Not because I loved you; oh, no! She loved you to the day of her death, after all the misery and suffering you had heaped upon her. No woman ever endured the anguish that she suffered throughout those hungry years. You kept her child from her. You denied him to her, even though you denied him to yourself. Why did you keep him from her? She was his mother. She had borne him; he was all hers. But no! It was your revenge to deprive her of the child she had brought into the world. You worked deliberately in this plan to crush what little there was left in life for her.

"You kept him with you, though you branded him with a name I cannot utter; you guarded him as if he were your most precious possession, and not a curse to your pride; you did this because you knew that you could drive the barb more deeply into her tortured heart. You allowed her to die, after years of pleading, after years of vain endeavour, without one glimpse of her boy, without ever having heard the word mother on his lips. That is what you did to my sister. For twelve long years you gloated over her misery. Man, man, how I hated you when I married you!" She paused, breathless.

"You are creating an excuse for your devilish conduct!" he exclaimed harshly. "You are like Matilde, false to the core. You married me for the luxury I could provide, notwithstanding the curse I had put upon your sister. I don't believe a word of what you are saying to———"

"Don't you believe that I am her sister?"

"You, yes; I must believe that. Why have I been so blind? You are the little Thérèse, and you hated me in those other days. I remember well the———"

"A child's despairing hatred because you were taking away the being she loved best of all. Will you believe me when I say that my hatred did not endure for long? When her happy, joyous letters came back to us filled with accounts of your goodness, your devotion, I allowed my hatred to die. I forgot that you had robbed me. I came to look upon you as the fairy prince, after all. It was not until she came all the way across the ocean and began to die before our eyes—she was years in dying—it was not until then that I began to hate you with a real, undying hatred."

"And yet you gave yourself to me!" he cried. "You put yourself in her place! In Heaven's name, what was to be gained by such an act as that?"

"I wanted to take Matilde's boy away from you," she hurried on, and for the first time her eyes began to waver. "The idea suggested itself to me the night I met you at the comtesse's dinner. It was a wonderful, a tremendous thought that entered my brain. At first my real self revolted, but as time went on the idea became an obsession. I married you, James Brood, for the sole purpose of hurting you in the worst possible way: by having Matilde's son strike you where the pain would be the greatest. Ah, you are thinking that I would have permitted myself to have become his mistress, but you are mistaken. I am not that bad. I would not have damned his soul in that way. I would not have betrayed my sister in that way. Far more subtle was my design. I confess that it was my plan to make him fall in love with me and in the end to run away with him, leaving you to think that the very worst had happened. But it would not have been as you think. He would have been protected, my friend, amply protected. He———"

"But you would have wrecked him; don't you see that you would have wrecked the life you sought to protect? How blind and unfeeling you were. You say that he was my son and Matilde's, honestly born. What was your object, may I inquire, in striking me at such cost to him? You would have made a scoundrel of him for the sake of a personal vengeance. Are you forgetting that he regarded himself as my son?"

"No; I do not forget, James. There was but one way in which I could hope to steal him away from you, and I went about it deliberately, with my eyes open. I came here to induce him to run away with me. I would have taken him back to his mother's home, to her grave, and there I would have told him what you did to her. If, after hearing my story, he elected to return to the man who had destroyed his mother, I should have stepped aside and offered no protest.

"But I would have taken him away from you in the manner that would have hurt you the worst. My sister was true to you. I would have been just as true, and after you had suffered the torments of hell, it was my plan to reveal everything to you. But you would have had your punishment by that time. When you were at the very end of your strength, when you trembled on the edge of oblivion, then I would have hunted you out and laughed at you and told you the truth. But you would have had years of anguish—years, I say."

"I have already had years of agony, pray do not overlook that fact," said he. "I suffered for twenty years. I was at the edge of oblivion more than once, if it is a pleasure for you to hear me say it, Thérèse."

"It does not offset the pain that her suffering brought to me. It does not counterbalance the unhappiness you gave to her boy, nor the stigma you put upon him. I am glad that you suffered. It proves to me that you secretly considered yourself to be in the wrong. You doubted yourself. You were never sure, and yet you crushed the life out of her innocent, bleeding heart. You let her die without a word to show that you———"

"I was lost to the world for years," he said. "There were many years when I was not in touch with———"

"But her letters must have reached you. She wrote a thousand of———"

"They never reached me," he said significantly.

"You ordered them to be destroyed?" she cried in sudden comprehension.

"I must decline to answer that question."

She gave him a curious, incredulous smile and then abruptly returned to her charge.

"When my sister came home, degraded, I was nine years of age, but I was not so young that I did not know that a dreadful thing had happened to her. She was blighted beyond all hope of recovery. It was to me, little me, that she told her story over and over again, and it was I to whom she read all of the pitiful letters she wrote to you. My father wanted to come to America to kill you. He did come later on to plead with you and to kill you if you would not listen to him. But you had gone—to Africa, they said. I could not understand why you would not give to her that little baby boy. He was hers, and———"

She stopped short in her recital and covered her eyes with her hands. He waited for her to go on, sitting as rigid as the image that faced him from beyond the table's end.

"Afterward my father and my uncles made every effort to get the child away from you, but he was hidden; you know how carefully he was hidden so that she might never find him. For ten years they searched for him, and you. For ten years she wrote to you, begging you to let her have him, if only for a little while at a time. She promised to restore him to you. You never replied. You scorned her. We were rich, very rich. But our money was of no help to us in the search for her boy. You had secreted him too well. At last, one day, she told me what it was that you accused her of doing. She told me about Guido Feverelli, her music-master. I knew him, James. He had known her from childhood. He was one of the finest men I have ever seen."

"He was in love with her," grated Brood.

"Perhaps. Who knows? But if so, he never uttered so much as one word of love to her. He challenged you. Why did you refuse to fight him?"

"Because she begged me not to kill him. Did she tell you that?"

"Yes. But that was not the real reason. It was because you were not sure of your ground."

"I deny that!"

"Never mind! It is enough that poor Feverelli passed out of her life. She did not see him again until just before she died. He was a noble gentleman. He wrote but one letter to her after that wretched day in this house. I have it here in this packet."

She drew a package of letters, tied with a white ribbon, from her bosom and laid it upon the table before him.

"But one letter from him," she went on. "I have brought it here for you to read. But not now. There are other letters and documents here for you to consider. They are from the grave. Ah, I do not wonder that you shrink and draw back from them. They convict you, James."

"Now I can see why you have taken up this fight against me. You—you knew she was innocent," he said in a low, unsteady voice.

"And why I have hated you, aïe? But what you do not understand is how I could have brought myself to the point of loving you."

"Loving me! Good Heaven, woman, what do you———"

"Loving you in spite of myself," she cried, beating upon the table with her hands. "I have tried to convince myself that it was not I, but the spirit of Matilde that had come to lodge in my treacherous body. I hated you for myself and I loved you for Matilde. She loved you to the end. She never hated you. That was it. The pure, deathless love of Matilde was constantly fighting against the hatred I bore for you. I believe as firmly as I believe that I am alive that she has been near me all the time, battling against my insane desire for vengeance. You have only to recall to yourself the moments when you were so vividly reminded of Matilde Valeska. At those times I am sure that something of Matilde was in me. I was not myself. You have looked into my eyes a thousand times with a question in your own. Your soul was striving to reach the soul of Matilde. Ah, all these months I have known that you love Matilde, not me. You loved Matilde that was in me. You———"

"I have thought of her, always of her, when you were in my arms."

"I know how well you loved her," she declared slowly. "I know that you went to her tomb long after her death was revealed to you. I know that years ago you made an effort to find Feverelli. You found his grave, too, and you could not ask him, man to man, if you had wronged her. But in spite of all that you brought up her boy to be sacrificed as———"

"I—I—am I to believe you? If he should be my son!" he cried, starting up, cold with dread.

"He is your son. He could be no other man's son. I have her dying word for it. She declared it in the presence of her God. Wait! Where are you going?"

"I am going down to him!"

"Not yet, James. I have still more to say to you, more to confess. Here! Take this package of letters. Read them as you sit beside his bed—not his death-bed, for I shall restore him to health, never fear. If he were to die I should curse myself to the end of time, for I and I alone would have been the cause. Here are her letters, and the one Feverelli wrote to her. This is her death-bed letter to you. And this is a letter to her son and yours. You may some day read it to him. And here—this is a document requiring me to share my fortune with her son. It is a pledge that I took before my father died a few years ago. If the boy ever appeared he was to have his mother's share of the estate, and it is not an inconsiderable amount, James. He is independent of you. He need ask nothing of you. I was taking him home to his own."

She shrank slightly as he stood over her. There was more of wonder and pity in his face than condemnation. She looked for the anger she had expected to arouse in him, and was dumbfounded to see that it was not revealed in his steady, appraising eyes.

"Your plan deserved a better fate than this, Yv—Thérèse. It was prodigious! I—I can almost pity you."

"Have you no pain, no regret, no grief?" she cried weakly.

"Yes," he said, controlling himself with difficulty. "Yes, I know all these and more." He picked up the package of letters and glanced at the superscription on the outer envelope. Suddenly he raised them to his lips and, with his eyes closed, kissed the words that were written there. Her head drooped and a sob came into her throat. She did not look up until he began speaking to her again, quietly, even patiently.

"But why should you, even in your longing for revenge, have planned to humiliate and degrade him even more than I could have done? Was it just to your sister's son that you should blight his life, that you should turn him into a skulking, sneaking betrayer? What would you have gained in the end? His loathing, his scorn. Thérèse, did you not think of all this?"

"I have told you that I thought of everything. I was mistaken. I did not stop to think that I would be taking him away from happiness in the shape of love that he might bear for someone else. I did not know that there was a Lydia Desmond. When I came to know my heart softened and my purpose lost most of its force. He would have been safe with me, but would he have been happy? I could not give him the kind of love that Lydia promised. I could only be his mother's sister to him. He was not in love with me. He has always loved Lydia. I fascinated him, just as I fascinated you. He would not have gone away with me, even after you had told him that he was not your son. He would not do that to you, James, in spite of the blow you struck him. He was loyal to Lydia and to himself."

"And what did he think of *you?*" demanded Brood scornfully.

"If you had not come upon us here he would have known me for who I am, and he would have forgiven me. I had asked him to go away with me. He refused. Then I was about to tell him the whole story of my life, of his life, and of yours. Do you think he would have refused forgiveness to me? No! He would have understood."

"But up to that hour he thought of you as — what shall I say?"

"A bad woman? Perhaps. I did not care. It was part of the price I was to pay in advance. I would have told him everything as soon as the ship on which we sailed was outside the harbour yonder. That was my intention, and I know you believe me when I say that there was nothing more in my mind. Time would have straightened everything out for him. He could have had his Lydia, even though he went away with me. Once away from here, do you think that he would ever return? No! Even though he knew you to be his father, he would not forget that he has never been your son. You have hurt him since he was a babe. Would he forget? Would he forgive? No! When you came into this room and found us, I was about to go down on my knees to him to thank him for saving me from my own designs. I realised then, as I had come to suspect in the past few months, that I had not counted on my own conscience.

"James, I—I would not have carried out my plan. I had faltered, and my cause was lost. What have I accomplished? Am I able to gloat over you? What have I wrought, after all? I weakened under the love she bore for you, I permitted it to creep in and fill my heart. Do you understand? I do not hate you now. It is something to know that you have worshipped her all these years. You were true to her. What you did long, long ago was not your fault. You believed that she had wronged you. But you went on loving her. That is what weakened my resolve. You loved her to the end, she loved you to the end. Well, in the face of that, could I go on hating you? You must have been worthy of her love. She knew you better than all the world. You came to me with love for her in your heart. You took me, and you loved her all the time. I am not sure, James, that you are not entitled to this miserable, unhappy love I have come to feel for you—my own love, not Matilde's."

"You are saying this so that I may refrain from throwing you out into the street———"

"No!" she cried, coming to her feet. "I shall ask nothing of you. If I am to go, it shall be because I have failed. I have been a blind, vainglorious fool. The trap has caught me instead of you, and I shall take the consequences. I have lost everything!"

"You have lost *everything*," said he steadily.

"'You despise me?'"

"I cannot ask you to stay here after this."

"But I shall not go. I have a duty to perform before I leave this house. I intend to save the life of that poor boy downstairs, so that he may not die believing me to be an evil woman, a faithless wife. Thank God, I have accomplished something! You know that he is your son. You know that my sister was as pure as snow. You know that you killed her, and that she loved you in spite of the death you brought to her. That is something."

Brood dropped into the chair and buried his face on his quivering arms. In muffled tones came the cry from his soul:

"They've all said that he is like me. I have seen it at times, but I would not believe. I fought against it resolutely, madly, cruelly! Now it is too late and I *see!* I see, I feel! You curse of mankind, you have driven me to the killing of my own son!"

She stood over him, silent for a long time, her hand hovering above his head.

"He is not going to die," she said at last, when she was sure that she had full command of her voice. "I can promise you that, James. I shall not go from this house until he is well. I shall nurse him to health and give him back to you and Matilde, for now I know that he belongs to both of you and not to her alone. Now, James, you may go down to him. He is not conscious. He will not hear you praying at his bedside. He———"

A knock came at the door—a sharp, imperative knock. It was repeated several times before either of them could summon the courage to call out. They were petrified with the dread of something that awaited them beyond the closed door. It was she who finally called out:

"Come in!"

Dr Hodder, coatless and bare-armed, came into the room.

CHAPTER XXII

The doctor blinked for a moment. The two were leaning forward with alarm in their eyes, their hands gripping the table.

"Well, are we to send for an undertaker?" demanded Hodder irritably.

Brood started forward.

"Is—is he dead?"

"Of course not, but he might as well be!" exclaimed the doctor. It was plain to be seen that he was very much out of patience. "You've called in another doctor and a priest, and now I hear that a Presbyterian parson is in the library. Hang it all, Brood, why don't you send for the coroner and undertaker and have done with it! I'm blessed if I— — —"

Yvonne came swiftly to his side.

"Is he conscious? Does he know?"

"Hodder, is there any hope?" cried Brood.

"I'll be honest with you, Jim. I don't believe there is. It went in here, above the heart, and it's lodged back here by the spine somewhere. We haven't located it yet, but we will. Had to let up on the ether for a while, you see. He opened his eyes a few minutes ago, Mrs Brood, and my assistant is certain that he whispered Lydia Desmond's name. Sounded that way to him, but, of course— — —"

"There! You see, James?" she cried, whirling upon her husband.

"I think you'd better step in and see him now, Jim," said the doctor, suddenly becoming very gentle. "He may come to again, and it may be the last time he'll ever open his eyes. Yes, it's as bad as that."

"I'll go," said Brood, his face ashen. "You must revive him for a few minutes, Hodder. There's something I've got to say to him. He must be able to hear and understand me. It is the most important thing in the— — —" He choked up suddenly.

"You'll have to be careful, Jim. He's ready to collapse. Then it's all off."

"Nevertheless, Dr Hodder, my husband has something to say to his son that cannot be put off for an instant. I think it will mean a great deal to him in his fight for recovery. It will make life worth living for him."

Hodder stared for a second or two.

"He'll need a lot of courage, and if anything can put it into him he'll make a better fight. If you get a chance, say it to him, Jim. If it's got anything to do with his mother, say it. He has moaned the word a dozen times———"

"It has to do with his mother!" Brood cried out. "Come! I want you to hear it, too, Hodder."

"There isn't much time to lose, I'm afraid," began Hodder, shaking his head. His gaze suddenly rested on Mrs Brood's face. She was very erect, and a smile such as he had never seen before was on her lips, a smile that puzzled and yet inspired him with a positive, undeniable feeling of encouragement.

"He is not going to die, Dr Hodder," she said quietly. Something went through his body that warmed it curiously. He felt a thrill, as one who is seized by a great, overpowering excitement.

She preceded them into the hall. Brood came last. He closed the door behind him after a swift glance about the room that had been his most private retreat for years.

He was never to set foot inside its walls again. In that single glance he bade farewell to it for ever. It was a hated, unlovely spot. He had spent an age in it during those bitter morning hours, an age of imprisonment.

On the landing below they came upon Lydia. She was seated on a window-ledge, leaning wearily against the casement. She did not rise as they approached, but watched them with steady, smouldering eyes in which there was no friendliness, no compassion. They were her enemies; they had killed the thing she loved.

Brood's eyes met hers for an instant, and then fell before the bitter look they encountered. His shoulders drooped as he passed close by her motionless figure and followed the doctor down the hall to the bedroom door. It opened and closed an instant later and he was with his son.

For a long time Lydia's sombre, piteous gaze hung upon the door through which he had passed and which was closed so cruelly against her, the one who loved him best of all. At last she looked away; her attention was caught by a queer, clicking sound near at hand. She was surprised to find Yvonne Brood standing close beside her, her eyes closed and her fingers telling the beads that ran through her fingers, her lips moving in voiceless prayer.

The girl watched her dully for a few moments, then with growing fascination. The incomprehensible creature was praying! To Lydia this seemed to be the most unnatural thing in all the world. She could not associate prayer with this woman's character; she could not imagine her having been in all her life possessed of a fervent religious thought. It was impossible to think of her as being even hypocritically pious.

Lydia began to experience a strange feeling of irritation. She turned her face away, unwilling to be a witness to this shallow mockery. She was herself innately religious. In her secret soul she resented an appeal to Heaven by this luxurious worldling; she could not bring herself to think of her as anything else. Prayer seemed a profanation on her scarlet lips.

Lydia believed that Frederic had shot himself. She put Yvonne down as the real cause of the calamity that had fallen upon the house. But for her, James Brood never would have had a motive for striking the blow that crushed all desire to live out of the unhappy boy. She had made of her husband an unfeeling monster, and now she prayed! She had played with the emotions of two men, and now she begged to be pardoned for her folly! An inexplicable desire to laugh at the plight of the trifler came over the girl, but even as she checked it another and more unaccountable force ordered her to obey the impulse to turn once more to look into the face of her companion.

Yvonne was looking at her. She had ceased telling the beads, and her hands hung limply at her sides. For a full minute, perhaps, the two regarded each other without speaking.

"He is not going to die, Lydia," said Yvonne gravely.

The girl started to her feet.

"Do you think it is your prayer, and not mine, that has reached God's ears?"' she cried.

"The prayer of a nobler woman than either of you or I has gone to the throne," said the other.

Lydia's eyes grew dark with resentment.

"You could have prevented all———"

"Be good enough to remember that you have said all that to me before, Lydia."

"What is your object in keeping me away from him at such a time as this, Mrs Brood?" demanded Lydia. "You refuse to let me go in to him. Is it because you are afraid of what———"

"There are trying days ahead of us, Lydia," interrupted Yvonne. "We will have to face them together. I can promise you this: Frederic will be saved for you. To-morrow, next day, perhaps, I may be able to explain everything to you. You hate me to-day. Everyone in this house hates me, even Frederic. There is a day coming when you will not hate me. That was my prayer, Lydia. I was not praying for Frederic, but for myself."

"For yourself? I might have known you———"

"You hesitate? Perhaps it is just as well."

"I want to say to you, Mrs Brood, that it is my purpose to remain in this house as long as I can be———"

"You are welcome, Lydia. You will be the one great tonic that is to restore him to health of mind and body. Yes, I shall go further and say that you are commanded to stay here and help me in the long fight that is ahead of us."

"I thank you, Mrs Brood," the girl was surprised into saying.

Both of them turned quickly as the door to Frederic's room opened and James Brood came out into the hall. His face was drawn with pain and anxiety, but the light of exaltation was in his eyes.

"Come, Lydia," he said softly, after he had closed the door behind him. "He knows me. He is conscious. Hodder can't understand it, but he seems to have suddenly grown stronger. He———"

"Stronger?" cried Yvonne, the ring of triumph in her voice. "I knew! I could feel it coming—his strength—even out here, James. Yes, go in now, Lydia. You will see a strange sight, my dear. James Brood will kneel beside his son and tell him———"

"Come!" said Brood, spreading out his hands in a gesture of admission. "You must hear it, too, Lydia. Not you, Thérèse! You are not to come in."

"I grant you ten minutes, James," she said with the air of a dictator. "After that I shall take my stand beside him and you will not be needed." She struck her breast sharply with her clenched hand. "His one and only hope lies here, James. I am his salvation. I am his strength. When you come out of that room again it will be to stay out until I give the word for you to re-enter. Go, now, and put spirit into him. That is all I ask of you."

He stared for a moment and then lowered his head. A moment later Lydia followed him into the room and Yvonne was alone in the hall. Alone? Ranjab was ascending the stairs. He came and stood before her and bent his knee.

"I forgot," she said, looking down upon him without a vestige of the old dread in her eyes. "I have a friend, after all."

CHAPTER XXIII

On a warm morning, toward the middle of June, Frederic and Lydia sat in the quaint, old-world courtyard, almost directly beneath the balcony of Yvonne's boudoir. He lounged comfortably, yet weakly, in the invalid-chair that had been wheeled to the spot by Ranjab, and she sat on a pile of cushions at his feet.

Looking at him, one would not have thought that he had passed through the valley of the shadow of death and was but now emerging into the sunshine of security. His face was pale, but there was a healthy gloss to the skin and a clear light in the eye.

For a week or more he had been permitted to walk about the house and into the garden, always leaning on the arm of his father or the faithful Hindu. Each succeeding day saw his strength and vitality increase, and each night he slept with the peace of a care-free child. He was filled with contentment; he loved life as he had never dreamed it would be possible for him to love it. There was a song in his heart and there was a bright star always on the edge of his horizon.

As for Lydia, she was radiant with happiness. The long fight was over. She had gone through the campaign against death with loyal, unfaltering courage; there had never been an instant when her staunch heart had failed her; there had been distress, but never despair. If the strain told on her it did not matter, for she was of the fighting kind. Her love was the sustenance on which she throve, despite the beggarly offerings that were laid before her during those weeks of famine. Her strong, young body lost none of its vigour; her splendid spirit gloried in the tests to which it was subjected, and now she was as serene as the June day that found her wistfully contemplating the results of victory.

Times there were when a pensive mood brought the touch of sadness to her grateful heart. She was happy and Frederic was happy, but what of the one who actually had wrought the miracle? That one alone was unhappy, unrequited, undefended. There was no place for her in the new order of things. When Lydia thought of her, as she often did, it was with an indescribable craving in her soul. She longed for the hour to come when Yvonne Brood would lay aside the mask of resignation and demand tribute;

when the strange defiance that held all of them at bay would disappear, and they could feel that she no longer regarded them as adversaries.

There was no longer a symptom of rancour in the heart of Lydia Desmond. She realised that her beloved's recovery was due almost entirely to the remarkable influence exercised by this woman at a time when mortal agencies appeared to be of no avail. Her absolute certainty that she had the power to thwart death, at least in this instance, had its effect not only on the wounded man, but on those who attended him.

Dr Hodder and the nurses were not slow to admit that her magnificent courage, her almost scornful self-assurance, supplied them with an incentive that otherwise might never have got beyond the form of a mere hope. There was something positively startling in her serene conviction that Frederic was not to die. No less a sceptic than the renowned Dr Hodder confided to Lydia and her mother that he now believed in the supernatural and never again would say "there is no God."

Hodder had gone to James Brood at the end of the third day and, with the sweat of the haunted on his brow, had whispered hoarsely that the case was out of his hands. He was no longer the doctor, but an agent governed by a spirit that would not permit death to claim its own. And somehow Brood understood far better than the man of science.

The true story of the shooting had long been known to Lydia and her mother. Brood confessed everything to them. He assumed all of the blame for what had transpired on that tragic morning. He humbled himself before them, and when they shook their heads and turned their backs upon him he was not surprised, for he knew they were not convicting him of assault with a deadly firearm. Later on the story of Thérèse was told by him to Frederic and the girl. He did his wife no injustice in the recital.

Frederic laid his hand upon the soft brown head at his knee and voiced the thought that was in his mind.

"You are wondering, as I am, too, what is to become of Yvonne after to-day," he said. "There must be an end, and if it doesn't come now, when will it come? To-morrow we sail. It is certain that she is not to accompany us. She has said so herself, and father has said so. So to-day must see the end of things."

"Frederic, I want you to do something for me," said Lydia earnestly. "There was a time when I could not have asked this of you, but now I implore you to speak to your father in her behalf. I love her, Freddy dear. I cannot help it. She asks nothing of any of us; she expects nothing, and yet she loves all of us. If he only would unbend toward her a little———"

"Listen, Lyddy dear. I don't believe it's altogether up to him. There is a barrier that we can't see, but they do, both of them. My mother stands between them. You see, I've come to know my father lately, dear. He's not a stranger to me any longer. I know what sort of a heart he's got. He never got over loving my mother, and he'll never get over knowing that Yvonne knows that *she* loved him to the day she died.

"We know what it was in Yvonne that attracted him from the first, and she knows. He's not likely to forgive himself so easily. He didn't play fair with either of them, that's what I'm trying to get at. I don't believe he can forgive himself any more than he can forgive Yvonne for the thing she set about to do.

"You see, Lyddy, she married him without love. She debased herself, even though she can't admit it even now. I love her, too. She's the most wonderful woman in the world. But she did give herself to the man she hated with all her soul and—well, there you are. He can't forget *that*, you know, and she can't. She loves him for herself now, and that's what hurts both of them. It hurts because they both know that he still loves my mother."

"She's his wife, however," said Lydia, with a stubborn pursing of the lips. "She didn't wrong him, and, after all, she's only guilty of—well, she isn't guilty of anything except being a sister of the girl *he* wronged."

"I'll have a talk with him if you think best," said he, an eager gleam in his eyes.

"And I with Yvonne," she said quickly. "You see, it's possible she is the one to be persuaded."

"Of course, you've observed that they never see one another alone," said he. "They never meet except when someone else is about. He rather resents the high-handed way in which she ordered him to stay away from me until I was safely out of danger. He says she saved my life. He says she performed a miracle. But he has never uttered a word of thanks or gratitude or appreciation to her. I'm sure of that, for she has told me so. And she is satisfied to go without his thanks."

"I see what you mean," she said with a sigh. "I suppose we just can't understand things."

"You've no idea how beautiful you are to-day, Lyddy," he cried suddenly, and she looked up into his glowing eyes with a smile of ineffable happiness. Her hand found his, and her warm, red lips were pressed to its palm in a hot, impassioned kiss. "It's great to be alive! Great!"

"Oh, it is," she cried, "it is!"

They might better have said that it is great to be young, for that is what it all came to in the analysis.

Later on Brood joined them in the courtyard. He stood, with his hand on his son's shoulder, chatting carelessly about the coming voyage, all the while smiling upon the radiant girl to whom he was promising paradise. She adored the gentle, kindly gleam in those one-time steady, steel-like eyes. His voice, too, of late was pitched in a softer key, and there was the ring of happiness in its every note. It was as if he had discovered something in life that was constantly surprising and pleasing him. He seemed always to be venturing into fresh fields of exploration and finding there something that was of inestimable value to his new estate.

Lydia left father and son after a few minutes, excusing herself on the ground that she wished to have a good, long chat with Yvonne. She did not delay her departure, but hurried into the house, having rather adroitly provided Frederic with an opening for an intercession in behalf of his lovely stepmother. Her meaning glance was not wasted on the young man.

He lost no time in following up the advantage.

"See here, father, I don't like the idea of leaving Yvonne out in the cold, so to speak. It's pretty darned rough, don't you think? Down in your heart you don't blame her for what she started out to do, and, after all, she's only human. Whatever happened in the past we—well, it's all in the past. She——"

Brood stopped him with a gesture.

"My son, I will try to explain something to you. You may be able to understand things better than I. I fell in love with her once because an influence that was not her own overpowered me. There was something of your mother in her. She admits that to be true, and I now believe it. Well, that something, whatever it was, is gone. She is not the same. Yvonne is Thérèse. She is not the woman I loved two months ago."

"Nor am I the boy you hated two months ago," argued Frederic. "Isn't there a parallel to be seen there, father? I am your son. She is your wife. You———"

"There was never a time when I really hated you, my son. I tried to, but that is all over. We will not rake up the ashes. As for my wife—well, I have tried to hate her. It is impossible for me to do so. She is a wonderful woman. But you must understand, on the other hand, that I do not love her. I did when she looked at me with your mother's eyes and spoke to me with your mother's lips. But she is not the same."

"Give yourself a chance, dad. You will come to love her for herself if only you will let go of yourself. You are trying to be hard. You———"

Again Brood interrupted. His face was pale, his eyes grew dark with pain.

"You don't know what you are saying, Frederic. Let us discontinue the subject."

"I want you to be happy, I want———"

"I shall be happy. I am happy. Have I not found out the truth? Are you not my beloved son? Are———"

"And who convinced you of all that, sir? Who is responsible for your present happiness, and mine?"

"I know, I know!" exclaimed the father in some agitation.

"You'll regret it all your life if you fail her now, dad. Why, hang it all, you're not an old man! You are less than fifty. Your heart hasn't dried up yet. Your blood is still hot. And she is glorious. Give yourself a chance. You know that she's one woman in a million, and she's yours! She has made you happy, she can make you still happier."

"No, I am not old. I am far younger than I was fifteen years ago. That's what I am afraid of—this youth I really never possessed till now. If I gave way to it now I'd—well, I would be like putty in her hands. She could go on laughing at me, trifling with me, fooling me to———"

"She wouldn't do that!" exclaimed his son hotly.

"I don't blame you for defending her. It's right that you should. You are forgetting the one important condition, however. She can never reconcile herself to the position you would put her in if I permitted you to persuade me that———"

"I can tell you one thing, father, that you ought to know, if you are so blind that you haven't discovered it for yourself. She loves you."

"You are very young, my boy." Brood shook his head and smiled faintly.

"What's to become of her? You are leaving her without a thought for her future. You———"

"I fancy she is quite capable of arranging her future. As a matter of fact, she had arranged it pretty definitely before this thing happened. Leave it to her, Frederic. It is impossible for me to take her away with us. It is not to be considered."

"All right, but bear this in mind: Lydia loves Yvonne, and she's heartbroken. Now we'll talk about her, if you like."

Lydia had as little success in her rather more tactful interview with Yvonne.

"Thank you, dear, I am satisfied," said she. "Everything has turned out as it should. The wicked enchantress has been foiled and virtue triumphs. Don't be unhappy on my account, Lydia. It will not be easy to say goodbye to you and Frederic, but—*là! là!* What are we to do? Now please don't speak of it again. Hearts are easily mended. Look at my husband—*aïe!* He has had his heart made over from top to bottom—in a rough crucible, it's true, but it's as good as new, you'll admit. In a way, I am made over, too. I am happier than I've ever been in my life. I'm in love with my husband, I'm in love with you and Frederic, and I am more than ever in love with myself. So there! Don't feel sorry for me. I shall have the supreme joy of knowing that not one of you will ever forget me or my deeds, good and bad. Who knows? I am still young, you know. Time has the chance to be very kind to me before I die."

That last observation lingered in Lydia's mind.

But despite her careless treatment of the situation, Yvonne awaited with secret dread the coming of that hour when James Brood would say goodbye to her and, instead of turning her away from his house, would go out of it himself without a single *command* to her. He would not tell her that it was no longer her home, nor would he tell her that it was.

CHAPTER XXIV

The next day came, bright and sweet.

The ship was to sail at noon.

At ten o'clock the farewells were being said. There were tears and heartaches, and there was fierce rebellion in the hearts of two of the voyagers. Yvonne had declined to go to the pier to see them off, and Brood was going away without a word to her about the future. That was manifest to the anxious, soul-tried watchers.

In silence they made their way out to the waiting automobile. As Brood was about to pass through the broad front door a resolute figure confronted him. For a moment master and man stared hard into each other's eyes, and then, as if obeying an inflexible command, the former turned to glance backward into the hallway. Yvonne was standing in the library door.

"*Sahib!*" said the Hindu, and there was strange authority in his voice. "Tell her, *sahib*. It is not so cruel to tell her as it would be to go away without a word. She is waiting to be told that you do not want her to remain in your home."

Brood closed his eyes for a second, and then strode quickly toward his wife.

"Yvonne, they all want me to take you along with us," he said, his voice shaking with the pent-up emotion of weeks.

She met his gaze calmly, almost serenely.

"But, of course, it is quite impossible," she said. "I understand, James."

"It is not possible," he said, steadying his voice with an effort.

"That is why I thought it would be better to say good-bye here and not at the pier. We must have some respect for appearances, you know."

He searched her eyes intently, looking for some sign of weakening on her part. He did not know whether to feel disappointed or angry at what he saw.

"I don't believe you would have gone if I had— —"

"You need not say it, James. You did not ask me, and I have not asked anything of you."

"Before I go," he said nervously, "I want to say this to you: I have no feeling of resentment toward you. I am able to look back upon what you would have done without a single thought of anger. You have stood by me in time of trouble. I owe a great deal to you, Yvonne. You will not accept my gratitude—it would be a farce to offer it to you under the circumstances. But I want you to know that I am grateful. You———"

"Go on, please. This is the moment for you to say that your home cannot be mine. I am expecting it."

His eyes hardened.

"I shall never say that to you, Yvonne. You are my wife. I shall expect you to remain my wife to the very end."

Now, for the first time, her eyes flew open with surprise. A bewildered expression came into them almost at once. He had said the thing she least expected. She put out her hand to steady herself against the door.

"Do—do you mean that, James?" she said wonderingly.

"You are my property. You are bound to me. I do not intend that you shall ever forget that, Yvonne. I don't believe you really love me, but that is not the point. Other women have not loved their husbands, and yet—yet they have been true and loyal to them."

"You amaze me!" she cried, watching his eyes with acute wonder in her own. "Suppose that I should refuse to abide by your—what shall I call it?"

"Decision is the word," he supplied grimly

"Well, what then?"

"You will abide by it, that's all. I am leaving you behind without the slightest fear for the future. This is your home. You will not abandon it."

"Have I said that I would?"

"No."

She drew herself up.

"Well, I shall now tell you what I intend to do, and have intended to do ever since I discovered that I could think for myself and not for Matilde. I intend to stay here until you turn me out as unworthy. I love you, James. You may leave me here feeling very sure of that. I shall go on caring for you all the rest of my life. I am not telling you this in the hope that you will say that you have a spark of love in your soul for me. I don't want you to say it now, James. But you will say it to me one day, and I will be justified in my own heart."

"I *have* loved you. There was never in this world anything like the love I had for you. I know it now. It was not Matilde I loved when I held you in my arms. I know it now. I loved *you*; I loved your body, your soul———"

"Enough!" she cried out sharply. "I was playing at love then. Now I love in earnest. You've never known love such as I can really give. I know you well, too. You love nobly, and without end. Of late I have come to believe that Matilde could have won out against your folly if she had been stronger, less conscious of the pain she felt. If she had stood her ground, here, against you, you would have been conquered. But she did not have the strength to stand and fight as I would have fought. To-day I love my sister none the less, but I no longer fight to avenge her wrongs. I am here to fight for myself. You may go away thinking that I am a traitor to her, but you will take with you the conviction that I am honest, and that is the foundation for my claim against you."

"I know you are not a traitor to her cause," he replied. "You are its lifelong supporter. You have done more for Matilde than———"

"Than Matilde could have done for herself? Isn't that true? I have forced you to confess that you loved her for twenty-five years with all your soul. I have done my duty for her. Now I am beginning to take myself into account. Some day we will meet again and—well, it will not be disloyalty to Matilde that moves you to say that you love me."

He was silent for a long time. When at last he spoke his voice was full of gentleness.

"I do not love you, Yvonne. I cannot allow you to look forward to the happy ending that you picture. You say that you love me. I shall give you the opportunity to prove it to yourself, if not to me. I order you, Thérèse, to remain in this house until I come to set you free."

She stared at him for a moment, and then an odd smile came into her eyes.

"A prisoner serving her time? Is that it, my husband?"

"If you are here when I return, I shall have reason to believe that your love is real, that it is good and true and enduring. I am afraid of you now. I do not trust you."

"Is that your sentence?"

"Call it that if you like, Thérèse."

"My keepers? Who are they to be? The old men of the sea——"

"Your keeper will be the thing you call love," said he.

"Do you expect me to submit to this———"

He held up his hand.

"I did not intend to impose this condition upon you by word of mouth. I was going away without a word, but you would have received from Mr Dawes a sealed envelope as soon as the ship sailed. It contains this command in writing. He will hand it to you, of course, but now that you know the contents it will not be necessary to———"

"And when you *do* come back, am I to hope for something more than your pardon and a release?" she cried.

"I will not promise anything," said he.

She drew a long breath and there was the light of triumph in her eyes. Laying her slim hand on his arm, she said:

"I am content, James. I am sure of you now. You will find me here when you choose to come back, be it one year or twenty. Now go; they are waiting for you. Be kind to them, and tell to them all that you have just told me. It will make them happy. They love me, you see."

"Yes, they *do* love you," said he, putting his hands upon her shoulders. They smiled into each other's eyes. "Good-bye, Thérèse. I *will* return."

"Good-bye, James. No, do not kiss me. It would be mockery. Good luck, and God speed you home again." Their hands met in a warm, firm clasp. "I will go with you as far as the door of my prison."

From the open door she smiled out upon the young people in the motor and waved her handkerchief in gay farewell. Then she closed the door and walked slowly down the hallway to the big library.

"He has taken the only way to conquer himself," she mused, half aloud. "He is a wise man, a very wise man. I might have expected this of him."

She pulled the bell-cord, and Jones came at once to the room.

"Yes, madam."

"When Mr Dawes and Mr Riggs return from the ship, tell them that I shall expect them to have luncheon with me. That's all, thank you."

"Yes, madam."

"By the way, Jones, you may always set the table for three."

Jones blinked. He felt that he had never behaved so wonderfully in all the years of service as he did when he succeeded in bowing in his habitual manner, despite the fact that he was "everlawstingly bowled over, so to speak."

"For three, madam. Very well."

A cold, blustery night in January, six months after the beginning of Yvonne's voluntary servitude in the prison to which her husband had committed her. In the big library, before a roaring fire, sat the two old men, very much as they had sat on the December night that heralded the approach of the new mistress of the house of Brood, except that on this occasion they were eminently sober. On the corner of the table lay a long, yellow envelope, a cablegram addressed to Mrs James Brood.

"It's been here for two hours, and she don't even think of opening it to see what's inside," complained Mr Riggs, but entirely without reproach.

"It's her business, Joe," said Mr Dawes, pulling hard at his cigar.

"Maybe someone's dead," said Mr Riggs dolorously.

"Like as not, but what of it?"

"What of it, you infernal—but, excuse me, Danbury, I won't say it. It's against the rules, God bless 'em. If anybody's dead, she ought to know it."

"But supposing nobody is dead."

"There's no use arguing with you."

"She'll read it when she gets good and ready. At present she prefers to read the letters from Freddy and Lyddy."

"Maybe it's from Jim," said his friend, a wistful look in his old eyes.

"I—I hope it is, by gee!" exclaimed the other, and then they got up and went over to examine the envelope for the tenth time. "I wish he'd telegraph or write, or do something, Dan. She's never had a line from him. Maybe this is something at last."

"What puzzles me is that she always seems disappointed when there's nothing in the post from him, and here's a cablegram that might be the very thing she's looking for, and she pays no attention to it. It certainly beats me."

"You know what puzzles me more than anything else? I've said it a hundred times. She never goes outside this here house, except in the garden, day or night."

"*Sh—h!*"

Mrs Brood was descending the stairs, lightly, eagerly. In another instant she entered the room.

"How nice the fire looks!" she cried. Never had she been more radiantly, seductively beautiful. "My cablegram, where is it?"

The old men made a simultaneous dash for the long-neglected envelope. Mr Dawes succeeded in being the first to clutch it in his eager fingers.

"Better read it, Mrs Brood," he panted, thrusting it into her hand. "Maybe it's bad news."

She regarded him with one of her most mysterious smiles.

"No, my friend, it is *not* bad news. It is good news; it's from my husband."

"But you haven't read it," gasped Mr Riggs.

"Ah, but I know, just the same." She deliberately slit the envelope with a slim finger and held it out to them. "Read it if you like."

They solemnly shook their heads, too amazed for words. She unfolded the sheet and sent her eyes swiftly over the printed contents. Then, to their further stupefaction, she pressed the bit of paper to her red lips. Her eyes flashed like diamonds.

"Listen! Here is what he says: 'Come by the first steamer. I want you to come to me, Thérèse.' And see! It is signed 'Your husband.'"

"Hurray!" shouted the two old men.

"But," she said, shaking her head slowly, "I shall not obey."

"What! You—you won't go?" gasped Mr Riggs.

"No!" she cried, the ring of triumph in her voice. She suddenly clapped her hands to her breast and uttered a long, deep sigh of joy. "No, I shall not go to him."

The old men stared helplessly while she sank luxuriously into a big chair and stuck her little feet out to the fire. They felt their knees grow weak under the weight of their suddenly inert bodies.

"He will come and unlock the door," she went on serenely. "Ring for Jones, please."

"Wha—what are you going to do?" Mr Dawes had the temerity to ask.

"Send a cablegram to my husband saying———"

She paused to smile at the flaming logs on the broad hearth, a sweet, rapturous smile that neither of the old men could comprehend.

"Saying—what?" demanded Mr Riggs anxiously.

"That I cannot go to him," she said, as she stretched out her arms toward the East.